Writing

From Inner World
to Outer World

Writing
From Inner World to Outer World

Barbara Fine Clouse

Youngstown State University

McGraw-Hill Book Company

New York   St. Louis   San Francisco   Auckland   Bogotá   Hamburg
Johannesburg   London   Madrid   Mexico   Montreal   New Delhi   Panama
Paris   São Paulo   Singapore   Sydney   Tokyo   Toronto

Writing: From Inner World to Outer World

1 2 3 4 5 6 7 8 9 0   DOCDOC   8 9 8 7 6 5 4 3 2

ISBN 0-07-011407-2

See Acknowledgments on page 367.
Copyrights included on this page by reference.

This book was set in Baskerville by Monotype Composition Company, Inc.
The editors were Phillip A. Butcher and David Dunham;
the designer was Merrill Haber;
the production supervisor was Diane Renda.
The cover photograph was taken by Peter Menzel/Stock, Boston;
the cover photo inset was taken by Suzanne Szasz/Photo Researchers, Inc.
The photo editor was Inge King.
R. R. Donnelley & Sons Company was printer and binder.

Part-Opening Photo Credits
The Bridge and The Outer World were taken by Elizabeth Hamlin/Stock, Boston.
The Inner World was taken by Suzanne Szasz/Photo Researchers, Inc.

Library of Congress Cataloging in Publication Data

Clouse, Barbara Fine.
    Writing, from inner world to outer world.

    Includes index.
    1. English language—Rhetoric. I. Title.
PE1408.C538   808'.042   82-6594
ISBN 0-07-011407-2   AACR2

To Denny, Greg, and Jeff — with love

Contents

Preface   **xiii**

The Inner World

Chapter 1

GETTING STARTED: Ideas about
Writing and Ideas for Writing   **3**

Ideas about Writing   **4**
Write What You Think   **6**
Discovering Ideas   **6**
    Freewriting   **6**
    Answering Questions   **6**
    Listing   **10**
    Letter Writing   **11**
    Keeping a Journal   **12**
    Talking to Others   **12**
    Using a Tape Recorder   **12**
A Final Word   **12**

Chapter 2

OBSERVING MORE CLOSELY:
Descriptive Writing   **13**

Reading Selection: "Central Park"   **14**
    Vocabulary Building:
      "Central Park"   **15**

    Vocabulary List: "Central Park"   **15**
    Questions for Discussion:
      "Central Park"   **16**
The Descriptive Writing Process:
The Need to Revise   **19**
The Descriptive Writing Process:
Selecting Detail   **20**
The Descriptive Writing Process:
Mood and Emotion   **21**
Getting Ready: Descriptive Writing
Practice   **22**
    Descriptive Writing Practice A   **22**
    Descriptive Writing Practice B   **23**
    Descriptive Writing Practice C   **23**
    Descriptive Writing Practice D   **23**
Grammar and Usage   **23**
    Economical Diction   **24**
      Exercise: Economical Diction   **24**
    Precise Diction   **26**
      Exercise: Precise Diction   **27**
    Clichés   **27**
      Exercise: Clichés   **28**
    A Word about Commas between
      Coordinate Modifiers   **29**
      Exercise: Commas between
       Coordinate Modifiers   **30**
Writing Assignment I   **31**
    Sample Descriptive List:
      "My Bedroom"   **32**
    Questions for Discussion:
      "My Bedroom"   **33**
Writing Assignment II   **34**

Writing the Paragraph   35
  The Topic Sentence   35
    Exercise: The Topic Sentence   36
  Supporting Detail   38
    Exercise: Relevant Supporting
    Detail   38
    Exercise: Adequate Supporting
    Detail   40
  The Closing   40
    Exercise: The Closing   41
  Paragraph Organization:
    An Illustration   42
    Exercise: A Descriptive
    Paragraph to Analyze   43
Writing Assignment III   45
  Questions to Answer before
  Submitting Your Paragraph   45
Writing Assignment IV   45
A Final Word   46

Chapter 3

DISCOVERING CAUSES: Writing
about Influences in Your Life   47

**Reading Selection: "Discovery of a
Father"**   47
  Vocabulary List: "Discovery of a
  Father"   51
  Questions for Discussion:
  "Discovery of a Father"   51
Getting Ready: Freewriting   53
    Exercise: Freewriting   54
The Multiparagraph Theme   55
Theme Organization   55
  Introductory Paragraphs:
    The Thesis   56
    Exercise: The Thesis   56
    Exercise: Relevance   57
  Narrowing the Thesis   58
    Exercise: Narrowing the Thesis   59
  Introductory Paragraphs:
    The Lead-In   60
    Exercise: The Lead-In and Thesis 63
  Body Paragraphs   63
    Exercise: The Topic Sentence   65
    Exercise: Supporting Detail   65
  Concluding Paragraphs   66
    Exercise: The Conclusion   67

  Outline of Theme Organization   67
A Sample Theme: "The Purse"   68
  Questions for Discussion:
  "The Purse"   69
**Grammar and Mechanics:
Why Bother?**   70
Grammar and Usage   71
  Punctuating Conversation   71
    Exercise: Punctuating
    Conversation   72
  A Word about Capitals   73
    Exercise: Capitals   73
  Sentence Fragments   74
  Correcting Sentence Fragments:
    Adding Missing Information   74
    Exercise: Correcting Fragments by
    Adding Missing Information   75
  Correcting Sentence Fragments:
    Joining the Fragment to an
    Existing Sentence   75
    Exercise: Correcting Fragments by
    Joining Them to Sentences   76
  Correcting Sentence Fragments:
    Changing Verb Forms   76
    Exercise: Correcting Fragments by
    Changing Verb Forms   77
  Finding and Correcting Fragments
  in Your Own Themes   77
Writing Assignment I   78
  Questions to Answer before
  Submitting Your Theme   78
Writing Assignment II   79
Writing Assignment III   79
A Final Word   79

Chapter 4

DISCOVERING SOLUTIONS: Writing
to Solve Problems and Clear up
Confusion   80

**Reading Selection: "Life for My
Child Is Simple, and Is Good"**   80
  Vocabulary List: "Life for My
  Child Is Simple, and Is Good"   81
  Questions for Discussion:
  "Life for My Child Is Simple,
  and Is Good"   82
Getting Ready: Freewriting   83

Getting Ready: Looking Within 83
The Difference between Speech and
Writing 85
Planning Your Writing: The Outline 86
   Outline Form for Planning the
   Theme 86
   Planning Your Writing: How to
   Fill in the Outline 88
Planning Your Writing: Twelve Steps
for Writing a Theme 89
Grammar and Usage 93
   Run-On Sentences 93
   Correcting Run-On Sentences:
   Using a Period and Capital
   Letter 93
      Exercise: Correcting Run-On
      Sentences 94
   Correcting Run-On Sentences:
   Using a Semicolon 95
      Exercise: Correcting Run-On
      Sentences 95
   Correcting Run-On Sentences:
   Using a Comma and Coordinate
   Conjunction 96
      Exercise: Correcting Run-On
      Sentences 97
   Correcting Run-On Sentences:
   Using a Subordinate Clause 98
      Exercise: Correcting Run-On
      Sentences 99
   Proofreading for Run-Ons 101
   A Word about Commas with
   Clauses 101
      Exercise: Commas with Clauses 101
   A Word about the Semicolon 102
      Exercise: The Semicolon 103
   Subject–Verb Agreement 103
   Compound Subjects Joined by *And* 105
   Compound Subjects Joined by *Or,*
   Nor, or *Either-Or, Neither-Nor* ... 105
   Subjects with Phrases 105
   Indefinite Pronouns Used as
   Subjects 106
   Collective Noun Subjects 107
   There Is, There Are 108
   Inverted Order 108
   Relative Pronouns as Subjects 108
      Exercise: Subject–Verb Agreement 109
   Tense Shift 110
      Exercise: Tense Shift 110

Writing Assignment I 111
   A Sample Theme: "Fear of Death" 111
   Questions for Discussion: "Fear of
   Death" 112
   Questions to Answer before
   Submitting Your Theme 114
Writing Assignment II 114
Writing Assignment III 115
Writing Assignment IV 116
A Final Word 117

The Bridge
Chapter 5

CLARIFYING AND STIMULATING THOUGHT: Persuasive Writing

CLARIFYING AND STIMULATING
THOUGHT: Persuasive Writing 121
Reading Selection: "How to Say
Nothing in Five Hundred Words" 122
   Vocabulary List: "How to Say
   Nothing in Five Hundred
   Words" 124
   Questions for Discussion: "How to
   Say Nothing in Five Hundred
   Words" 125
Reading Selection: "Strike Out Little
League" 126
   Vocabulary List: "Strike Out Little
   League" 128
   Questions for Discussion: "Strike
   Out Little League" 128
Reading Selection: "Away with Big-
Time Athletics" 130
   Vocabulary List: "Away with Big-
   Time Athletics" 133
   Questions for Discussion: "Away
   with Big-Time Athletics" 134
Getting Ready: Gathering Support 135
Tips for Handling the Persuasive
Theme 136
      Exercise: Tips for Handling the
      Persuasive Theme 139
Writing Strategies 141
Grammar and Usage 146
   Transitional Words and Word
   Groups 146
      Exercise: Transitions 149

A Word about Commas with
   Interrupters   **151**
      *Exercise: Commas with
         Interrupters*   **152**
Writing Assignment I   **153**
   A Sample Theme: "Give Me the
      Home Life"   **153**
   Questions for Discussion: "Give
      Me the Home Life"   **154**
   Questions to Answer before
      Submitting Your Theme   **156**
Writing Assignment II   **156**
Writing Assignment III   **157**
A Final Word   **157**

A Word about Commas and
   Introductory Phrases   **181**
      *Exercise: Commas with
         Introductory Phrases and
         Relative Clauses*   **181**
A Word about the Colon, Dash,
   and Parentheses   **182**
The Colon   **182**
The Dash   **183**
Parentheses   **183**
      *Exercise: Commas, Semicolons,
         Colons, Dashes, and
         Parentheses*   **184**
**Reading Selection: "How TV
Violence Damages Your Children"**   **184**
Writing Assignment I   **190**
   Questions to Answer before
      Submitting an Essay Exam   **190**
Writing Assignment II   **191**
A Final Word   **191**

The Outer World

Chapter 6

WORKING AGAINST THE CLOCK:
Writing Essay Examination Answers
and In-Class Themes

                                        161

**Reading Selection: "Rah! Rah!
SELL! SELL!"**   **161**
   Vocabulary List: "Rah! Rah!
      SELL! SELL!   **163**
**Getting Ready: Pretend You Are
the Instructor**   **164**
**Tips for Handling the Essay
Examination**   **164**
      *Exercise: Two Essay Exam
         Answers to Study*   **168**
**Becoming Proficient at Writing Essay
Examination Answers**   **171**
**Eight Steps for Writing the In-Class
Theme**   **171**
Practicing the In-Class Theme   **173**
Grammar and Usage   **174**
   Coordination   **174**
      Exercise: Coordination   **176**
   Subordination   **176**
      Exercise: Subordination   **178**
   Relative Clauses   **179**
   A Word about Commas and
      Relative Clauses   **180**
      *Exercise: Commas and
         Relative Clauses*   **180**

Chapter 7

COMMUNICATING EFFECTIVELY:
Writing for Your Audience

                                        192

**Reading Selection: From *The
Autobiography of Malcolm X***   **193**
   Vocabulary List: From *The
      Autobiography of Malcolm X*   **195**
   Questions for Discussion: From
      The Autobiography of Malcolm X **195**
**Getting Ready: Improving
Communication in One Situation**   **197**
**Getting Ready: Improving
Communication with Those
Closest to Us**   **198**
Audience   **199**
   Sample Paragraphs: "Never Ride
      with Strangers"   **199**
   Questions for Discussion: "Never
      Ride with Strangers"   **200**
      *Exercise: The Message Sent and
         the Message Received*   **201**
Grammar and Usage   **204**
   Building Your Vocabulary   **204**
   Agreement of Pronouns and
      Referents in Number   **206**
      Exercise: Choosing Pronouns   **207**

Agreement of Pronouns and
Referents in Person 208
Exercise: Choosing Pronouns 209
Other Pronoun Problems:
Ambiguous Reference, Remote
Reference, and Implied
Reference 210
*Exercise: Ambiguous, Implied,
and Remote Reference* 211
Dangling and Misplaced Modifiers 212
*Exercise: Dangling and
Misplaced Modifiers* 213
Sentence Variety 214
Exercise: Sentence Variety 216
A Word about the Apostrophe 217
Exercise: The Apostrophe 219
Writing Assignment I 219
Questions to Answer before
Submitting Your Theme 220
Writing Assignment II 221
Three Sample Letters 222
Questions for Discussion:
Three Sample Letters 224
Writing Assignment III 226
Writing Assignment IV 226
A Final Word 227

Chapter 8

UNDERSTANDING OTHERS: Writing about People

228

Reading Selection: "Birthday Party" 229
Vocabulary List: "Birthday Party" 230
Questions for Discussion:
"Birthday Party" 230
Reading Selection: "The Monster" 231
Vocabulary List: "The Monster" 234
Questions for Discussion:
"The Monster" 235
Getting Ready: Role Playing 236
Getting Ready: Trying to Understand 237
Grammar and Usage 239
Parallelism 239
Parallelism: Items in a Series 239
Parallelism: Items Compared or
Contrasted 240
Exercise: Parallelism 242
A Word about Commas in a Series 243

A Word about Commas for Clarity 244
A Word about Commas for
Emphasis or Contrast 244
Exercise: The Comma 245
Writing Assignment I 245
Questions to Answer before
Submitting Your Theme 246
Writing Assignment II 247
Sample Theme: Role Playing 247
Writing Assignment III 249
Writing Assignment IV 250
Writing Assignment V 250
A Final Word 252

Chapter 9

INFORMING AND BECOMING INFORMED: Writing and Research

253

**Reading Selection: "Should Instant
Replay Cameras Aid in Officiating
Football Games?"** 254
Vocabulary List: "Should Instant
Replay Cameras Aid in
Officiating Football Games?" 259
Questions for Discussion: "Should
Instant Replay Cameras Aid in
Officiating Football Games?" 259
Getting Ready: Choosing a Topic 261
**The Research Paper: Ten Steps to
Follow When Writing a Research
Paper** 262
Exercise: Narrowing the Topic 265
Progress Check: Narrowing the
Topic 266
Progress Check: The Working
Bibliography 267
Progress Check: The Preliminary
Outline 268
Paraphrasing 269
Quoting 269
*Exercise: Paraphrasing and
Quoting* 271
Progress Check: Note Taking 273
Progress Check: The Final Outline 273
**What to Notice about a Theme Using
Research Material** 277
The Six Sins of Research Writing 282

Questions to Answer before
Submitting Your Theme   **282**
Using Research Material   **282**
A Final Word   **282**

Chapter 10

GETTING AND KEEPING A JOB:
Writing at Work   **284**

**Getting Ready: How Much Writing
Will You Have to Do?**   **284**
**Reading Selection: "How to Write a
Letter That Will Get You a Job"**   **286**
Vocabulary List: "How to Write a
Letter That Will Get You a Job"   **289**
Questions for Discussion: "How to
Write a Letter That Will Get
You a Job"   **289**
Writing Assignment I   **290**
**The Role of Grammar and Usage in
Business Writing**   **290**
Frequently Confused Words   **291**
*Exercise: Frequently Confused
Words*   **296**
The Letter of Application   **297**
A Sample Application Letter   **297**
Résumés   **299**
A Sample Résumé   **299**
Writing Assignment II   **301**
Business Letters   **303**
A Business Letter and Envelope   **302**
About the Heading   **303**
About the Inside Address   **304**
About the Salutation   **304**
About the Body   **304**
About the Closing   **304**
About the Signature   **305**
About the Envelope   **305**
Writing Assignment III   **305**
Committee Reports   **306**
Formal Reports   **307**
*Exercise: Informational and
Analytical Reports*   **308**

A Sample Formal Report   **308**
Writing Assignment IV   **310**
A Final Word   **310**

APPENDIXES

A   Vocabulary List   **311**
**B   Proofreading, Revising, and
Editing Checklist**   **314**
Revising: Organization   **314**
Revising: Content   **315**
Editing: Style   **315**
Proofreading: Grammar and
Usage   **316**
**C   A Selected List of General
Reference Works**   **317**
**D   A Selected List of Bibliographies
and Indexes**   **319**
E   How to Make Bibliography Cards   **332**
Sample Bibliography Forms for
Books   **333**
Sample Bibliography Forms for
Periodicals   **335**
**F   How to Write Footnotes and
End Notes**   **337**
Sample Note Forms: Books   **338**
Sample Note Forms: Periodicals   **339**
**G   Sample End Note and
Bibliography Pages**   **341**
H   Additional Exercises   **346**
Sentence Fragments   **346**
Run-On Sentences   **349**
Subject-Verb Agreement   **351**
Tense Shift   **352**
Transitions   **354**
Coordination   **356**
Subordination   **358**
Pronouns and Referents   **361**
Dangling and Misplaced Modifiers   **362**
Parallelism   **364**
Acknowledgments   **367**
Index   **369**

Preface

Several years ago a student in one of my composition classes raised his hand and asked a question. Why, he demanded to know, did he have to take a writing course? He already knew (he was sure) that he could write well enough to survive college and handle any routine writing tasks that might come up on the job. So he needed an explanation: Why did he have to spend his time, energy, and money in my class learning to do better what he could already do adequately?

Well the question surprised me, not because it was bold or impertinent or facetious—for it was none of these. The question surprised me because it had never come up before. No one had ever asked me why it is important to write. Yet it is a valid question. Surely students *should* understand why writing and writing courses are valuable.

It was at the moment the student asked his question that the idea for this book came to me. It was then I realized that while many texts do a fine job of teaching students *how* to write, few texts explain why students *should* write. This book does both. It treats the writing principles traditionally within the realm of freshman composition and also explains the real usefulness of writing.

To do this, I have set up each chapter so that it focuses on at least one reason for writing. This reason for writing provides the touchstone for the chapter, so students learn how to incorporate writing into their lives on a regular basis to do such things as achieve insight, solve problems, and understand people and influences in their lives. However, students are also required to write papers that respect the traditional conventions, and they are instructed in how to do this.

The teacher's manual that accompanies this text details its distinguishing characteristics. There are three characteristics, however, that I would like to mention here. First, every effort was made to ensure that the writing tasks move progressively from the less complex to the more complex. Thus, students begin with list writing, move to paragraph writing, and then on to theme writing. Second, I have worked to integrate grammar and usage explanations so that these discussions are logically placed. For example, run-on sentences are explained in the chapter that demonstrates how writing can clear up confusion. This is logical because run-on sentences can be a source of confusion. I believe that when students see how grammar and usage relate to specific writing tasks, the points are more readily learned, so whenever possible, I explain grammar and usage where they emerge naturally from a required writing task or from a reason for writing under consideration. Third, the organization principle for the chapters is the movement from the inner world to the outer world, thereby reflecting the fact that writing tasks move from the introspective and experiential to the more outer-directed and objective.

As you use this text, you will probably discover things you like and areas that could be strengthened. Please write to me with your reactions and suggestions. I will be most interested in and grateful for your comments.

There are many who have helped and encouraged me along the way. Mary Louise Quisenberry typed and proofread the manuscript with great care and concern. Her editing suggestions were always astute, and her understanding of this project made her an invaluable sounding board. I am most grateful to Barbara Brothers, Chairman of the Youngstown State University English Department, who not only encouraged me, but made available the resources of the department. To Gratia Murphy, Coordinator of Composition at Y.S.U., I owe much. Her ideas about writing instruction have influenced me and this book in large measure. So many of the English faculty at Y.S.U. have helped me. Joy DeSalvo and Barbara Flinn tested some of the material in their classrooms and helped me get the bugs out. Their help was essential. John Lough, Stephen Sniderman, James Henke, Richard Shale, John Mason, and Bonnie Huffman were always there for me and enormously supportive.

I owe a special thanks to June Siegel of New York City Community College, Thomas Miles of West Virginia University, and Larry McDoniel of St. Louis Community College at Meramec. They studied the manuscript carefully in its various stages, provided many helpful suggestions, and when necessary guided me back on course. I thank them along with Jay Balderson of Western Illinois University, Kenneth Krauss of John Jay College of Criminal Justice, Janet McReynolds of Southern Illinois University at Edwardsville, Mark Rollins of Ohio University, and Dale Ross of Iowa State University. And, of course, I am grateful to my students, whose contributions to this book go beyond the writing samples all the way to inspiration.

I must also say thank you to my parents, for it was they who instilled in me the love of learning.

Finally, to my husband, Denny, I owe the most because he cleared away all the obstacles. Without his support, interest, help, and understanding I could not have written this book.

Barbara Fine Clouse

Writing
From Inner World
to Outer World

The Inner World

Chapter **1**

Getting Started:

Ideas about Writing and Ideas for Writing

If you think writing is a skill you need in order to succeed in college, you're right. If you think writing is a skill you need in order to perform well on the job, you're right again. However, if you think writing is important and useful only at school and work, you're wrong. Writing is a skill that can help you in many areas of your life. That's one thing this book will show you. There are chapters here to demonstrate that writing can help you solve problems, work through confusion, come up with new ideas, and observe more of the world. There are chapters to show you how writing can help you understand people better and communicate more clearly. And yes, there are chapters to show you how to use writing to succeed in school and on the job.

But this book does more than explain how you can use writing in different areas of your life. It also explains what you should do in order to write well. You will learn all the points about grammar, usage, and organization you need in order to construct a piece of writing you can feel proud of. In addition, you will learn ways to approach your writing and develop ideas so you can proceed in an orderly fashion.

Perhaps you are a student who enjoys writing. If so, this book will help you sharpen your skills and discover many uses for writing so you can enjoy it even more. Perhaps you are a student who is uncomfortable writing because you never understood writing principles. If so, this book will help you master the points you need so you can come to feel confident in your ability to write. No matter what kind of writer you are now, and no matter how you feel about writing, this book will help you learn to write better, at the same time it explains why you should.

3

IDEAS ABOUT WRITING

Over the years I've come to understand a few things about learning how to write and taking a writing course. I call these understandings my "ideas about writing," and I'd like to share them with you so you can approach your learning with the proper awareness.

Idea 1. A writing class is different from many other classes.   You see, when you learn how to write, you are learning a skill. This means you are learning how to do something just as if you were learning how to play the piano, shoot par golf, or cook Greek dishes. In many other classes, such as history and psychology, you are not asked to learn a skill; instead, you are asked to learn the content of books and lectures and take tests that show whether you have remembered the material. A writing class is a *skill* course because you must learn to do something. Many other classes are *content* courses because you are asked to remember things.

Idea 2. It takes time to learn any skill, including writing.   Try to remember that slow, steady progress must be your goal. It is most unlikely that your improvement will be dramatic and sudden. After all, you can't learn how to play the piano after one or two lessons and a few hours of practice. The same is true for becoming a skilled writer. It takes time because the process is gradual. If you try to make each piece of writing you do just a bit better than the one that came before, you will accomplish your goal, one step at a time. If you expect overnight results, then you are sure to be disappointed.

Idea 3. A person learning to write must expect to make mistakes.   We all make mistakes. Even when we know how to do something well and we've been doing it for a long time, we still make mistakes once in a while. Even professional writers make mistakes. What you must remember is that mistakes have their good side because we can learn from them. Each time you make a mistake, you should study it until you understand it and learn how to overcome it. In that way your mistakes can be part of the learning process. If you can learn from an error so you do not repeat it, you have turned that error to your advantage. You have learned something. Remember, you are expected to make mistakes because you are learning—not to mention the fact that you are human.

Idea 4. Sometimes, as fast as a person learns to correct some mistakes, new ones come along to take their place.   This is a normal part of learning a skill, so don't be discouraged if it happens to you. As you progress, you will be learning more things, so naturally there will be more that can go wrong. However, if you tackle your problem areas one at a time, eventually you will get to the point where most of your mistakes are out of the way, and your writing is relatively error-free.

Idea 5. Writing is hard work.   If you ever feel you're the only one who struggles with a writing task, let me tell you that nothing could be farther from the truth. Writing is *not* easy. Everyone—even the professional writer—strains and sweats over the page from time to time. Sure there are some who have an easier time than others, but the writing process is complex, and often difficult. Keep in mind that the successful writer is not the person who writes *easily;* the successful writer is the one who writes *well.* And writing well is frequently tough work. I wish you could have seen me struggling with the words in this book; then you would realize writing isn't always easy. But I have found that all the hard work is worthwhile, and I'm sure you will come to feel the same way. One other thing: Usually when people say they find writing easy, it means that they aren't doing a very good job of it. There's just no getting around the fact that writing well is often hard work. There is good news, however. As you get more experience and practice, you will discover that not only are you getting better, but writing is getting easier.

Idea 6. Students who have had writing problems in the past should not feel discouraged.   It's time to forget the past because this is a whole new beginning, a chance to learn the things you didn't know before. After all, if you already knew everything there was to know about writing, you wouldn't need this course, and you'd be wasting your time and money by taking it. Don't spend your energy feeling bad if you have had trouble with writing; instead, feel optimistic and determined because now you will learn the skills you need.

Idea 7. Learning to write has its ups and downs.   As you work and learn, there will be many times when you will feel good about your progress. You will recognize that you are learning and improving, and this will give you satisfaction. But I must be honest with you. There will also be moments when things won't go as well as you would like. At these times you may feel a bit discouraged or frustrated, but this is quite normal. So if you hit a low point, don't feel alone. Even experienced writers have their discouraging or frustrating moments. However, if frustration mounts too high, it can interfere with the learning process. If this happens to you, talk to your instructor. Let your teacher help ease you up from this low spot so you can go forward.

Idea 8. Getting a graded paper back should be a learning experience.   To make it a learning experience, I suggest you take time to reread your work and read your instructor's comments. Then make sure that you understand everything your teacher has written and make sure that you agree with everything he or she has written. Also, be sure that you know how to correct any weaknesses that are noted and be sure that you know how to repeat any strengths that are noted in future writings. If you don't understand a comment, don't agree with a comment, or don't know how to correct a weakness or repeat a strength, you should ask questions until you do understand. Only in this way can you profit from the evaluation of your work and go on to improve. It is also a good idea to keep a list of the mistakes you make so you have an idea of your problem areas. In that way, when you write, you can pay special attention to your particular weaknesses.

WRITE WHAT YOU THINK

Very often students make two serious mistakes when they are faced with a writing assignment. First, they believe they are better off if they try to figure out what the instructor wants to hear and then try to deliver that. Well, I'd like to clear up that mistaken idea right away. Your teachers are not the least bit interested in reading what *you* think they want. But your teachers are most anxious to learn what *your* ideas are.

The second mistake students make is believing that they don't have anything worthwhile to say. That's just not so. You are an interesting person with interesting experiences and ideas. Your thoughts are important and worth being written about. That's one reason writing teachers like their work: Each time they read a set of papers, they are exposed to the thoughts, feelings, and experiences of many different, interesting people. So don't disappoint your teacher; write what *you* think.

DISCOVERING IDEAS

Often students believe that when they have a writing assignment, all the ideas they need should somehow jump magically into their brains. I'm afraid it doesn't work that way. If you're lucky, one or two ideas may occur to you right away. But it's also possible to draw a blank and not be able to think of anything to say.

Fortunately, there are things writers can do to stimulate their thinking and come up with ideas. These ways of discovering ideas are called *prewriting*. Below are explanations of some common prewriting activities. You should always try one or more of these activities as the first step of any writing assignment. Many of them are explained throughout this book, but they are grouped together here for easy reference.

Freewriting

Freewriting is timed writing. You sit down for a period of time, perhaps fifteen minutes, and write on a subject. You do not stop writing for any reason. You don't even pause. As you write, do not try to decide if your ideas are good or not. Also, do not worry about spelling, grammar, punctuation, organization, or neatness. Just put down in any way you can every idea that occurs to you. If you run out of ideas, write anything: famous sayings, the alphabet, names of your family members—anything. After a while, new ideas will come to you, and you can put them down. After several minutes of freewriting (I've found fifteen minutes to work well), I'm sure you will discover you have written at least one idea that you can refine and develop for your theme. Below is an example of freewriting done for a theme about the advantages of college life. The underlined ideas are the ones the student felt could be developed and used in the theme.

Free Writing

Subject, the advantages of college life. I don't have to do work from 7:00 till 9:00 or all day as a bricklayer. Now I use my head instead of my back ABCDEF I like the freedom of being on my own. I meet all kinds of new people and new Ideas of people ABCDEFGHIJKLMNOPQRSTUVW My parents are pleased about me going to school. While I go to skool I can look forward to the proffesion I want to do. There are so many new experiences. My teachers are all good. I like the challenge of some of the classes I hope I make it. I'm stuck. I'm stuck. What should I say? OH Help. I'm more close to my girlfriend because she goes to college. I am the first one out of my family to go to college. I like the building ABCDDEFGHI I like the freedom the teachers give you. And how they don't care what you do not like stupid high school I like all the time I get to do my homework. I like the simple fact that school is relaxing compared to bricklaying and I can relase and not work as hard I don't know what to write anymore. I'm cold. I'm tired. ABC—123—Do re mi—I like BS'n with mister Gross and I like learning about health and things about the body and jerms with Mrs. Sabo I like getting good grades on my english papers in english because I never did good in english because I couldn't sple opps—spell. Now my mind is woundering agian I want to go skiing in Colorado again I love it out there I'm going to move out there. Before I got on that plane to go home I said, "I'm going to come back someday. I like the ski club up at college. Next year I'm going to join and I'm going to do a lot of activities next year.

Notice that when the student did his freewriting, he did not concern himself with grammar, usage, spelling, or punctuation. Also notice that when he ran out of ideas, he wrote whatever came into his mind until new ideas on the subject occurred to him. Still, the student was able to come up with several ideas that could be included in his theme.

What did the student do with these ideas? Well, first he decided which ones to include in his writing. He decided to have one paragraph on not having to do physical labor, one paragraph on the challenge of college, and one paragraph on being close to his girlfriend. Then he did three more freewritings, one on each paragraph subject. These additional freewritings gave the student most of the ideas he needed to complete his theme.

Answering Questions

Very often you can discover ideas by asking yourself the right questions and then putting the answers in writing. The answers may well contain ideas you can shape and develop in your theme. Below is a list of questions you might try answering. Not all the questions will be useful for a particular assignment, so you will have to decide which questions should be answered.

What happened?

When did it happen?

Why did it happen?

How did it happen?

To whom did it happen?

Who did it? (Who is responsible?)

Why did that person do it?

What was the result?

Where did it happen?

How did people feel?

How long did it take?

Could it happen again?

What did it look (sound, smell, feel, taste) like?

How do you know?

What is your reaction to it?

What kind of person was involved?

What does it mean?

What are the good points?

What are the bad points?

What other things is it like?

What other things is it different from?

How is it made?

How is it used?

How is it done?

What are its parts?

What happened first (second, third)?

Why is it important?

What if it hadn't happened?

What if it didn't exist?

Below is a list of questions that have been answered to stimulate ideas for a theme about a problem experienced in college.

What happened?
    I couldn't find my 8:00 o'clock physics class.

When did it happen?
    The first day of classes at 8:00 A.M.

Why did it happen?
    The room was changed and I was not notified.

Who is responsible?
    The university, because it didn't send me a letter about the change.

Why did the university do it?
    It didn't get my name on the class list in time because I registered late.

What was the result?
    I was embarrassed and made to feel bad because I was half an hour late to class.

How did people feel?
    The instructor thought I was unreliable and uninterested because I was late. He told me to be careful in the future because he didn't like being distracted by people coming in late.

Could it happen again?
    Yes, if the university makes the same mistake.

What was my reaction?
    Embarrassment and anger.

What does it mean?
    The university isn't as organized as it should be.

Why is this important?
    A student shouldn't be hassled and made to look bad because the university can't get its act together.

What if it hadn't happened?
    I would have been on time and I wouldn't have had to spend the rest of the term trying to improve the first impression I made on my instructor.

The question–answer technique can often be combined successfully with freewriting. Many writers like to do freewriting and then answer questions on some of the ideas their freewriting produced.

Listing

Another useful prewriting activity is listing. To do this you list the main ideas you have on a subject. Below is a list of main ideas for a theme about how college is different from high school.

More freedom in college

More work in college

More problems in college

More fun in college

After you have your list of ideas, do some more listing. This time, though, list the subpoints that come to mind for each of the main ideas in your first list. If you have four major points in the first list, you would go on to write four more lists. Five main points in the first list would mean five more lists, and so on. The next set of lists might look something like this:

More Freedom in College
To cut classes
To select courses
To select instructors
To decide when to take classes

More Work in College
Instructors expect better work
Instructors assign more homework
The material is harder to learn

More Problems in College
Budgeting time
Getting tuition and book money
Adjusting to being away from family and friends
Making friends
Staying on top of the work
Doing for myself what my parents used to do for me

More Fun in College
Football games
Fraternity and sorority parties
Dorm get-togethers
Intramural basketball

After listing the ideas under your major points, you will have quite a few ideas that can be developed in a theme. You may decide to use all of them or only some of them. You may also decide to freewrite on some of the ideas in your list or answer questions about them. Perhaps you will want to do both.

Letter Writing

Sometimes it is useful to pretend you are writing a letter to a friend on the subject of your theme. Let's say, for example, that you must write a theme about how you feel about college life, and you are having trouble coming up with ideas. Try writing a letter to someone you know well and tell that person how you feel about college life. Because you may be more relaxed writing to a friend than for an instructor, the ideas may come more easily. Then take the ideas from the letter and develop them in your theme. Below is a "letter" written to a friend on the theme subject of the advantages of joining a sorority.

Dear Maggie,

I wanted to let you know how things are going for me. I love school, mostly because of the sorority I joined. The girls are fantastic. They're all friendly and willing to help. You can't imagine what a great feeling it is to walk across campus and see so many people to say hi to. I really felt lonely before I joined because I didn't know anyone. Now I know so many super people. I've met a lot more guys, too, through the sorority. We're always having mixers with the fraternities. The guys are pretty sharp.

The sorority does a lot of community service work that we're proud of. We raised $500 for the Heart Association, and now we're working to collect enough money for a seeing-eye dog for the Society for the Blind. We help the university too by working at freshman orientation to help the new students.

I guess the best part, though, is the feeling of closeness and belonging I get. It's so great to know that there are forty other people who care about me and will help me if I need it. If you get the chance, Maggie, try to join a sorority.

Love,
Sue

If Sue were to go back over her letter to Maggie, she would find several ideas that she could shape and develop to include in a theme about the advantages of joining a sorority. She may even want to freewrite on those ideas, answer questions, or do some listing.

Keeping a Journal

Journal writing can be an interesting and rewarding experience. Each day you take some time to record in a notebook your thoughts and feelings about anything significant you observed or were involved in that day. A journal doesn't tell so much *what* happened as it explains how you felt about or reacted to what happened. You can write about something that troubled, pleased, angered, or amused you. A journal has many uses. For one, it can come in handy when you need ideas for a theme; you can look through your journal for ideas to include in your writing.

Talking to Others

When you are trying to think of ideas, it can be helpful to talk to other people and find out what they think. The ideas of others can often trigger your own thinking on a subject. Of course, you do not want your writing to include only what other people think. Instead, you want to use other people's thoughts as a starting point—something that motivates you to come up with ideas. This technique can be particularly effective when combined with one of the other prewriting activities.

Using a Tape Recorder

Speaking is easier than writing. For this reason, you may find it easier to come up with ideas if you speak your thoughts into a tape recorder rather than write them down. If you try this, just begin talking and follow the freewriting technique. When you run out of ideas, say anything until new thoughts put you back on the track. Play back the tape and write down the ideas you hear that sound like ones that can be developed in writing. Once again, this is an activity that can be combined successfully with one of the other prewriting techniques.

A FINAL WORD

Writing isn't easy, and there may be times when you feel a bit frustrated. But as you learn, you will find that the writing process does become easier. Each mistake you overcome, each idea you discover and develop, will reward you with a sense of accomplishment and pride that can only come from knowing that you are getting better. It will take some time and practice, but one step at a time, you will grow to be a better writer than you have ever been before. And just as this chapter suggested ways to discover ideas to write about, the rest of this book will help you discover how to write those ideas effectively.

Chapter 2

Observing More Closely:
Descriptive Writing

This is a book about writing. It's a book about *how* to write and it's a book about why you *should* write. You will find that each chapter has two purposes—to explain what to do in order to write well and to explain some important ways you can use writing both in and out of the classroom.

This chapter is about descriptive writing—how to do it and why it's worthwhile. Let's start with why it's worthwhile. Descriptive writing can help us to become more aware of our surroundings by sharpening our powers of observation. Let's face it; the world we live in is often hectic. The frantic pace that forms so much of our routine makes it seem impossible to linger over sights and sounds, to enjoy them. As students, you find yourselves crossing campus frequently. But your attention may be on making it to class on time or on tomorrow's midterm exams, so you don't notice many of the interesting things along the way.

And how quickly our routines numb us to our surroundings. We may pass a certain way so often that we no longer notice what's around us—"looking but not seeing" we often call it. How many times have you been somewhere you visit often, pulled up short, and said, "I've never noticed that before. Has it always been there?" Yes, it has. You were just too rushed or too numb to your surroundings to be a careful observer.

But what a shame it is to be in the middle of so much that can stimulate and excite you and miss so much of it. Yet that can be changed, and writing can help. The next pages will demonstrate that descriptive writing is valuable because it can teach you to observe more carefully and thus improve the quality of your life by making you more aware.

READING SELECTION:
"Central Park"

As a first step to learning to be a better observer, read the following piece by John Updike.

Central Park

On the afternoon of the first day of spring, when the gutters were still heaped high with Monday's snow but the sky itself was swept clean, we put on our galoshes and walked up the sunny side of Fifth Avenue to Central Park. There we saw:

Great black rocks emerging from the melting drifts, their craggy skins glistening like the backs of resurrected brontosaurs.

A pigeon on the half-frozen pond strutting to the edge of the ice and looking a duck in the face.

A policeman getting his shoe wet testing the ice.

Three elderly relatives trying to coax a little boy to accompany his father on a sled ride down a short but steep slope. After much balking, the boy did, and, sure enough, the sled tipped over and the father got his collar full of snow. Everybody laughed except the boy, who sniffled.

Four boys in black leather jackets throwing snowballs at each other. (The snow was ideally soggy, and packed hard with one squeeze.)

Seven men without hats.

Twelve snowmen, none of them intact.

Two men listening to the radio in a car parked outside the Zoo; Mel Allen was broadcasting the Yanks–Cardinals game from St. Petersburg.

A tahr (Hemigragus memiacus) pleasantly squinting in the sunlight.

A yak with its back turned.

Empty cages labelled "Coati," "Orang-outang," and "Ocelot."

A father saying to his little boy, who was annoyed almost to tears by the inactivity of the seals, "Father (Father Seal, we assumed) is very tired; he worked hard all day."

Most of the cafeteria's out-of-doors tables occupied.

A pretty girl in black pants falling on them at the Wollman Memorial Rink.

"BILL AND DORIS" carved on a tree. "REX AND RITA" written in the snow.

Two old men playing, and six supervising, a checkers game.

The Michael Friedsam Foundation Merry-go-round, nearly empty of children but overflowing with calliope music.

A man on a bench near the carrousel reading, through sunglasses, a book on economics.

Crews of shinglers repairing the roof of the Tavern-on-the-Green.

A woman dropping a camera she was trying to load, the film unrolling in the slush and exposing itself.

A little boy in aviator goggles rubbing his ears and saying, "He really hurt me." "No, he didn't," his nursemaid told him.

The green head of Giuseppe Mazzini staring across the white softball field, unblinking, though the sun was in its eyes.

Water murmuring down walks and rocks

and steps. A grown man trying to block one rivulet with snow.

Things like brown sticks nosing through a plot of cleared soil.

A tire track in a piece of mud far removed from where any automobiles could be.

Footprints around a KEEP OFF sign.

Two pigeons feeding each other.

Two showgirls, whose faces had not yet thawed the frost of their makeup, treading indignantly through the slush.

A plump old man saying, "Chick, chick," and feeding peanuts to squirrels.

Many solitary men throwing snowballs at tree trunks.

Many birds calling to each other.

One red mitten lying lost under a poplar tree.

An airplane, very bright and distant, slowly moving through the branches of a sycamore.

Vocabulary Building:
"Central Park"

There are two chief reasons for working to build your vocabulary. First, you cannot fully appreciate and enjoy a piece such as "Central Park" if you do not know the meanings of all the words you read. Second, when you build your vocabulary, you increase the storehouse of words available to you as you write and speak. This will make both writing and speaking more satisfying to you because you will be able to express exactly what you mean better. After all, it is *words* that convey ideas. So the more words you know, the more ideas you can express.

Happily, it is not hard to increase your vocabulary. But is does involve a degree of patience and dedication. It involves looking up the words you're unsure of in a dictionary and making an honest effort to use those words over and over again until they become a natural part of your word storehouse.

So let's begin right away. In the spaces provided below, list all the words from "Central Park" that you cannot define. Then check a dictionary and write a brief definition next to each word. Of course, most words have several definitions. But you need only write the meaning that you think is the one used in "Central Park." Next, reread the piece and notice how much more you understand it and enjoy it once you know all the words.

Finally, select two of the new words on your list that you think you can use comfortably in your speech and writing. Write these in the vocabulary building list in Appendix A. Each day or two, review this list and make an effort to use the words you find there in your speech and writing.

Vocabulary List:
"Central Park"

(Example) emerging—rising _____ _____

_____ _____

_____   _____
_____   _____
_____   _____
_____   _____

Questions for Discussion:
"Central Park"

The following questions about "Central Park" are meant to point out some things about descriptive writing. You can write your answers in the spaces provided.

1. Which of Updike's descriptions do you like best? Why?

_____

_____

_____

_____

_____

2. So often Updike uses simple vocabulary, the kinds of words we may use every day. Yet he achieves a certain vividness because the simple words he uses are so precise (exact). Notice, for example, the expressiveness of the simple word "nosing" in "Things like brown sticks nosing through a plot of cleared soil." What other words strike you as being simple yet precise and expressive?

_____   _____

_____   _____

_____   _____

3. A *modifier* is a descriptive word or word group. Sometimes when people write descriptions, they think they must heap modifier upon modifier to make the point. The effect is not always satisfactory; it can result in something like this:

The light-green, four-door, chrome-trimmed, Cadillac with spacious, plush, dark-green fabric interior.

Notice that Updike avoids this kind of stringiness. Instead of stringing many modifiers together, he often writes something like this:

Twelve snowmen, none of them intact.

What other phrases like this can you find, and what makes them interesting descriptions?

_____

_____

_____

_____

_____

4. When Updike does use more modifiers, he does so effectively. This is because he chooses the perfect descriptive words, words that are precise. Examine the first piece of description in the list. What are the descriptive words or modifiers? Why do they work so well?

_____

_____

_____

_____

_____

5. An *image* is a mental picture, something seen, heard, felt, tasted, or smelled in the mind. When Updike compares the "great black rocks" to brontosaurs, he creates for us a mental image, a picture in our minds of what the rocks looked like. In the spaces provided, describe a bit of the mental image you get from the descriptions that follow.

a. "A policeman getting his shoe wet testing the ice."

_____

_____

_____

b. "The snow was ideally soggy, and packed hard with one squeeze."

_____

_____

_____

c. "Two old men playing, and six supervising, a checkers game."

_____

_____

_____

d. "Two pigeons feeding each other."

_____

_____

_____

6. When Updike refers to the statue of Mazzini "staring," he is using a technique called *personification*—giving living qualities to something not alive. A statue, in reality, cannot "stare." Only people and animals, which are alive, can do this. What other examples of personification do you find in this piece?

_____   _____

_____

7. Reread the introduction. Notice that Updike is writing about the first day of spring. Also notice that even though it is spring and sunny, galoshes (boots) are needed and snow is in the gutters. Many of Updike's descriptions are of snow and winter, and many are of thaw and spring. In column I, list the snow/winter descriptions. In column II, list the thaw/spring descriptions. If you wish, write only enough of each description to make it clear which one you are referring to.

I	II
1. _____	1. _____
_____	_____
2. _____	2. _____
_____	_____
3. _____	3. _____
_____	_____
4. _____	4. _____
_____	_____
5. _____	5. _____
_____	_____

6. _____   6. _____

  _____   _____

7. _____   7. _____

  _____   _____

8. _____   8. _____

  _____   _____

9. _____   9. _____

  _____   _____

10. _____   10. _____

  _____   _____

11. _____   11. _____

  _____   _____

12. _____   12. _____

  _____   _____

8. When writing description, a person cannot possibly record *everything* noticed. A writer must select certain details to include and leave out the rest. However, a careful writer has a *plan* for that selection. A careful writer selects details because they fulfill the plan. Take another look at your response to question 7 and then record below what you judge to be Updike's plan for his selection of detail.

_____

_____

_____

9. We become aware of our surroundings through our five senses— seeing, hearing, tasting, smelling, touching. Which of the five senses does Updike use? Are there any he could—or should—have used but did not?

_____

_____

THE DESCRIPTIVE WRITING PROCESS: THE NEED TO REVISE

You can't really expect that the first time you try to record an observation you will get it "just right"—get it down in a way that accurately reflects what you noticed. Just as with most any writing, descriptive writing will involve you in revision. (You can be sure that Updike did *his* share of revising too.) Often descriptive writing calls for a series of refinements. You will find yourself writing and rewriting, shaping phrases and changing words until you're satisfied that you have captured your observation in just the right way.

Furthermore, when you write descriptively, you will often want to record your reaction to or feeling about what you have observed. And this, too, will involve you in revision. Let's look at an example to illustrate this point about revision. At my home I can see a weeping willow tree from my living room window. My first effort to describe this tree might result in this:

a fat weeping willow with drooping branches

As I examine this description I want to revise it because the word *fat* doesn't express for me the "fullness" that I see. So I'll try again:

a lush weeping willow with drooping branches

There, that's better—but I'm still not satisfied. All weeping willows have drooping branches, so that last word group doesn't please me. I think I'd like to express the idea of "drooping branches" in a fresh way. Here goes:

a lush weeping willow with branches reaching mournfully to the grass below

I like it. It accurately reveals what I see from my window, and it has the advantage of expressing a mood—mournful. It took me three efforts and a fair amount of thought to arrive at a description that pleased me. It may take you that many tries too—or it could take you even more. But that's okay, because each time we revise, we must examine closely what we are observing. Each examination means another close observation, and each observation makes us ever more aware. And that's a good thing.

THE DESCRIPTIVE WRITING PROCESS: SELECTING DETAIL

There's one other thing to keep in mind when you write description: It is most unlikely that you will be able to or even want to describe *all* of what you notice. Certainly Updike made no effort to describe every detail of New York's Central Park. As a writer, Updike had a decision to make. He had to decide what to describe and what to leave out. So how did Updike make his decision? Well, he had a plan—a plan of selection. He planned to select details that contrasted the spring melting with what was left of winter's snow and ice (see questions 7 and 8 on pp. 18–19).

As a writer, you will face the very same decision Updike did. You, too, will need a plan for selecting detail. Such a plan will serve two purposes. The first purpose is practical. The plan will make your job as writer easier because it will determine what details you should include (the ones related to your plan). This, of course, gives you less material to deal with and makes your writing more manageable.

The second purpose is related to the fact that descriptive writing can improve the quality of your life by making you a better observer. When you write using a plan for detail selection, you must do more than just observe closely. You must also observe with an eye toward seeing how things relate to each other. You must look for patterns, for the common link among things. Otherwise you have just a random, disconnected list of observations. True, that isn't bad. But how much more interesting, even exciting, it is to notice connections. And when you do notice relationships, your observations have more meaning. This discovery of relationships helps us order our experiences and give them meaning.

THE DESCRIPTIVE WRITING PROCESS: MOOD AND EMOTION

A writer cannot describe everything, so a writer needs a plan for detail selection. Now let's be realistic. Updike is a talented professional writer. What makes him so good is that he can come up with a plan for detail selection as clever as contrasting spring thaw and winter chill. But we aren't all Updikes. If we were, we'd all be turning out publishable stuff like crazy. Yet even if the publishers aren't racing to our doors, we do still share with Updike the need for a plan for detail selection. What's the solution? It's focusing on a mood or emotion.

After careful observation, you may discover a plan for detail selection. Perhaps, like Updike, you will settle on contrast as a unifying relationship. Or perhaps you will find that certain details are related by patterns of growth, or shades of lighting, or stages of decay, or degrees of activity. Or you may not be able to find a single plan for detail selection such as these. If this is the case, don't worry. You can decide how you *feel* about what you are observing and let that feeling form your plan.

If what you are observing makes you depressed, let depression be your plan for detail selection and describe only those things that are depressing. Just be sure that your descriptions convey the sense of depression. The same holds true for any mood or emotion: cheerfulness, hostility, tension, optimism—whatever. Describe only the elements that convey the mood or emotion you have focused on, and write your descriptions in ways that convey that mood or emotion.

To understand the difference mood and emotion can make, examine the following two descriptions:

> As I entered the kitchen, the hearty aroma of steaming cabbage filled the air.
>
> As I entered the kitchen, the powerful stink of boiling cabbage overcame me.

In each description, the writer's attitude toward the smell of cooking cabbage is obvious. See the difference mood and emotion can make?

GETTING READY: DESCRIPTIVE WRITING PRACTICE

So far I've mentioned that descriptive writing is valuable because it helps us become more aware of what is around us. This increased awareness enriches our lives. I've also pointed out that descriptive writing involves us in a series of revisions, and this, too, improves our powers of observation. Furthermore, I have explained the need for a plan for detail selection in order to give both our observations and our writing an order and added meaning.

Now it's time to practice descriptive writing. As you do the exercises in this book, keep in mind that writing is a *skill*. Learning any skill takes practice. The exercises are meant to give you that practice so you can improve your writing. After all, you can't learn how to play tennis just reading a book on the subject. You must get on the court and practice. It's the same with writing—you must practice.

Descriptive Writing Practice A

As a class, go to some spot on campus, either indoors or out. Examine your surroundings; study closely what there is around you. Then write five descriptive phrases or sentences, drawing on a different sense for each one. Taste may be a bit tricky, but give it a try. (Perhaps you are chewing gum.) For now, it is not necessary to develop a plan for detail selection.

After everyone has completed a list, you should share your descriptions with each other. Talk about what has been written in terms of accuracy of description and precise (exact) word choice. (Remember how precise Updike is?) Applaud what pleases you and explain why you like what you do; suggest improvements where you note they are in order.

Remember, the goal here is to get some practice observing and recording. The exact words to convey what you notice will not necessarily come easily. You will have to do some fishing and some revising. But your search for the best words will lead you to closer examination of what is around you—and that is how writing helps you become a keener observer.

Descriptive Writing Practice B

Look again at the descriptive phrases or sentences you wrote for Practice A. Some or all of them may not satisfy you yet. They may not be as precise or as nicely stated as you would like. To give you some practice with revision, you should revise at least two of your phrases to make them more to your liking. You might want to consider some of the suggestions your classmates made.

Descriptive Writing Practice C

To understand the use of mood and emotion in descriptive writing, try this. Pair up with a classmate and go together to the same spot on campus. After observing for a time, each partner should write five descriptive phrases or sentences. However, one of you should convey liking the spot, and the other, disliking it. Next, return to class. Pairs should read their descriptions so everyone can discuss the difference mood and attitude can make.

Descriptive Writing Practice D

This writing practice is meant to give you some experience forming a plan for detail selection. Once again, go to some spot on campus. This time, try to select a place where there are many people who are doing things (the cafeteria, the library, a lounge, the admissions office). Observe for a while and decide on a plan for detail selection. Write out that plan (if necessary, it can be a mood, attitude, or emotion). Then write five descriptions, but make sure each of them is related to the plan.

Now here's something interesting to try. While at the same place, form a second, different plan for detail selection and write it down. Then write five different descriptions, making sure the descriptions fit the plan. You can describe the same things you did before but in a different way, or you can describe different things.

GRAMMAR AND USAGE

Whenever you write, you must select your words carefully for the effect they will produce in the mind of the reader. As the writer, you are in control. You have the power to choose words on the basis of the kind of impact you are after. Among other things, you should remember to use words economically, and choose specific words over general ones. Also, you should avoid clichés. These three points are explained below.

Economical Diction

Diction refers to word choice. Writers should avoid extra words, rarely using three words when two will do just as well. That is what *economical diction* means. Always give your readers the courtesy of acknowledging how valuable their time is by trimming word waste. Also, do not weaken the impact of your ideas by using extra words that do not add meaning. This will only detract from the quality of your thought by causing readers to grow annoyed at the unnecessary extras. An eye to economical diction should not discourage you from using modifiers, however. Just proofread your work carefully, looking for unnecessary words and ways to state your thoughts economically without disturbing style and flow.

Economical diction is a principle that applies to any writing, not just description. Therefore, you always want to weed out unnecessary words, regardless of the kind of writing you are doing. Why, then, do I bring up a discussion of economical diction now, when descriptive writing is the issue? For this reason: Although word choice is always important, at no time is it more critical than when you are writing descriptively. Consider "Central Park" once again. The wonderful mental pictures (see p. 17) that Updike creates are a direct result of his careful, always economical, word selection.

When the descriptive writing process was discussed, I mentioned the need for several revisions. It is while revising that you work to achieve economy; weeding out unnecessary words is one way you refine your writing. Thus, in the early stages of your writing, concentrate on getting everything down any way you can. Only later, when you revise to improve the effect of your words, do you trim away word waste. In this way, you need not think about too much all at once.

EXERCISE:
Economical Diction

To give yourself practice trimming excess words, revise the following sentences in the spaces provided.

Sample original: Freshman composition courses are designed to teach students how to write their thoughts down on paper better.

Sample revision: Freshman composition courses are designed to teach students to write better.

Explanation: "their thoughts down on paper" was eliminated because it is implied in the word *write*. Can we write anything that is not thought? Do we write "up?" Unless you like writing graffiti on public restroom walls, don't you usually write on paper? "How" was eliminated because it contributes no additional meaning to the sentence.

1. The audience watched with fascination as the magician made his lovely assistant disappear from view.

_____

_____

2. Anyone who attacks the mayor, who happens to be a personal friend of mine, will have me to deal with.

_____

_____

3. Until such time as she has her own income, Jan is forced to live with her parents.

_____

_____

4. In my opinion I think that in today's modern world it is very essential that all women are aware of the laws and legislation protecting their rights.

_____

_____

5. The reason why I was so angry is that Hank dented my car, a sporty Camaro that is blue in color.

_____

_____

6. Trembling, Kate entered the Dean's office and said, "The thing which I want to talk to you about is my grades."

_____

_____

7. The cafeteria, which is located in the student union building, serves an assorted variety of food at a moderate, reasonable price.

_____

_____

8. Whenever anyone, no matter who he was, needed extra help, he could count on Coach Tate to provide assistance and lend a helping hand with the troublesome problem.

_____

_____

9. Walter was asked to speak before the Lions Club on the extremely fascinating issue of whether or not instant voter registration is a good thing or a bad thing from the economic standpoint and the political standpoint.

_____

_____

10. It is my earnest desire and wish that all people will come to live in peace and that all people will respect each other, not only for their likenesses of many kinds but for all of their many differences as well.

_____

_____

Precise Diction

As you know, diction means word choice. _Precise diction_ refers to selecting exact words with very specific meanings. When examining "Central Park," I noted that Updike uses a simple vocabulary, but his vocabulary is quite expressive because it is so precise (see p. 16). I also pointed out that Updike creates clear mental images (see p. 17). He is able to do so _because_ his diction is so precise. Precise diction, therefore, is important when you are writing descriptively because it allows you to express yourself as exactly as possible in order to help your reader form a clear mental image.

In order to be precise, you will need to pass over vague, general words in favor of more precise, specific ones. Notice, for example, the following two sentences.

The car went down the street.

The bright yellow Corvette streaked down the narrow, tree-lined street.

The second sentence creates a clearer image because the general words _car_ and _went_ were replaced by the precise _Corvette_ and _streaked_. Also, the precise modifiers _bright, yellow, narrow,_ and _tree-lined_ help create more vividness.

I have one note of caution and one note of advice for you. I caution you to avoid stringing modifiers as you strive for precision (see pp. 16–17), and I advise you to get your descriptions down the best way you can at first. As you revise, you can reshape your descriptions to make them more precise. You would be unfair to yourself if you expected perfectly precise descriptions on the first try. Remember, even Updike must have revised before he was satisfied.

EXERCISE:
Precise Diction

Below is a list of general words. For each one supply more specific words to convey a more vivid mental image. Remember to avoid stringiness and revise until you are satisfied that you've done your best.

Sample general word: room

Sample specific phrase: the cheery, sun-filled kitchen with its delightful aroma of freshly baked bread

1. dog _____   2. basement _____

_____   _____

_____   _____

3. baby _____   4. book _____

_____   _____

_____   _____

5. water _____   6. candy _____

_____   _____

_____   _____

7. ring _____   8. flower _____

_____   _____

_____   _____

9. chair _____   10. blind date _____

_____   _____

_____   _____

Clichés

Clichés are phrases that at one time were highly expressive but have come to be so overworked they are tired and dull. They are phrases like "cold as ice," "turn over a new leaf," and "all in a day's work." Generally it is unwise to use clichés because they can suggest that the writer does not care enough to find a fresher, more expressive way to convey ideas. Hence clichés can detract from even the worthiest ideas.

Because clichés are so dull and so familiar, most readers tend to pass over them quickly without thinking much about their meaning. As a result, they are usually a weakness in any writing, but they are a particularly serious problem in description, where they fail to provide clear mental images.

EXERCISE:
Clichés

Below is a list of commonly used clichés. Pick five of them or use ones you think of and rewrite below the thoughts behind them in fresh, interesting, descriptive sentences. Remember the principles of economical and precise diction.

Sample cliché: old as the hills

Sample revision: The broken-down boat James wanted to buy was so old I half expected to see "Mayflower" carved on its cracked and peeling bow.

black as night
white as snow
in the same boat
hard as nails
old as the hills
hard as a rock
sadder but wiser
last but not least
the calm before the storm
like pulling teeth
right as rain
cold as ice
nip in the bud
the last straw
brown as a berry
tried and true
bite the bullet

cold, cruel world
free as a bird
smell a rat
wise as an owl
cut and dried
smooth as silk
fresh as a daisy
American as apple pie
raining cats and dogs
no rhyme or reason
eat your heart out
not knowing which way is up
good as gold
drunk as a sailor
fat as a horse
better late than never

1. Cliché: _____

   Revision: _____

   _____

2. Cliché: _____

   Revision: _____

   _____

3. Cliché: _____

   Revision: _____

   _____

4. Cliché: _____

   Revision: _____

   _____

5. Cliché: _____

   Revision: _____

   _____

A Word about Commas between Coordinate Modifiers

Because there are more rules for placement of the comma than for any other punctuation mark, many students feel insecure about using this mark. They fear they cannot keep all the rules straight. Happily, it is really not difficult to master comma usage, especially if the rules are learned a few at a time. That is how you will learn them in this book. Since for your descriptive writing you will want to use modifiers (descriptive words), a good comma rule to discuss at this point is the use of commas to separate coordinate modifiers.

Coordinate modifiers are those that read sensibly and naturally when joined by *and*.

Coordinate modifiers: the *sweaty* and *grimy* marathon runner
the *smooth* and *graceful* gymnast

Modifiers that are not coordinate cannot be joined sensibly and naturally with *and*.

Noncoordinate modifiers: the *sweet old* lady
the *delicious pepperoni* pizza
a *green hardtop Ford* sedan

The comma rule, then, goes like this: When modifiers can be joined by *and,* place a comma between them. Otherwise don't use one. In other words, you can think of the comma between coordinate modifiers as a replacement for the *and.*

Examples: the *sweaty, grimy* marathon runner
the *smooth, graceful* gymnast
quickly, recklessly driving down the street

Note: If you separate coordinate modifiers with *and,* do not use a comma.

Occasionally you may wish to use more than two coordinate modifiers. In such a case, commas are used wherever *and* could be placed to separate the modifiers.

Example: The mangy, wet, shivering mutt whined piteously to be let in.

Another way to tell if modifiers are coordinate is this: If the modifiers can be rearranged without creating something that sounds "off," they are coordinate. For example, "the *sweaty, grimy* marathon runner" can be changed to "the *grimy, sweaty* marathon runner," which sounds fine, so the modifiers are coordinate.

EXERCISE:
Commas between Coordinate Modifiers

Below are phrases that contain pairs of modifiers. In the spaces provided use each phrase in a sentence. If the modifiers are coordinate and not separated by *and,* use a comma. Otherwise no comma is needed.

1. the cold hungry child

_____

_____

2. the dry cracked paint

_____

_____

3. the tart apple pie

_____

_____

4. slowly cautiously climbing the ladder the painter
(Hint: Let the seven words begin your sentence.)

_____

_____

5. the excited happy girl

_____

_____

6. excitedly happily the girl
(Hint: Let these four words begin your sentence.)

_____

_____

7. the fragrant pear tree

_____

_____

8. the fragrant blossoming pear tree

_____

_____

9. the expensive three-piece suit

_____

_____

10. the worn and useless sofa

_____

_____

WRITING ASSIGNMENT I

Now that you have read "Central Park," tried your hand at some descriptive
writing practice, and studied some grammar and usage points, you are ready

for the first writing assignment of this chapter. To use writing as a tool to help you become a better observer, go someplace that you visit regularly but feel you have not really noticed fully because of the numbing effects of familiarity and routine or because you have not really stopped long enough to observe. Take paper and pen with you and record a descriptive list in the fashion of Updike's. Here are some hints:

1. You might try your bedroom, your doctor's office, the street in front of your house, the campus library or cafeteria, a view from a roof, a bus terminal, a supermarket, a gas station, or someplace you are employed.

2. Plan your visit when you have plenty of time to observe and write in a relaxed fashion. You should not fight the clock on this one.

3. Use a dictionary and thesaurus, but be sure you understand the meanings of any words you pull from these sources. These books should be used only when you cannot think of the "right" word. They should not be overused or your paper will lack your own distinctive style.

4. Do not forget to provide an introductory paragraph, as Updike does. Your introduction should reveal your plan for detail selection.

5. Strive to give your reader a clear mental picture of what you are describing.

6. Remember to convey mood or attitude in your descriptions or select details clearly related to your plan.

7. Select details carefully, since you cannot describe everything.

8. Remember that you will need to revise and refine, perhaps several times. As you do this, remember to avoid clichés and be economical and precise. Also remember commas between coordinate modifiers.

9. Use as many of the senses (taste, touch, sight, hearing, and smell) as you can.

10. Before you write, examine the student paper below and answer the questions that follow it.

Sample Descriptive List: "My Bedroom"

Below is a sample descriptive list written by a student for you to study. The questions that follow it are meant to point out the details of descriptive writing discussed in this chapter.

My Bedroom

I woke up early one Saturday morning alarmed by my mother's voice ringing, "Sandy, it's time to get up! Don't forget you have cleaning to do!" I groaned, peered out over the covers, and was heartened by the sight of my comforting room. There I noticed:

My spicy red rug blanketing the cold wooden floor.

An AM–FM radio squelching all silence with its blaring rock music.

A small brown ashtray lurking nearby, hoarding old cigarette butts and tabs from Coca Cola cans.

Ladybugs swarming over an apple-green quilted bedspread.

A snapshot of Tony taken in perfect range.

Four cream-colored walls fondly hugging the room.

A Tootsie Roll bank, full of copper candy.

Big Bird on the face of an alarm clock, his double-jointed arms pointing to the numbers eight and twelve.

Unwanted chemistry and calculus books strewn about the desk.

A beer bottle, pretending to be a vase, holding a bouquet of withered jonquils.

Scattered newspaper and magazine clippings, yellowing with age, suspended by multicolored pins on a cork surface.

A pane trembling as an exhausted WRTA bus lumbers past my window.

A bottle of Windsong, half-full, its sweet scent lingering.

An irritating scratch at my door that introduces a little poodle dressed in a coat of cotton.

A calendar hiding the chipped paint on the wall while announcing important dates with scribbles of blue ink.

A dirty blue tennis shoe estranged from its mate.

A green antique rocking chair, the throne of Raggedy Ann, with her servants Snoopy, Tweety, and Cookie Monster at her feet.

A red wicker wastebasket overflowing with the crumpled efforts of a college English student.

Questions for Discussion:
"My Bedroom"

"My Bedroom," written by a student, is a fine piece of descriptive writing. The author demonstrates her awareness of the principles of descriptive writing, which is one reason the piece is so enjoyable. As one last reminder of these principles, answer the following questions.

1. What is the author's plan for detail selection?

_____

_____

2. Are there any details that do not fit the plan? If so, what are they?

_____

_____

3. Cite ten examples of precise diction.

_____   _____

_____   _____

_____   _____

_____   _____

_____   _____

4. Cite four examples of good mental images.

_____

_____

_____

_____

5. Does the author use a simple vocabulary? Give two examples.

_____

_____

6. Does the author string modifiers?

_____

7. Cite two examples of personification.

_____

_____

8. Are there any clichés? If so, what are they?

_____

_____

9. To which of the senses does the author refer?

_____

_____

WRITING ASSIGNMENT II

To further train yourself to observe closely, try writing a one-page description of a simple, commonplace object—one you are so familiar with that you have become numb to its various qualities. In your description, do not mention the object's name or the name of any of its parts. For example, if you are describing a flower, you may not mention "flower," "daisy," "stem," or "petal." Nor may you refer to an item's function. You cannot, when describing a rubber ball, mention that it is used to play catch.

Then trade papers with someone, and each of you try to determine what the other has described. A successful paper is one that vividly describes, using all the relevant senses, in such a way that the reader determines what has been described. Here are some possible objects to describe. Draw from this list or choose something else.

a bowl of spaghetti	a step stool	a book
a hairbrush	a safety razor	a finger
a shoe	a lamp	a popsicle
a salt shaker	a stick of gum	an envelope
a garden rake	a skillet	a key

WRITING THE PARAGRAPH

As a unit of composition, the paragraph is relatively uncomplicated. In fact, it is made up of only three parts: the topic sentence, the supporting detail, and the closing. Because of this simple structure, you will have little difficulty understanding paragraph design and organization.

The Topic Sentence

The topic sentence is the sentence in your paragraph that lets your reader know what your paragraph is about. Just as you needed a plan for detail selection when you wrote your descriptive list, so, too, you must have a plan when you write a paragraph. If you don't have such a plan, you will not have a system for deciding which details to include in your paragraph and which ones to leave out. A topic sentence, then, should present two things: It should state what your paragraph is about (your subject), and it should present how you feel about your subject (your plan).

A topic sentence can come pretty much anywhere in a paragraph, but many student writers feel it is easiest to make it the first sentence. A topic sentence placed first is also frequently appreciated by the reader because it lets that person know immediately what is in store. After all, how many of us want to read something if we have no idea what the subject matter is? For these reasons, I suggest placing the topic sentence first. Later, as you become more skilled, you can experiment with different placements.

There is one final point to make about topic sentences: Keep your subject and your feeling about your subject narrow enough so that you have something manageable to deal with. It would be hard, for example, to write a paragraph with a topic sentence such as "I always loved New York State." New York is a pretty big state, and if there are many things you love about it, your paragraph would be unreasonably long. So be good to yourself and select a subject and feeling that you can handle in a single paragraph. Something like this will do: "I always found the workers in Manhattan's garment district fascinating to watch."

EXERCISE:
The Topic Sentence

Read the topic sentences below. In the spaces provided, indicate whether each one is acceptable or not. If a topic sentence is not acceptable, indicate why not and rewrite it to make it acceptable.

Example: Everything about college life excites me.
unacceptable because it is too broad

Revision: A college football game can be quite exciting.

1. My grandmother's house always depressed me.

_____

_____

_____

2. For a vacation Yellowstone Park is an interesting and relaxing place to visit.

_____

_____

_____

3. My supervisor's office is utterly disorganized.

_____

_____

_____

4. Nowhere can you find a more hectic place than our kitchen at 7:00 A.M.

_____

_____

_____

5. After spending a week in Florida, I'm convinced that it is the most beautiful state we have.

_____

_____

_____

6. Our street after dark is wonderfully peaceful and lovely.

_____

_____

_____

7. The back of Rick's van is every bit as filthy as his room.

_____

_____

_____

8. In only ten minutes my two-year-old turned his bedroom into a scene of devastation.

_____

_____

_____

9. A Las Vegas gambling casino is the height of confusion and excitement.

_____

_____

_____

10. The inside of Leslie's refrigerator should be condemned by the board of health.

_____

_____

_____

11. This is what the inside of my closet looks like.

_____

_____

_____

12. It reminded me of a castle from the Middle Ages.

_____

_____

_____

Supporting Detail

The supporting detail is all the information in your paragraph, all the sentences, that explain or defend or develop or clarify your topic sentence. These are the sentences, the detail, that support your topic sentence.

It is important to make sure that all your supporting detail is _relevant_ to your topic sentence. That is, your support must clearly relate to the subject and how you feel about your subject. Remember, your topic sentence tells your reader what your paragraph is about. If you stray from your topic sentence, your reader may well become confused and annoyed.

Not only must your supporting detail be relevant, it must also be _adequate_. This means that you must supply enough detail to develop your topic sufficiently. If you neglect to provide enough supporting detail, your reader will surely come away from your paragraph feeling most unsatisfied and let down because you never quite made the point you said you would in your topic sentence.

EXERCISE:
Relevant Supporting Detail

Below are some topic sentences, followed by some ideas to be developed and used as supporting detail. Circle any ideas you judge not to be relevant. If all the ideas are relevant to the topic sentence, do not circle anything.

Example: After dark, my basement reminds me of something out of an old horror movie.

a. The single naked bulb casting eerie shadows on the walls and ceiling.

b. The moan of the dehumidifier sounding frighteningly human.

c. The bikes leaning against the far wall, reminding me of pleasant spring afternoons when I cycle in the park.

d. Every creak of the house, somehow magnified, sending a shiver through me.

e. The shirts hanging from a single clothesline appearing ready to reach out and grab me if I turn my back.

Explanation: Idea c is not relevant because it refers to a happy time in spring rather than an eerie moment in the basement.

1. On Christmas morning, our living room was overflowing with excitement.
   a. The children ripping open their packages.
   b. The baby squealing with enthusiasm.
   c. Dad singing carols.
   d. Mom in the kitchen making pancakes and sausages.
   e. Our boxer, Duke, chasing bits of paper and ribbon.

2. The sight of Andy's kitchen was enough to make anyone nauseous.
   a. Grease on the counter.
   b. Dried food on the floor.
   c. Heaps of dirty dishes in the sink.
   d. Smell of sour milk.
   e. Wild flowers in a vase on the kitchen table.

3. The instant I entered Dr. Weston's waiting room, I was surprised at how unlike the typical dentist's office it was.
   a. Rock music playing.
   b. A picture of the parts of a tooth on the wall.
   c. Early American furniture.
   d. No one wearing white clothes.
   e. A TV for patients to watch.

4. If you are looking for an Italian restaurant with plenty of atmosphere, visit Antonio's.
   a. Red-checkered tablecloths.
   b. Candles in wine bottles.
   c. Waiters with Italian accents.
   d. Smell of garlic.
   e. Strolling violinists.

5. After waiting five minutes in the personnel office, I could tell it was a very busy place.
   a. Secretaries walking briskly back and forth.
   b. Desks covered with important-looking papers.
   c. Phones ringing constantly.
   d. Many people coming in and going out.
   e. A copying machine standing idle.

EXERCISE:
Adequate Supporting Detail

The following paragraph lacks adequate supporting detail. Read it and then answer the questions that follow.

A Boring Class

The students in Dr. Zenner's political science class show all the classic signs of boredom. A blond in the back has her book propped up to hide the blushing rose nail polish she is carefully applying. The jock next to her (you can tell he's a jock by his muscles and the gym bag at his feet) is openly reading *Sports Illustrated*. Even "the brain" up front has stopped taking notes and is leaning her head against her writing hand and looking disinterested. After three years at this school, I have yet to find anyone who enjoys Dr. Zenner's class.

1. How do you feel when you finish this paragraph? Why?

_____

_____

_____

2. List below ideas for supporting detail that could be added to make this an adequately developed paragraph.

_____

_____

_____

_____

_____

_____

The Closing

The closing is the last sentence or two of your paragraph. It should bring your paragraph to a satisfying finish by doing one or a combination of the following:

1. Restating the main idea in a new way
2. Resolving an issue
3. Creating a final impression
4. Relating the main idea to another related idea

Use the closing to tie off your paragraph in some sensible way. Never does a writer want to hit the brakes and end abruptly because the reader will be left hanging. I'm sure you've seen a movie or TV show that did not have a satisfactory ending. Remember how frustrated and uncomfortable you felt as a result? Well, these are the feelings you want to spare your reader by closing off your paragraph neatly.

EXERCISE:
The Closing

Read the student paragraphs "My Awakening" on page 42 and "A Rainy View" on page 43. In the spaces provided below write two different closings for each paragraph. Then examine the closings you have written and the ones the student authors wrote. Decide which of the endings is the best and explain why you believe as you do.

1. "My Awakening": First Closing

_____

_____

_____

_____

Second Closing

_____

_____

_____

_____

2. "A Rainy View": First Closing

_____

_____

_____

Second Closing

_____

_____

_____

_____

42

3. Best Closing for "My Awakening"

_____

_____

_____

_____

4. Best Closing for "A Rainy View"

_____

_____

_____

_____

Paragraph Organization:
An Illustration

The one-paragraph theme is organized in this way:

Topic sentence
↓
Supporting detail
↓
Closing

To illustrate the organization and development of a one-paragraph theme, here is a descriptive paragraph written by a college freshman. Various parts of the paragraph are pointed out for you to study.

My Awakening

Today while sitting in my cabin in the woods, I became aware, for the first time in my life, of all the wondrous things that lived and grew around me. _[Topic sentence tells what paragraph is about and conveys writer's feeling about the subject.]_ Looking out my own small window, I saw a great myriad of life. There was a rabbit loping along, its lopears dragging through the snow. In a small tree hung an opossum seemingly unaware of its precarious position. I heard a faint, almost undetectable foot tread on the roof. It was a fox squirrel running from the roof to a tree nearby. His eyes met mine, and he looked at me as though asking why I sat inside on a day like this. I heard a rustle out near my woodpile. I put on my clothes and decided to go out to investigate. Once outside I saw an awesome sight. It was a doe with her young fawn searching for something to eat. I stepped toward them. The doe bolted. The fawn remained. It must not have learned to fear man as its parents had. I sighed; here no one had spoiled the plan God had for us all to live in harmony with one another. The fawn showed no fear of man, the creature that stalks it so feverishly. *[Supporting detail is relevant and adequate. Notice the precise, economical diction and the delightful mental images.]* I found a beauty that few will ever find, for nothing could possibly equal the splendor I discovered in my own small nook in nature's world. *[Closing leaves a final impression and restates idea of topic sentence in a new way.]*

EXERCISE:
A Descriptive Paragraph to Analyze

Read the paragraph below written by a student and answer the questions that follow.

A Rainy View

My view from a fourth-floor window of the Ward Beecher Science Building on Friday proved that the very soggy and bleak day was miserable for everyone. Crossing campus in a bright blue jacket was a coed, trying to fight the overpowering wind that was slowing her down. Her umbrella was turned inside out by an unexpected gust. A twinge of pity came over me as I watched a slumping elderly lady slowly inch her way up the steps as the rain beat down on her mercilessly. As the pounding drops threw themselves against the window pane, as if demanding to be allowed inside, I noticed a well-dressed businessman carrying a briefcase, fleeing toward Jones Hall. Water from the weather-beaten roof above was flowing past the window like a rushing waterfall, partially obscuring my view. Three girls were hurrying from the library, frantically trying to open their umbrellas so as not to get drenched. They passed a small police scooter carefully making its way down the wet, sloppy walk between the library and Jones Hall. Parking, too, was difficult, as many students discovered. They all raced for the Wick Avenue parking deck, only to get tangled in the snarl of traffic that always develops when the weather turns bad. I noticed a bright, cherry-red sports car streaking down a partially flooded side street, splashing surprised pedestrians as it passed. Many tardy students were straggling into class soaked. As I gazed out the window, I heard in the background the sound of a teacher lecturing to a classroom of students made restless by the gloom of the day. Finally, classes were over, and students pushed to get to the doors. They had made it through the last day of the week despite the pouring rain.

1. What is the topic sentence of this paragraph?

_____

_____

_____

2. What subject does the topic sentence present?

_____

3. What does the topic sentence say is the writer's feeling about the subject?

_____

4. Is the supporting detail relevant to both the topic and mood given in the topic sentence? If so, explain how. If not, state which details are not relevant.

_____

_____

_____

_____

5. Is there enough detail to develop the topic adequately? Explain why you feel as you do.

_____

_____

_____

6. Give three examples of precise diction.

_____

_____

_____

7. Give three examples of economical diction.

_____

_____

_____

8. Is there anything about the supporting detail you would change? If so, what?

_____

_____

_____

9. What is the closing of this paragraph?

_____

_____

_____

10. Is the closing effective? Why? Or why not?

_____

_____

_____

11. If you were the teacher, what comments would you make on this paragraph?

_____

_____

_____

WRITING ASSIGNMENT III

For your first descriptive paragraph assignment, turn the descriptive list you wrote modeled after "Central Park" into a descriptive paragraph. To do this, you may wish to add certain details and omit others. Before you hand your theme in, be sure you can answer yes to the questions below.

Questions to Answer before Submitting Your Paragraph

1. Does your paragraph have a topic sentence that mentions what you are describing (subject) and how you feel about what you are describing?
2. Is your support adequate? Do you have enough of it to develop your topic sentence satisfactorily?
3. Is all your support relevant? Does all of it pertain to the subject and attitude of the topic sentence?
4. Do you have a satisfactory closing?
5. Is your diction precise, economical, and free of clichés?
6. Have you used commas between coordinate modifiers?
7. Have you read over your theme slowly and carefully at least twice, looking for errors?

WRITING ASSIGNMENT IV

For this theme pretend you work in the public relations office of your college or university. Assume you have been asked by your boss to write a one-paragraph description of some appealing feature of your campus to include in a pamphlet that will be mailed to area high schools. The purpose of the pamphlet is to encourage seniors to apply for admission to your school. You might describe a favorite spot in the student union, an attractive garden area, the library reference room, the bookstore browsing area, a class in session, or some other spot that might make your school sound attractive to a prospective freshman. Before handing in your work, be sure you can answer yes to the questions following the previous assignment.

A FINAL WORD

Descriptive writing is valuable because it forces us to search for just the right word to convey our observations accurately. Interestingly, this attempt at precision leads us to a closer examination of our surroundings. The result is that we become even more aware. And since we pass this way but once, what a pity not to see, hear, smell, taste, and touch as much of life as possible. Even while caught up in our routine and hectic lives, we can observe once we have trained ourselves to do so. Now that you have done some descriptive writing and sharpened your powers of observation, let those powers serve you. From time to time, do some more descriptive writing to stay sharp. By writing descriptively you should learn to observe. Now put that learning to use in your lives: Notice what is around you!

Chapter 3

Discovering Causes:
Writing about Influences in Your Life

We are what we are for many reasons. We are born with certain traits that cause us to act in certain ways; our parents, teachers, and friends have affected us dramatically; our experiences are responsible for various positive and negative influences on us; our goals and dreams motivate us. In short, all we have known in the past, all we are currently experiencing, and all we hope to achieve in the future join to influence us every moment.

So varied are the influences in our lives, so complex are the relationships among these influences, that it is not always easy to sort out and understand the factors at work. Yet we should all attempt such sorting and understanding if we are to understand and accept ourselves. And here writing can help. This chapter will demonstrate that by writing about influences in our lives, we can come to understand them better. This understanding, in turn, can improve the quality of our lives by leading to self-awareness. It can also help us cope with, take advantage of, overcome, or accept those influences that help shape us.

READING SELECTION:
"Discovery of a Father"

Your first step toward learning to use writing to understand influences in your life is to read "Discovery of a Father" by Sherwood Anderson. As you read, notice that Anderson explains how he came to an understanding of a major influence in his life—his father.

Discovery of a Father
Sherwood Anderson

One of the strangest relationships in the world is that between father and son. I know it now from having sons of my own.

A boy wants something very special from his father. You hear it said that fathers want their sons to be what they feel they cannot themselves be, but I tell you it also works the other way. I know that as a small boy I wanted my father to be a certain thing he was not. I wanted him to be a proud, silent, dignified father. When I was with other boys and he passed along the street, I wanted to feel a glow of pride: "There he is. That is my father."

But he wasn't such a one. He couldn't be. It seemed to me then that he was always showing off. Let's say someone in our town had got up a show. They were always doing it. The druggist would be in it, the shoe-store clerk, the horse doctor, and a lot of women and girls. My father would manage to get the chief comedy part. It was, let's say, a Civil War play and he was a comic Irish soldier. He had to do the most absurd things. They thought he was funny, but I didn't.

I thought he was terrible. I didn't see how Mother could stand it. She even laughed with the others. Maybe I would have laughed if it hadn't been my father.

Or there was a parade, the Fourth of July or Decoration Day. He'd be in that, too, right at the front of it, as Grand Marshal or something, on a white horse hired from a livery stable.

He couldn't ride for shucks. He fell off the horse and everyone hooted with laughter, but he didn't care. He even seemed to like it. I remember once when he had done something ridiculous, and right out on Main Street, too. I was with some other boys and they were laughing and shouting at him and he was shouting back and having as good a time as they were. I ran down an alley back of some stores and there in the Presbyterian Church sheds I had a good long cry.

Or I would be in bed at night and Father would come home a little lit up and bring some men with him. He was a man who was never alone. Before he went broke, running a harness shop, there were always a lot of men loafing in the shop. He went broke, of course, because he gave too much credit. He couldn't refuse it and I thought he was a fool. I had got to hating him.

There'd be men I didn't think would want to be fooling around with him. There might even be the superintendent of our schools and a quiet man who ran the hardware store. Once, I remember, there was a white-haired man who was a cashier of the bank. It was a wonder to me they'd want to be seen with such a windbag. That's what I thought he was. I know now what it was that attracted them. It was because life in our town, as in all small towns, was at times pretty dull and he livened it up. He made them laugh. He could tell stories. He'd even get them to singing.

If they didn't come to our house they'd go off, say at night, to where there was a grassy place by a creek. They'd cook food there and drink beer and sit about listening to his stories.

He was always telling stories about himself. He'd say this or that wonderful thing happened to him. It might be something that made him look like a fool. He didn't care.

If an Irishman came to our house, right away father would say he was Irish. He'd tell what county in Ireland he was born in. He'd tell things that happened there when he was a boy. He'd make it seem so real that, if I hadn't known he was born in southern Ohio, I'd have believed him myself.

If it was a Scotchman, the same thing happened. He'd get a burr into his speech. Or he was a German or a Swede. He'd be anything the other man was. I think they all knew he was lying, but they seemed to like him just the same. As a boy that was what I couldn't understand.

And there was Mother. How could she stand it? I wanted to ask but never did. She was not the kind you asked such questions.

I'd be upstairs in my bed, in my room above the porch, and Father would be telling some of his tales. A lot of Father's stories were about the Civil War. To hear him tell it he'd been in about every battle. He'd known Grant, Sherman, Sheridan and I don't know how many others. He'd been particularly intimate with General Grant so that when Grant went East, to take charge of all the armies, he took Father along.

"I was an orderly at headquarters and Sam Grant said to me, 'Irve,' he said, 'I'm going to take you along with me.'"

It seems he and Grant used to slip off sometimes and have a quiet drink together. That's what my father said. He'd tell about the day Lee surrendered and how, when the great moment came, they couldn't find Grant.

"You know," my father said, "about General Grant's book, his memoirs. You've read of how he said he had a headache and how,

when he got word that Lee was ready to call it quits, he was suddenly and miraculously cured.

"Huh," said Father. "He was in the woods with me.

"I was in there with my back against a tree. I was pretty well corned. I had got hold of a bottle of pretty good stuff.

"They were looking for Grant. He had got off his horse and come into the woods. He found me. He was covered with mud.

"I had the bottle in my hand. What'd I care? The war was over. I knew we had them licked."

My father said that he was the one who told Grant about Lee. An orderly riding by had told him, because the orderly knew how thick he was with Grant. Grant was embarrassed.

"But, Irve, look at me. I'm all covered with mud," he said to Father.

And then, my father said, he and Grant decided to have a drink together. They took a couple of shots and then, because he didn't want Grant to show up potted before the immaculate Lee, he smashed the bottle against the tree.

"Sam Grant's dead now and I wouldn't want it to get out on him," my father said.

That's just one of the kind of things he'd tell. Of course, the men knew he was lying, but they seemed to like it just the same.

When we got broke, down and out, do you think he ever brought anything home? Not he. If there wasn't anything to eat in the house, he'd go off visiting around at farm houses. They all wanted him. Sometimes he'd stay away for weeks, Mother working to keep us fed, and then home he'd come bringing, let's say, a ham. He'd got it from some farmer friend. He'd slap it on the table in the kitchen. "You bet I'm going to see that my kids have something to eat," he'd say, and Mother would just stand smiling at him. She'd never say a word about all the weeks and months he'd been away, not leaving us a cent for food. Once I heard her speaking to a woman in our street. Maybe the woman had dared to sympathize with her. "Oh," she said, "it's all right. He isn't ever dull like most of the men in this street. Life is never dull when my man is about."

But often I was filled with bitterness, and sometimes I wished he wasn't my father. I'd even invent another man as my father. To protect my mother I'd make up stories of a secret marriage that for some strange reason never got known. As though some man, say the president of a railroad company or maybe a Congressman, had married my mother, thinking his wife was dead and then it turned out she wasn't.

So they had to hush it up but I got born just the same. I wasn't really the son of my father. Somewhere in the world there was a very dignified, quite wonderful man who was really my father. I even made myself half believe these fancies.

And then there came a certain night. Mother was away from home. Maybe there was church that night. Father came in. He'd been off somewhere for two or three weeks. He found me alone in the house, reading by the kitchen table.

It had been raining and he was very wet. He sat and looked at me for a long time, not saying a word. I was startled, for there was on his face the saddest look I had ever seen. He sat for a time, his clothes dripping. Then he got up.

"Come on with me," he said.

I got up and went with him out of the house. I was filled with wonder but I wasn't afraid. We went along a dirt road that led down into a valley, about a mile out of town, where there was a pond. We walked in silence. The man who was always talking had stopped his talking.

I didn't know what was up and had the queer feeling that I was with a stranger. I don't know whether my father intended it so. I don't think he did.

The pond was quite large. It was still raining hard and there were flashes of lightning followed by thunder. We were on a grassy bank at the pond's edge when my father spoke, and in the darkness and rain his voice sounded strange.

"Take off your clothes," he said. Still filled with wonder, I began to undress. There was a flash of lightning and I saw that he was already naked.

Naked, we went into the pond. Taking my hand, he pulled me in. It may be that I was too frightened, too full of a feeling of strangeness, to speak. Before that night my father had never seemed to pay any attention to me.

"And what is he up to now?" I kept asking myself. I did not swim very well, but he put my hand on his shoulder and struck out into the darkness.

He was a man with big shoulders, a powerful swimmer. In the darkness I could feel the movements of his muscles. We swam to the far edge of the pond and then back to where we had left our clothes. The rain continued and the wind blew. Sometimes my father swam on his back, and when he did he took my hand in his large powerful one and moved it over so that it rested always on his shoulder. Sometimes there would be a flash of lightning and I could see his face quite clearly.

It was as it was earlier, in the kitchen, a face filled with sadness. There would be the momentary glimpse of his face, and then again the darkness, the wind and the rain. In me there was a feeling I had never known before.

It was a feeling of closeness. It was something strange. It was as though there were only we two in the world. It was as though I had been jerked suddenly out of myself, out of my world of the schoolboy, out of a world in which I was ashamed of my father.

He had become blood of my blood; he the strong swimmer and I the boy clinging to him in the darkness. We swam in silence, and in silence we dressed in our wet clothes and went home.

There was a lamp lighted in the kitchen, and when we came in, the water dripping from us, there was my mother. She smiled at us. I remember that she called us "boys." "What have you boys been up to?" she asked, but my father did not answer. As he had begun the evening's experience with me in silence, so he ended it. He turned and looked at me. Then he went, I thought, with a new and strange dignity, out of the room.

I climbed the stairs to my room, undressed in darkness and got into bed. I couldn't sleep and did not want to sleep. For the first time I knew that I was the son of my father. He was a storyteller as I was to be. It may be that I even laughed a little softly there in the darkness. If I did, I laughed knowing that I would never again be wanting another father.

Vocabulary List:
"Discovery of a Father"

In Chapter 2, I explained the importance of vocabulary building (see p. 15). As you did for "Central Park," record below the words from "Discovery of a Father" that you are unsure of. Next to each word, write the dictionary definition that corresponds to the way the word is used in the story. Finally, pick two words you want to work into your speech and writing and put these on your vocabulary list in Appendix A.

_____   _____

_____   _____

_____   _____

_____   _____

Questions for Discussion:
"Discovery of a Father"

1. Circle the words in the list below that you believe describe how Anderson viewed his father at the beginning of the story.

admirable	good with money	undignified
foolish	unlike other fathers	hard working
a clown	like other fathers	irresponsible
entertaining	an embarrassment	silly

2. Mention four things the father did that caused Anderson to feel the way he did about his father.

_____

_____

_____

_____

_____

3. In what ways did Anderson's father and Anderson's feelings about his father influence the boy early in the story?

_____

_____

_____

_____

_____

4. Can you think of a time when the behavior of one of your parents caused you to feel or act in a certain way? Describe your parent's behavior and how it influenced your feelings or actions.

_____

_____

_____

_____

_____

5. At the end of the story, Anderson comes to view his father differently from the way he did earlier. What event prompted Anderson to change his view?

_____

6. Have you ever viewed a person one way only to have something happen that changed your opinion? Describe your view before and after you changed your mind and explain what caused you to change your view.

_____

_____

_____

_____

_____

_____

_____

7. Circle the words in the list below that describe how Anderson viewed his father during and after the swim.

sad	a storyteller	ashamed
foolish	strong	childish
dignified	powerful	a clown
masterful	loving	quiet

8. In the last paragraph Anderson says, "For the first time I knew that I was the son of my father." What do you judge this line to mean?

_____

_____

_____

_____

9. At the end of the story, Anderson recognizes that his father influenced his life in one particular, significant way. What is this influence?

_____

_____

_____

_____

GETTING READY: FREEWRITING

So often students say to me, "I don't know what to write." Each time I hear those words, the student speaks them as though he or she were the only person ever to suffer the pain of staring at a blank page and waiting for an idea to come. Sure, needing an idea and not having one leap into your brain is frustrating. But let me assure you that every writer—whether professional or unpublished, teacher or student, experienced or inexperienced—knows the frustration of having the brain step out to lunch just when it's time to begin a writing project.

Sometimes if you sit long enough, an idea strikes you. But let's be realistic. Sometimes you sit for a long time and nothing occurs to you. When this happens, it's time to meet the problem head-on and take action. It's time to do something to stimulate your brain.

Whenever you find yourself at a loss for something to write, and just sitting back and thinking doesn't help, try *freewriting.*

Freewriting works like this: Select a topic or use one you have been assigned. Then on a blank sheet of paper begin writing about that topic and continue doing so for a solid fifteen minutes. Now here is the most important point: *Do not for any reason stop writing.* Instead, write any and every idea that pops into your head without pausing to evaluate whether the ideas are good ones or bad ones. If it occurs to you, write it down. If you run out of ideas, write down the alphabet, the multiplication tables, even "I don't know what to write" or "I feel lousy today," but do not stop writing. Soon new ideas will strike you, and you can write them down. Do not worry about such things as grammar, spelling, and form.

Continue in this fashion for the full fifteen minutes. Then read what you have (and it will probably cover about two pages). In there somewhere you will most likely discover the seeds of several excellent ideas that can be expanded for development in a theme. Underline these ideas. Keep in mind that freewriting is intensely personal. No one will view your work but you, so feel free to write even the most private thoughts. You must be uninhibited and relaxed while freewriting to allow a free flow of ideas.

For many people, one freewriting such as this provides enough raw material to begin a first draft. Others, however, find it necessary to do a second freewriting. If you are in this second group, select all or some or even just one of your underlined ideas in the first freewriting and do a second freewriting, following the same procedure. When finished, again underline worthy ideas. Between the two writings, you should have enough material to use as the basis for a first draft. For an example of freewriting see p. 7.

EXERCISE:
Freewriting

In "Discovery of a Father" Anderson reveals his understanding of the influence his father had on him. Because of this influence, Anderson grew to be a storyteller, just as his father was. In addition, Anderson explains how one event caused him to see his father differently. As it was for Anderson, parents have had a significant influence on most of us. Also as it was for Anderson, we often reach a point where we see our parents in a new light and change our opinion of them. This change of heart can affect how we think, feel, and act.

It is therefore important to examine the influence our parents have had on us as we work to use writing to help us understand influences in our lives. As one step toward this goal, and to get some practice freewriting, freewrite about some part of the relationship you have (or had) with one of your parents and the effect it has had on you.

To get maximum benefit from the exercise, remember the ground rules: Write without stopping for a full fifteen minutes and do not evaluate the worth of your ideas. I believe when you read the results, you will be pleased to discover at least one fine idea worthy of development in a theme. Underline this and any other such idea you find. Be sure to save your freewriting; it will be useful later when you do one of the assignments in this chapter.

THE MULTIPARAGRAPH THEME

As a unit of composition, the one-paragraph theme has its uses. However, the one-paragraph theme also limits the writer severely. There's only so much you can say when you're given only one paragraph to say it in. Of course, at times you *can* cover your subject just fine in one paragraph. But more often, as a writer you would be frustrated if you had to confine yourself to a single paragraph all the time. For this reason, I believe you will welcome mastering the organization of the multiparagraph theme, for it will allow you to express yourself more freely and completely. You can explore your subject more fully, follow your ideas into several related areas, and most importantly, enjoy the luxury of having the boundaries pushed back so you can really develop your thoughts.

THEME ORGANIZATION

In this chapter you will be asked to write your first multiparagraph theme, so this is a good point to pause to discuss one standard organization of such a theme. Typically, a multiparagraph theme has the following parts:

Introduction (first paragraph)

Body paragraphs (central paragraphs)

Conclusion (final paragraph)

Each of these three parts has its own function. Your introduction prepares your reader for your statement of the subject or purpose of your theme and then provides that statement. Your body paragraphs develop, discuss, explain, prove, or support the stand you take in your statement of subject or purpose.

Your conclusion brings the theme to a satisfying finish by providing your reader with a distinct sense of closing.

Introductory Paragraphs:
The Thesis

The introductory paragraph of a multiparagraph theme has two parts: the lead-in and the thesis. Let's turn our attention first to the thesis.

When you studied paragraph writing in Chapter 2, you learned that a paragraph should have a statement indicating the subject of your writing and how you feel about your subject. Well, the same is true when you write a multiparagraph theme. You should have a sentence or two that informs your reader of your subject and your feeling about your subject. This statement comes in the introduction and is called the *thesis*.

The thesis statement is important to a well-organized theme because it is the focus for all that you write—everything in your theme must relate to your thesis. Actually, a thesis is a form of contract between writer and reader. When you state your thesis, you are guaranteeing your reader an accurate preview of things to come and assuring that person that everything that follows will relate to the subject and feeling noted in the thesis. If ever you stray from your thesis, you create a serious writing problem: lack of relevance. Think of your thesis, then, as your plan for detail selection. All your detail will be selected on the basis of whether it fits in with the subject and feeling given in the thesis.

EXERCISE:
The Thesis

Below are some thesis statements. Some are acceptable because they mention both the subject and the feeling about the subject. Others are not acceptable because they fail to mention either the subject or the feeling. If the thesis is acceptable write "OK" in the blank. If the thesis is unacceptable, rewrite it to make it satisfactory.

Example:	Last August Dad lost his job.
Revision:	When Dad lost his job last August, I realized how much the family had come to depend on him.
Explanation:	The first topic sentence does not indicate any feeling about the subject. The revision includes such a feeling.

1. One day my dad and I went skydiving together.

_____

_____

2. Dad's stinginess over the years helped make me the miser I am today.

_____

_____

3. The night I found Mother crying in the kitchen, I realized she was not the unfeeling person I had always thought she was.

_____

_____

4. In 1976, Dad and I went to the Super Bowl.

_____

_____

5. I'll always remember that day.

_____

_____

EXERCISE:
Relevance

Below are some sample thesis statements followed by ideas to include in themes with those thesis statements. Circle the ideas that should not be included in the themes because they would create relevance problems.

Example: At one time I considered my mother to be the world's champion nag.

a. She constantly bugged me about my school work.

b. She continually reminded me about things I had not forgotten.

c. In all fairness, I must say that my dad did his share of nagging, too.

d. When I married, Mother called me every day to be sure I had done all my housekeeping chores.

Idea c is not relevant because Dad's nagging is not the issue—Mother's is.

1. Dad's drinking problem was the cause of my severe childhood depression.

a. I was afraid to have friends over, so I was always lonely.

b. Mother coped as well as she could, but mostly she pretended everything was all right.

    c. Once I tried to commit suicide because there seemed to be no hope that my dad would ever be like my friends' fathers.

    d. Holidays were particularly glum because Dad drank more than ever.

2. If ever there was an unselfish woman, Mom was the one.

    a. When Dad was unemployed, she refused to go to work because she felt her children needed her.

    b. Mom rarely spent money on herself, preferring instead to buy things for us kids.

    c. Once Mom stayed up all night sewing a costume for me so I would have a chance to win first prize at a Halloween party.

    d. For meals, Mom cooked only the family's favorite foods, disregarding her own preferences.

3. My father's generosity has been an inspiration to me.

    a. Dad never hesitates to lend money to a needy friend or relative.

    b. Never has he pressured anyone for repayment of a loan.

    c. Once when Dad was short of cash, he was embarrassed to seek a loan.

    d. Dad gives of his time as freely as he gives of his money.

Narrowing the Thesis

Almost always, a good piece of writing treats its subject in detail. That is, for writing to be successful, it must be done in enough depth to leave the reader feeling satisfied that all the important points have been developed sufficiently. Because of this, it's easy to see the wisdom of the following rule: It's better to treat a narrow subject in depth than a broad subject in a shallow manner. With this in mind, let's discuss narrowing the thesis.

Remember, the thesis reveals the subject of your writing and your feeling about the subject. Remember, too, these points must be narrowed so that you can treat them in detail. This idea is not really new to you. When you studied paragraph writing, you learned that your subject had to be manageable.

Examine the following thesis:

Now I realize that Dad's love of nature, his concern for others, and his need to succeed have influenced me in many ways.

The writer stuck with this thesis would have quite a large writing task. That person would have to discuss the father's love of nature, his concern for others, *and* his need to succeed. In addition, that writer would have to explain all the many ways these traits were an influence. In the first place, it would be hard to provide adequate detail for such a broad subject and feeling. In the second place, the writer attempting to cover this thesis would most likely end up running out of steam and providing only a surface treatment of each element—and how dull that would be for the reader, and how useless for the writer. So be sure to tailor a thesis for yourself that can be developed adequately in a reasonable number of words.

EXERCISE:
Narrowing the Thesis

Below is a list of thesis statements. Write "OK" in the space provided if the thesis is narrow enough. Rewrite the ones that are not narrow enough to make them more manageable.

Sample thesis: Many of Mom's habits are ones I now see in myself.

Sample revision: After being exposed to Mom's love of plants for eighteen years, I now find myself majoring in botany.

Explanation: If Mom and the writer share quite a few habits, it would be difficult to write about all of them.

1. If only my father had praised me on occasion, I'm sure I wouldn't be so lacking in self-confidence today.

_____

_____

2. It's because of Mom's constant nagging that I have the habits I do.

_____

_____

3. After living with Ken for one year, I came to see he was not the easygoing guy I had always admired.

_____

_____

4. The fact that Mom worked and was never home accounts for many of my feelings and actions.

_____

_____

5. When Jan betrayed my trust in her, my view of human nature changed dramatically in at least a dozen ways.

_____

_____

6. It wasn't until Sis and I worked together on the charity bazaar that I understood just how compassionate she can be.

_____

_____

7. Professor Altman's frequent encouragement prompted my love of biology.

_____

_____

8. Aunt Jennifer and Uncle Tod were always so kind, sympathetic, and understanding after Dad's death that I emerged from the tragedy a wiser, stronger, and more determined person.

_____

_____

9. My tenth-grade English teacher showed me the kind of teacher I did not want to be.

_____

_____

10. The night I learned of David's accident, I realized just how much he meant to me.

_____

_____

Introductory Paragraphs:
The Lead-In

The thesis statement is one part of an introductory paragraph. It is generally easiest to place the thesis at the end of your introduction, although it can appear in the beginning or middle.

When the thesis appears at the end of the introduction, several sentences usually come before it. These sentences are known as the _lead-in_ because they "lead in" to the thesis or pave the way for it. Actually, the lead-in is an appealing feature of the longer theme format. It gives you the opportunity to ease your reader into your thesis. You can work your reader up to your thesis gradually. That is so much nicer than jumping right in with your statement of purpose, which you have to do when you are writing a single-paragraph composition. Furthermore, and perhaps most importantly, an interesting lead-in can spark your reader's interest and curiosity.

The lead-in can be handled in one of several ways or in a combination of ways. Below are sample lead-ins for a theme with some variation of the thesis, "I was twelve years old before I understood that my mother was young once."

1. Provide Background Information.   I remember that during my early years it never occurred to me that my mother had a childhood. Sure, I had heard Mom make occasional references to her youth, but somehow I could never imagine her as someone my own age. Like most children, I assumed that my mother had always been an adult and therefore could not understand the heart and mind of a child. In fact, I was twelve years old before I understood that my mother was young once.

2. Explain the Significance the Topic Has for the Writer.   Now that I am a mother, it helps me to understand my child's attitude toward me if I recall my own childhood attitude toward *my* mother. For example, whenever my young son treats me as some ancient being who doesn't understand youth, I recall that I was twelve before I realized my mother was young once.

3. Explain the Significance Your Topic Has for the Reader.   If you are a parent confused and frustrated by your child's actions (and what parent isn't from time to time?), I urge you to look back on your own youth for insight into the child's mind. For example, if you cannot convince your youngster that you *do* understand because you were young once, remember how long it took you to realize that your parents had a childhood. For my part, I was twelve before I understood that my mother was young once.

4. Provide a Related Anecdote.   Not too long ago my five-year-old son approached me with a question. "Mommy," he began seriously, "before I was here, whose mommy were you?" Nate's question made me realize that children have a hard time appreciating that their parents weren't always parents. His question also reminded me that I was twelve before I understood that my mother was young once.

5. Ask a Question That Will Be Answered.   Why is it that children are convinced their parents don't understand them? Perhaps this is because children are slow to realize that their parents also experienced the pleasures and pains of youth. I know that I was twelve before I realized that my mother was young once.
     Note: The answer to your question need not appear in the introduction. It can be in the body or conclusion of your theme.

6. State a Problem That Will Be Solved.   Often parents cannot convince their children that they understand the problems of youth. "I understand, honey; it happened to me too when I was your age," parents say in an effort to comfort. But it is a useless effort that generally earns the disbelieving reply, "But it was different then." Perhaps frustrated parents can take heart in the knowledge that although they can't convince their children that they were young and had similar experiences, as time passes kids do come to understand this one way or another. I know that it was not until I was twelve that I realized that my mother really was young once.
     Note: The solution need not appear in the introduction. It can be in the body or conclusion of your theme.

7. Use a Quotation.   "Youth," it has been said, "is wasted on the young." This saying refers to the fact that young people do not have the necessary awareness to appreciate their condition. Indeed, it is true that children lack many understandings. I recall that I was twelve before I realized that my mother was young once.

8. Provide a Meaningful Fact.   Juvenile delinquency has long been a fact of American life, but lately it has assumed new and frightening dimensions. Whereas in the past the juvenile delinquent was occupied with such things as stealing hub caps and skipping school, now the youngster is involved in hard drugs, arson, assault, and even murder. Some experts attribute this trend to a decline in American family life. Parents, they say, do not have enough influence over their children. However, I often wonder if parents really can influence their children sufficiently when most children cannot believe that their folks are sympathetic to their cause. I recall, for instance, that for years I could not believe that my mother understood me; hence, I discounted any advice she gave. It wasn't until I was twelve that I realized my mother did understand because she had been young once.

9. Give an Example.   I remember when I was a young child I'd get the same warning from my mother every night at the dinner table. "Eat everything on your plate," she would order. Her reason followed quickly: "When I was a child during the Depression, we never had enough to eat." I recall that her explanation never meant much to me because I couldn't think of my mother ever being *any* kind of a child, let alone a hungry one. It wasn't until I was twelve that I understood that my mother was young once.

10. Supply a Definition.   Childhood is that period of life when you have a one-sided view of parents as nothing more than rule makers. The child has no concept of parents ever having a life apart from their lawmaking roles. The onset of adolescence, then, can be targeted as the time the child recognizes that parents have a past. In my case, I was twelve before I realized that my mother was young once.

Note: Deciding on a lead-in for your theme is not a matter of selecting one of the above approaches randomly. Rather, you should choose the type of lead-in that best suits the purpose and style of your theme. Regardless of the lead-in you select, the typical introductory paragraph is structured in this way:

Lead-in
↓
Thesis

EXERCISE:
The Lead-In and Thesis

Compose a narrow thesis statement about one of your parents and an influence he or she had on your life. Before doing this, you may want to consult the freewriting that you did earlier. Then write two different kinds of lead-ins for your thesis.

Thesis: _____

_____

Lead-in 1: _____

_____

_____

_____

_____

_____

_____

Lead-in 2: _____

_____

_____

_____

_____

_____

_____

Body Paragraphs

In your body paragraphs you support, develop, discuss, explain, or prove your thesis. The number of body paragraphs you use will depend on the lengths you must go to in order to develop your thesis adequately and the number of aspects of your thesis you plan to discuss. However, you should have at least two body paragraphs. Otherwise, you would do better to use a one-paragraph theme format.

Typically, each body paragraph is composed of two parts: the topic sentence and the supporting detail. The *topic sentence* of a body paragraph informs the reader of what that paragraph will be about and what aspect of the thesis will be developed. This means that each body paragraph will have a different topic sentence presenting a different aspect of the thesis to be discussed. Like the thesis, the topic sentence obligates the writer to include only supporting detail that is relevant to it. That is, a body paragraph may include only detail that is relevant to both the topic sentence for that paragraph and the thesis.

While you studied paragraph writing in Chapter 2, you learned the importance of supplying detail that is relevant to your topic sentence. This is still true when you write the body paragraphs—the detail in each paragraph must relate to its topic sentence. Also in Chapter 2 you learned about the need to supply adequate detail. This also holds true when you write body paragraphs; there must be enough detail to satisfy the reader that the idea in the topic sentence has been developed satisfactorily.

Probably the easiest organization for body paragraphs is to begin with the topic sentence and then move to the supporting detail in this way:

Topic sentence

Supporting detail

Supporting detail

Supporting detail

Note: How much supporting detail is required depends on how much discussion is needed to develop the topic sentence adequately.

When I give students a writing assignment, usually someone asks, "How many body paragraphs should there be?" I always tell this student the same thing I'll tell you now: It is impossible for me to predict the number of body paragraphs a writer will need because this number will vary from writer to writer and from subject to subject. You see, how many body paragraphs you write is determined by how many points you want to make to support your thesis. If you have three main points to make, then you will need a separate body paragraph for each; four main points will lead to four body paragraphs, and so on.

Keep three things in mind, however. First, the principle of adequate detail also applies to your thesis. That is, you must provide enough detail in enough body paragraphs to satisfy your reader that you have covered your subject. Second, not only must the detail in each body paragraph be relevant to the topic sentence, but the detail and the topic sentence must also be relevant to the thesis. Finally, although no one can tell you for sure the number of body paragraphs you will need, I can tell you the fewest you can have: You should have at least two body paragraphs. If you have only one body paragraph, you are developing only one point. If that is the case, you might as well use the one-paragraph theme format.

EXERCISE:
The Topic Sentence

On the basis of the thesis you wrote for the previous exercise, compose three relevant topic sentences that could be used in body paragraphs to develop your thesis in a theme. You may want to consult your freewriting.

Topic sentence 1 _____

_____

Topic sentence 2 _____

_____

Topic sentence 3 _____

_____

EXERCISE:
Supporting Detail

At the top of each column below, write one of the topic sentences you composed for the previous exercise. Then under each topic sentence, list down the column the ideas you could use for detail to support the topic sentence. Be careful that your detail is both adequate and relevant. Once again, you may want to consult your freewriting for ideas.

Topic Sentence	**Topic Sentence**	**Topic Sentence**
_____	_____	_____
_____	_____	_____
_____	_____	_____
Supporting Detail	**Supporting Detail**	**Supporting Detail**
_____	_____	_____
_____	_____	_____
_____	_____	_____
_____	_____	_____
_____	_____	_____

Concluding Paragraphs

The conclusion of your theme is most important because it forms the last impression your reader gets. As is the case with introductions, conclusions can be handled in a variety of ways. Regardless of the way you choose, be sure you create the sense that your essay has come to a close. Below are some different approaches to the conclusion of a theme with the thesis, "I was twelve years old before I understood that my mother was young once."

1. Restate the Thesis in a New Way.   Yes, it is true that it took me twelve years to realize that my mother had a childhood. But once I understood that, I also understood that Mom was what she was largely because of experiences she had as a child.

2. Summarize the Main Points of Your Essay.   For many years Mom and I did not get along. I refused to believe she understood me, and therefore I paid little attention to what she said. But when I learned that spring of my twelfth year that Mom did understand because she had been like me once, I tried to follow her advice. Since then, we have had a smooth, happy relationship.

3. Introduce a New Idea That is Related to Your Thesis.   Although it took me twelve years to understand that my mother was once young, I hope my own child will come to that realization far sooner. Yet I must be realistic. Some things just take time.

4. Give Your Thesis or Main Points a Larger Application.   It is too much to expect young children to recognize that their parents were once young. However, as children mature, they will come to understand that their parents are people with a past. When this point is reached, parents and children can enjoy a richer relationship.

5. Mention any Conclusion or Discovery That Can Be Drawn from Your Theme.   It is really too bad that I did not recognize sooner that my mother had experienced much of what I did. It would have saved countless arguments between us.

6. Try to Solve a Problem You Have Raised.   If young children don't realize that their parents speak from the firsthand experience of their own youths, how can parents convince their children of their wisdom? The answer lies in the trust that must be established in the family. If children have learned to trust their folks, they will heed them, whether or not they understand the source of their knowledge.

EXERCISE:
The Conclusion

Write two different, but suitable, conclusions for a theme that uses the thesis, topic sentences, and supporting detail you composed in the previous exercises.

Conclusion 1 _____

_____

_____

_____

_____

_____

_____

_____

Conclusion 2 _____

_____

_____

_____

_____

_____

_____

_____

Outline of Theme Organization

The outline form for a theme organized in the fashion described in this chapter looks like this:

I. Introduction
    A. Lead-in
    B. Thesis
II. Body paragraph
    A. Topic sentence
    B. Supporting detail
    C. Supporting detail
    D. Supporting detail
       (Use as much supporting detail as necessary to develop topic sentence.)

III. Body paragraph
  A. Topic sentence
  B. Supporting detail
  C. Supporting detail
  D. Supporting detail
     (Use as many body paragraphs as necessary to develop thesis.)
IV. Conclusion

A SAMPLE THEME:
"The Purse"

The following theme tells how the writer, like Anderson, came to change her view of a parent. As you read it, observe the introduction (lead-in and thesis), body paragraphs (topic sentences and supporting details), and conclusion. Then answer the questions that follow the theme.

The Purse

Throughout my youth the words I recall my mother speaking most frequently were, "When I was your age. . . ." These words usually prefaced one of her stories about her childhood, and the stories usually concluded with some advice for me. Yet despite the frequency of Mom's when-I-was-your-age lectures, I was unable to envision my mother as a child. Her stories with their morals were usually lost on me, because no matter how often Mom talked about being my age, I never believed she had been. It wasn't until I was twelve that I understood that my mother *was* young once.

What happened to change my mind began one spring day of my twelfth year when Mom and I went shopping downtown at a local department store. We had been at it for hours, and I was pretty tired when Mom made her last purchase and headed for the clerk behind a cash register.

I lingered behind and listlessly sifted through some items heaped on a sale table. I came across a purse. It was pink and plastic and without a handle—clutch bags we called them then. It had a heavy metal zipper across the top and two snap closures in front. I was crazy about it. Seizing the purse, I ran to Mother to show her. "Please," I pleaded, "may I have it?" It was just the sort of bag all the girls were carrying. "No," Mom said, "we've spent quite enough money today. And besides, you have a purse." I could tell arguing was useless, so I replaced the bag and rejoined my mother. I was sad as we headed for the elevator, but I do not recall showing it.

I was surprised, however, by what happened next. We reached the elevator, and Mom pushed the down button. Then she did a puzzling thing. She turned, took my hand, and walked me back across the floor. When we reached the sale table, she picked up the bag, found a clerk, and paid for it. As she handed me the bag, she said, "When I was your age, there was a purse I desperately wanted. But it was the Depression, and there was no money." As we walked once again toward the elevator, I remember that I did not feel happy that I had my purse. Instead I felt very sad that Mother had not gotten hers.

It was then, when my mother bought me that pink, plastic purse that I realized she really *had* been young once. Suddenly all her when-I-was-young-once stories had meaning for me. If Mom had been my age, then she did understand me and have valuable advice to offer. This marked a turning point in our relationship. After that I listened to Mom more carefully and tried to heed her words. I rebelled less, and mostly I came to appreciate my situation more. After all, I got my purse, but she didn't get hers.

I don't know why that particular event made me realize my mother had a youth when earlier ones hadn't. Perhaps I had finally matured enough to understand. But I do know that I'll always treasure that purse—not so much as a purse but as a symbol.

Questions for Discussion:
"The Purse"

1. How did the writer view her mother before she got her purse?

_____

_____

2. How did this view affect the writer?

_____

_____

3. How did the writer view her mother after she got her purse?

_____

_____

4. How did this changed view affect the writer?

_____

_____

_____

5. What type of lead-in is used in this theme?

_____

6. What is the thesis?

_____

_____

7. What is the topic sentence for each body paragraph?

a. _____

_____

b. _____

_____

c. _____

_____

d. _____

_____

8. Are all the topic sentences relevant to the thesis?

_____

9. Is the support for each topic sentence relevant and adequate?

_____   _____

10. What kind of conclusion is used? Explain why you do or do not find it effective.

_____

_____

GRAMMAR AND MECHANICS: WHY BOTHER?

It is not unusual for students to view grammar and mechanics as just a lot of rules to learn. There are even those who see these rules as something English teachers have mastered but a great mystery to almost everyone else. Yet nothing could be more wrong. To understand this, it is first necessary to appreciate the role grammar and mechanics play.

If you were at a fancy restaurant with a date you wanted to impress, surely you would not pick up your bowl and loudly slurp down your soup. If you did this, you would create a bad impression. Similarly, when you write you try to create the best possible impression in the mind of your reader. Here using the appropriate grammar and mechanics can help you. In fact, you can consider the rules for grammar and mechanics a kind of writing etiquette, just as you consider your table manners a social etiquette.

Interestingly, any etiquette develops largely from convention—agreement about what is acceptable. Also interestingly, convention and etiquette are always changing. Not too long ago, it was quite improper for a woman to ask a man for a date. We all know how that convention has changed. Well, conventions governing grammar and mechanics have changed too. For example, at one time it was improper to begin a sentence with *and*, but today this rule has been relaxed.

So there you have it. If you think of grammar and mechanics as conventions subject to change, as a writing etiquette, you can relax with the conventions and try to regard them as the things we do because they are expected and because ignoring them can create a bad impression. However, do not think that these rules are without purpose. Just as social etiquette is meant to make interaction between people smoother, writing rules are geared to make communication between writer and reader clearer. Keep this in mind as you study the grammar sections in this book.

GRAMMAR AND USAGE

In this chapter you will learn about punctuating conversation and capitalizing words that refer to relatives. In addition, you will learn how to avoid sentence fragments.

Punctuating Conversation

In "Discovery of a Father" Anderson uses conversation. Look back at the story and find where he does this. Notice that the use of conversation adds a certain vividness and liveliness to the writing. In the theme you will be asked to write soon, you too may wish to use some conversation, especially since you will be writing about another person and what that person has to say may be important in your theme. Therefore you need to know how to punctuate direct quotations.

How you punctuate someone's exact words depends upon where in the sentence these words come. If the quotation comes at the end of a sentence, the sentence looks like this:

When Hal arrived home three hours late, Dad shouted, *[comma before Dad's exact words; quotation marks noting beginning of his exact words; first word of quotation is capitalized]* "Go straight to your room, young man." *[quotation marks note end of quotation and period inside quotation marks]*

If the quotation comes at the beginning of a sentence, the sentence looks like this:

"If you wait five minutes, we can all leave together." *[quotation marks note beginning of quotation; first word of quotation capitalized; comma at end of quotation; quotation marks note end of quotation]* he suggested. *[period at end of sentence]*

If you choose to break up your quotation, the sentence looks like this:

"Be careful crossing that street," *[quotation marks note beginning of quotation; comma and quotation marks where quotation is interrupted]* my aunt cautioned, "because there's a great deal of traffic on it." *[comma after words noting who spoke; quotation marks again where conversation picks up; no capital letter since it is mid-conversation; quotation marks where quotation ends; period inside quotation marks]*

If only your quotation is a question, place the question mark inside the quotation marks.

Kathy asked, "How soon will we be there?"

However, if the whole sentence forms a question, place the question mark outside the quotation marks.

Did your father really say, "There's no chance that I'll buy you a motorcycle"?

It is conventional to use quotation marks when exact thoughts are written, as in this example:

When the baseball crashed through Mr. Turner's garage window, Jerry thought, "Now I'm going to get it."

Note: Be careful to use quotation marks only when exact words or thoughts are written. Although it is tempting to use quotation marks in the following sentence, to do so would be considered incorrect.

No quotation marks here:

I told Dad that I would not go.

EXERCISE:
Punctuating Conversation

Punctuate the following sentences according to the rules for punctuating conversation. Watch capitalization. Some sentences are correct, and one is tricky—it can be handled in two ways.

1. Watch out for that second turn explained Mark because it's easy to miss.
2. I can't be there at noon, but I'll come as soon as I can Martha apologized.
3. Janet told Hank that the final exam was making her a nervous wreck.
4. My history instructor told the class study chapters six through ten for Thursday.
5. My history instructor told the class to study chapters six through ten for Thursday.
6. If I arrive before you Joan promised I'll save you a seat.
7. Alone in the woods, I thought this is really living.
8. Be back before noon Sam cautioned or you'll miss lunch.
9. The young artist wondered why is it I'm never satisfied with my paintings.
10. Is it true that Danielle said Peter is the last man I'd marry?

A Word about Capitals

You will be writing your next theme about one of your parents, so a word about capitalizing words used to refer to relatives is in order here. When such a word is used in place of a person's name, capitalize it. If the word is just showing a relationship, don't use a capital letter.

Example:	I was quite nervous about asking my father for permission to go to Florida with some friends.
Example:	When I told Father I totaled the car, I thought he would throw me out of the house.
Explanation:	In the first example, *father* is used with *my*. Hence the father's name (such as Herb) cannot be substituted or you would get *my Herb*. In the second example, *Herb* can be substituted for *Father* to retain a smooth sentence, so *Father* is capitalized.

EXERCISE:
Capitals

In the sentences below, circle the letters that should be capitalized.

1. Janet explained to dad that her midterm grades were low because she was worried about grandma's operation.

2. I often wonder how my dad managed to work two jobs all those years and still find time to coach my softball team.

3. I'll ask father if we can use his van for the trip, but I doubt that he will let us because my aunt is moving that day and she will probably need it.

4. Tell mother I'll be home late and not to worry because grandfather will be with me.

5. By the time I got to my mother's home, sis was furious; she had been waiting for an hour for me to drive her to our cousin's lake.

Sentence Fragments

The writer has an obligation to express his or her message as clearly as possible, with no stumbling blocks or distractions to confuse, annoy, or lose the reader. One way the writer achieves clarity is to use the sentence. The sentence is an aid because it tells the reader where ideas start and stop. The reader sees a capital letter and knows the expression of an idea has begun. He or she follows along the words until a period or other end mark of punctuation indicates that the expression of that particular idea in that particular way has ended. Thus sentences help the reader sort out ideas in order to understand the message more easily. But we all know this, which raises still another point about sentences—they are conventional and expected. Because sentences are conventional and expected, writers run the risk of confusing or alienating their readers if they do not use them.

So much for the reader. Now what about the writer? Remember, this chapter is about using writing to help you understand influences in your life. It's certainly easy to see that it would be pretty hard to understand *anything* if we couldn't tell where one idea stopped and another began. So once again, the sentence is important for establishing where ideas begin and end because the writer needs to know the boundaries of his or her ideas so they can be examined, clarified, sorted out, interrelated, and *understood* more readily.

But sometimes writers think they are using sentences when they are not. Instead, they are writing sentence fragments. A *sentence fragment* is a group of words that is being presented as a sentence (because it has a capital letter at the beginning and a period or other end punctuation at the end). However, it is not really a sentence because it lacks a complete thought. A group of words that lacks a complete thought generally leaves the reader hanging on for more—although "more" never comes.

Fragment: When Dad walked into the room. (We're left waiting for more because the thought is incomplete.)

Sentence: When Dad walked into the room, everyone yelled, "Surprise!" (The thought is complete; there is no feeling that more should follow.)

Correcting Sentence Fragments:
Adding Missing Information

Some word groups are fragments because they lack the information that would complete the thought. To make a fragment a sentence, the missing information must be supplied.

Fragment: Knowing that Beth is always late.

Sentence: Knowing that Beth is always late, I set our departure time an hour earlier than necessary.

EXERCISE:
Correcting Fragments by Adding Missing Information

Add information to the following fragments to make them sentences.

Example: Before leaving for our vacation.

Revision: Before leaving for our vacation, we told the police and our neighbors that we would be gone.

1. After eating six pepperoni pizzas.

_____

2. Beside the yellow Corvette parked at the curb.

_____

3. Knowing I had to pass the final to pass the course.

_____

4. When my best friend gave up smoking.

_____

5. Who looked like King Kong.

_____

Correcting Sentence Fragments:
Joining the Fragment to an Existing Sentence

Some fragments can be eliminated by joining them to sentences that appear either before or after them.

Sentence and fragment: Jonathan and Mike were best friends. Until they began to date the same girl.

Fragment eliminated: Jonathan and Mike were best friends until they began to date the same girl.

EXERCISE:
Correcting Fragments by Joining Them to Sentences

Eliminate the fragments by joining them to sentences.

Example: As we crossed campus talking to each other. Jerry and I lost track of the time.

Revision: As we crossed campus talking to each other, Jerry and I lost track of the time.

1. My best friend is Fred Thompson. A fellow who enjoys swimming.

_____

_____

2. After class we hurried to The Pub. A place where a student can forget the troubles of school life.

_____

_____

3. Working together on the Spring Weekend project. Chris and Kate became best friends.

_____

_____

4. On a stormy day Benjamin Franklin experimented with a kite. Because he wanted to show the similarity of lightning and electricity.

_____

_____

5. We'll take Sue with us. If she arrives by nine.

_____

_____

Correcting Sentence Fragments:
Changing Verb Forms

Sometimes a word group is a fragment because its verb is in the wrong form. To correct such a fragment, change the verb to its appropriate form.

Fragment: Martha forgetting her purse on the table.

Sentence: Martha forgot her purse on the table.

EXERCISE:
Correcting Fragments by Changing Verb Forms

Correct the following fragments by changing verb forms.

Example: My older brother believing that he can accomplish anything if he works hard enough.

Revision: My older brother believes he can accomplish anything if he works hard enough.

1. One reason *Star Wars* is so popular being it appeals to our sense of fun.

_____

_____

2. Everyone recognizing the problem of pollution.

_____

_____

3. The grass parched by the hot sun.

_____

_____

4. The students listening attentively in class.

_____

_____

Finding and Correcting Fragments in Your Own Themes

Sometimes finding fragments in your own themes is tricky. This is because when a fragment appears next to a sentence, a quick reading makes the fragment *seem* to convey a complete thought although in fact the thought is completed by a sentence next to the fragment. A quick reading of the following paragraph, for example, could lead you to overlook the fragment.

The character played by John Travolta in *Saturday Night Fever* is an interesting one. During the week he has little power and status. Yet on weekends his dancing ability makes him important and admired at the local discotheque. In one scene, for example, when Travolta walks into the discotheque. Everyone steps aside to let him pass. [*Did you find the fragment? It's the next to last word group.*]

Because it is sometimes easy to overlook fragments in our own work, those of us who write them need a special way to proofread for them. The two-finger proofing method usually works well. If writing fragments is your problem, proof your themes an extra time, looking only for fragments. Place your left index finger below the first capital letter signifying a sentence beginning. Then move your right index finger across the words until you come to an end mark of punctuation. Examine the word group between your fingers to be sure it expresses a complete thought. If it does not, revise the fragment to a sentence, using one of the three methods explained. If the word group is a complete thought, move your left finger to the next capital marking a sentence beginning and move your right finger to the next end punctuation. Examine that word group for a complete thought. Continue in this manner to the end of your theme. Time-consuming? Yes, but two-finger proofing is an excellent way to catch those fragments, so it's worth the time.

WRITING ASSIGNMENT I

So far in this chapter you have read "Discovery of a Father," done some freewriting, learned theme organization, and studied fragments, some punctuation, and capitalization. Now it is time to write a theme that will help you understand one important influence in your life. You are to discuss *one* aspect of your relationship with *one* of your parents, being sure to discuss fully what that aspect is and what effect that aspect has on you today.

For example, a student once described how his father always demanded perfection of him. He discussed his repeated tries to perform to his father's standards and the resulting frustration he felt at his father's disapproval of his attempts. Then the student explained the lack of self-confidence and fear of failure he has to this day as a result of his father's demands. (Incidentally, this student later reported that he gained much insight into the source of his problems and some ideas about how to solve them as a result of his writing.)

By now you probably realize that many of the exercises you have done in this chapter will help you write this theme. Go back to the thesis, lead-ins, topic sentences, detail, and conclusions you wrote in the earlier exercises and put these together to form your first draft. Then refine what you have by improving any way you can, adding or taking out detail, shaping sentences, and so on. Also, check your freewriting for ideas to include.

Questions to Answer before Submitting Your Theme

1. Do you have an introduction with a narrow thesis and a lead-in?
2. Do your body paragraphs have topic sentences relevant to the thesis?
3. Is your detail relevant to the topic sentence of the paragraph it appears in?
4. Is your conclusion effective?
5. Have you checked your diction for economy and precision?

6. Have you avoided clichés?

7. Have you used commas with coordinate modifiers?

8. Have you punctuated conversation correctly?

9. Have you used capitals for titles of relatives used like names?

10. Have you avoided fragments?

11. Have you tried to use some new words from your vocabulary list?

12. Have you proofread carefully for careless errors?

13. Have you checked spellings?

WRITING ASSIGNMENT II

For this assignment, write a theme discussing how you view one of your parents differently now from the way you did at some point in the past. (Or discuss how you viewed one of your parents at some point in the past differently from the way you did in the more distant past.) Be sure to discuss what effect the changed view has had on you. You might also want to mention what prompted the change. The sample theme in this chapter (see p. 68) illustrates this assignment.

WRITING ASSIGNMENT III

Obviously, parents are not the only significant influence in our lives. Other people have had great impact on us, too. Also, situations and events have influenced us. For this assignment, pick one event that has had an effect on you. Explain what the event was, the effect it had on you, and why you believe the event influenced you as it did. The event you select can be an encounter with someone, a news story you read or heard, a happy or sad occasion in your family, a change in schools, a movie you saw, a book you read, a scene you witnessed—just about anything. Don't forget the help freewriting can provide.

A FINAL WORD

Understanding influences in our lives leads to self-awareness and self-acceptance—two keys to mental and emotional well-being. Writing can help us achieve this understanding, so why not take time out to write about those things that shape and motivate you? Of course, writing by itself may not lead to ultimate self-understanding, but it surely will provide many valuable insights.

Chapter 4

Discovering Solutions:
Writing to Solve Problems
and Clear up Confusion

Sometimes life seems to get so complicated, doesn't it? It almost seems that one day we're all carefree kids on summer vacation, and the next day we wake up to find we're grown and face serious problems, difficult decisions, doubts, and confusion. What career to choose, what courses to take, what bills to pay, whether to get married, whether to have children, where to live, what job offer to accept—these are so few of a long list of concerns we all must deal with. Of course, this is all part of maturing. And fortunately, we come to realize that although the problems get trickier in adulthood, the rewards and satisfactions become greater. Nevertheless, we all have periods in our lives when our doubts and confusion seem overwhelming. There are times when some problems just seem impossible to solve.

Confusion and problems are a natural part of living. Still, they can make for unhappiness—or, at the very least, a degree of unpleasantness. So what's the solution? Sometimes things straighten out by themselves if we sit back and wait. Other times we must work to iron things out. Then there are those times when we must get help. The help may come from a friend, relative, religious leader, or trained counselor. Or, believe it or not, sometimes writing can help. Sometimes you can use writing to help order the confusion in your life and solve some of your problems. That is what I plan to demonstrate to you in this chapter.

READING SELECTION:
"Life for My Child Is Simple, and Is Good"

The following poem by Gwendolyn Brooks is interesting for two reasons. First, it points out the contrast between the uncomplicated life of the child and the more complex life of the adult. Second, the poem notes how fears can hold us back and keep us from experiencing life fully. When you finish the poem, take a moment to consider your own fears and whether they hold you back and complicate your life.

Life for My Child Is Simple, and Is Good
Gwendolyn Brooks

Life for my child is simple, and is good.
He knows his wish. Yes, but that is not all.
Because I know mine too.
And we both want joy of undeep and unabiding things,
Like kicking over a chair or throwing blocks out of a window
Or tipping over an icebox pan
Or snatching down curtains or fingering an electric outlet
Or a journey or a friend or an illegal kiss.
No. There is more to it than that.
It is that he has never been afraid.
Rather, he reaches out and lo the chair falls with a beautiful crash,
And the blocks fall, down on the people's heads,
And the water comes slooshing sloppily out across the floor.
And so forth.
Not that success, for him, is sure, infallible.
But never has he been afraid to reach.
His lesions are legion.
But reaching is his rule.

Vocabulary List:
"Life for My Child Is Simple, and Is Good"

In the spaces below, write the words that you are not sure you know the meanings of. Then check a dictionary and write a brief definition next to each word. Finally, select one or two words to add to your vocabulary list in Appendix A. Work to use these and all the words on your vocabulary list so you will become comfortable with them.

_____   _____

_____   _____

_____   _____

Questions for Discussion:
"Life for My Child Is Simple, and Is Good"

1. The title of the poem and the first line are the same. Both seem to imply that the simple life of the child is the good life. Do you believe it's true that the simple life of children is a good one? Explain.

_____

_____

_____

2. In what ways is the life of the child in the poem simple and good?

_____

_____

_____

3. Do you believe that it's also true for adults that the simple life is a good one? Explain your view.

_____

_____

_____

4. Both the speaker and the child "want joy of undeep and unabiding things." What do you take this to mean?

_____

_____

_____

5. Does the speaker—or any adult—experience the "joy of undeep and unabiding things" very often? Why or why not?

_____

_____

_____

6. In what way is the speaker different from the child?

_____

7. What is it that the child does not fear?

_____

8. What is it that the speaker fears? Is this fear shared by many adults?

_____

_____

9. Does the author consider success to be very important? What *does* she consider important?

_____

_____

10. What is it that makes the child's life simple and good?

_____

_____

GETTING READY: FREEWRITING

"I just don't know what's bothering me." If you're like the rest of us, you've said these words more than once over the years. It's often true that we can feel troubled but be unsure of just why it is we feel that way. Sometimes if we wait long enough, the answer will come—and sometimes it won't. Sometimes it's a good idea not to wait but to work to get at the source of the difficulty. If you want to do this, try freewriting. Just sit down for fifteen minutes and write about your feelings of discomfort. Follow the procedure described in Chapter 3 (see p. 53). When you are done, you may well discover that you have written things that explain why you are bothered. If now is one of those times you feel disturbed without quite knowing why, try some freewriting.

GETTING READY: LOOKING WITHIN

Sometimes when life seems complicated, it gets hard for us to figure out what the best course of action is. Even if we can figure out what we want, we can't always determine the best path to follow in order to get it. As one step toward seeing how writing can help you order confusion, you will do some very personal writing based on careful soul-searching. Because this writing is so personal, you will not be asked to share it with your instructor. This should free you of any hesitancy you might have about recording the results of some honest, in-depth soul-searching.

To get the maximum benefit from this assignment, you must be totally honest with yourself and make an earnest effort to look within and record accurately what you find. If you do so, the results will be meaningful.

The assignment will be completed in stages, and you will need several sheets of paper. Follow precisely the steps below.

1. Find some quiet place where you are comfortable thinking and look within yourself to discover the things you want out of life. You may find answers as vague as "happiness" or as specific as "marriage to Ruth."

2. On the basis of what you have discovered in step 1, decide on your three most important life goals. These may be anything from the very specific "master's degree in electrical engineering from Florida State University" to the more general "freedom to go my own way." Write these three goals down, each at the top of a separate sheet.

3. Next, think carefully about why these goals are important to you. Below each written goal, state in at least a paragraph why that goal is important to you. In the process of evaluating and writing the importance of your goals, you may change your mind about them. If so, the assignment has already helped you order a portion of your life. Simply rethink and substitute another goal for the discarded one and write why this one is important to you.

4. Now consider specifically how you plan to work to achieve your goals. Below your statement about the importance of each goal, plot how you plan to achieve it. Be sure to be very specific. For example, the steps for getting a master's degree in electrical engineering might look like this:
   a. Study very hard in undergraduate school to maintain a 3.5 average.
   b. Write Florida State now to get graduate school catalog to be sure I meet or can work to meet all entrance requirements.
   c. Cultivate good personal and academic relationships with major professors to earn their support, advice, and recommendations.
   d. Join student auxiliary to electrical engineering professional association now.
   e. In June of junior year, write for application.
   f. In summer between junior and senior years, get job to earn money to visit Florida State.
   g. In September of senior year complete and mail applications.
   h. During Christmas break of senior year, visit Florida State to speak to admissions officers.

5. On the basis of the nature of your goals and what you have determined you must go through in order to achieve them, decide in percentage terms what your chances for success are. For example, if your present grade point average is 2.6, and you must bring it up to a 3.5 for

graduate school at Florida State, you might consider your chance for admission at 60 percent against. Write down both your chances for realizing your goals and why you estimate your chances as you do.

6. As the last step, write down for each goal what you plan to do in the event you do not reach it. You may wish to indicate a substitute goal you will strive for or another way to attempt achieving the original goal. Or you could decide to abandon the goal and concentrate your energies on other existing goals. Regardless, try to be as realistic as possible.

You will now have before you master plans for three goals very important to you. Both the plans and the thinking through to decide on goals should contribute much to ordering your life and overcoming obstacles hindering your progress. Furthermore, the writing of this assignment may have clarified much that formerly existed more as vague notion than clear plan. Good luck to you as you work toward your life goals.

THE DIFFERENCE BETWEEN SPEECH AND WRITING

For quite some time now—longer than you can even remember—you have been speaking your language easily and well to communicate effectively. Without much conscious strain, you convey ideas, desires, needs, fears, likes, dislikes, and many other thoughts quite clearly. So don't ever sell yourself short; you know a great deal about your language, and you use that knowledge readily all day long, day after day. And the language skills you use so often and so well you can bring to your writing to communicate just as effectively as you do with speech. However, there are some differences between speech and writing, and you should be aware of them.

First, our speech typically does not need to be as well organized as our writing. When we speak, our listener can always interrupt to ask a question if the flow of our ideas is confusing or if the connection between thoughts isn't understood. Also, the listener can ask for an explanation if we don't express ourselves quite clearly. When we write, however, we can't add needed explanations if the reader is confused—in fact, we may not even know the reader is confused—so we must labor to ensure clarity and tight organization. Second, those who listen to our speech have the benefit of our tone of voice, facial expressions, and gestures. This is not the case with writing, so we must rely on such things as carefully chosen words, correct paragraphing, and carefully chosen detail to be understood. Finally, those who listen to our speech are generally less demanding than those who read our writing. Hence we must pay stricter attention to grammar and usage conventions as writers than as speakers.

It is true that writing makes greater demands on us than speaking, but this should not cause us undue worry. Instead, it means that when we write, we should plan carefully. The next sections of this chapter will suggest some ways you can do that planning. Interestingly, they present ways you can bring some order to your writing and to the writing process—just as this chapter is about how writing can bring some order to your life. Thus, order is something you can bring to your writing *and* take away from it.

PLANNING YOUR WRITING: THE OUTLINE

You can use writing to help plan your life (as you did when you wrote about your goals), but you must also plan your writing. The best way to plan your writing is to outline. In the last chapter you wrote one form of outline, although it was not called such. When you wrote a thesis, selected an approach to the lead-in, wrote topic sentences in columns, listed ideas in the columns to develop those topics, and chose an approach to the conclusion, you were really writing one form of the outline. Planning in this fashion is one way to ensure a well-organized, adequately developed theme.

You are probably also familiar with the outline that has Roman numerals, letters, and numbers. This kind of outline can work very well, but there is another useful way to outline that you may find easier. The form for this outline appears below. To use it as a way of planning your theme, you fill in the blanks with phrases and/or sentences that indicate what you will write in your theme.

Outline Form for Planning the Theme

Introductory Paragraph

   1. Opening comments that form lead-in _____

_____

_____

   2. Thesis statement _____

_____

_____

First Body Paragraph

    1. Topic sentence _____

_____

    2. Supporting detail _____

_____

_____

Second Body Paragraph

    1. Topic sentence _____

_____

_____

    2. Supporting detail _____

_____

_____

Third Body Paragraph

    1. Topic sentence _____

_____

_____

    2. Supporting detail _____

_____

_____

Conclusion

_____

_____

_____

Note: The number of body paragraphs will vary. Be sure, however, that you have at least two.

Planning Your Writing:
How to Fill in the Outline

Of course, before you can outline, you must know what ideas you wish to cover in your theme. I suggest that you come up with these ideas by using one of the prewriting techniques discussed in Chapter 1. Then put your points in the outline. If some of them don't fit, discard them. If you need more detail, add it. You might have to outline several times before you come up with something that works. But don't worry. That's the way it is for most of us.

There is more than one procedure you can follow when using the outline form on pp. 86–87. One way works like this:

1. Settle on a tentative thesis and write it in the outline.
2. List the ideas you wish to include on a separate sheet.
3. Examine the list and form topic sentences that will allow you to discuss these ideas.
4. Write these topic sentences in the outline.
5. Take the ideas on your list and place them in the outline under the appropriate topic sentences.
6. Stop and examine your outline. Check to be sure that all your topic sentences are relevant to the thesis.
7. Check to be sure all your support is relevant to the appropriate topic sentence.
8. Make sure your detail is adequate.
9. More than likely you will find some problems that need correcting. Change or rearrange detail, alter topic sentences or the thesis, add or take out ideas, and do whatever else may be necessary.
10. Once you are satisfied with the thesis and the outline of your body paragraphs, fill in the introduction and conclusion sections of the outline.

Now you are ready to write a first draft. Remember, the outline is the plan for the essay. Like so many "best laid plans," it may require reworking once the first draft is begun. Despite the most careful planning, writers sometimes decide to change things mid-draft. That's fine. Don't be so rigid that you force your theme to conform to an outline when altering the outline would make for a better theme. Finally, do not underestimate the value of an outline. To write without one is very much like constructing a building without a blueprint.

PLANNING YOUR WRITING: TWELVE STEPS FOR WRITING A THEME

In general, the person who jumps into a theme with no plan runs a great risk of turning out an unsatisfactory product—or at least work that is not as good as it could be. Most writers need a procedure to follow, a plan of attack. Of course, this plan varies among writers, but you might try the twelve-step plan described below. It is one that many writers use successfully. Actually, it is an outlining procedure of sorts, but it is also much more, for it takes you from the stages before writing all the way to proofreading. As was the case when outlining was discussed, this procedure is meant to bring some order to the writing process. And order is something we can bring to writing as well as something we can take away from it.

Step 1. Empty Your Head.   Once you have a general idea of what you want to write, the first thing you should do is a form of prewriting called emptying the head. To do it, you simply jot down in list form any and every idea that occurs to you without pausing to evaluate the worth of these ideas. Emptying your head serves two purposes. First, it helps generate ideas much the same way freewriting does. Second, it forces you to record those ideas before you run the risk of forgetting them. (If you have difficulty coming up with ideas for your list, try freewriting or another prewriting activity first.)

Step 2. Cross Out and Add.   When your list of ideas is complete, review it. Cross out those ideas you consider unworthy or don't want to use for whatever reason. Add any ideas that occur to you.

Step 3. Form Your Preliminary Thesis.   On the basis of the ideas now on your list, form a preliminary thesis statement for your theme. This thesis is called preliminary because it is probably not the one you will include in the finished product. Rather, it is a tentative working model that will guide your thinking in these early stages. The preliminary thesis can even be something like, "This theme is about _____." Once it is thought out, write it at the top of another sheet of paper.

Step 4. Group Related Ideas.   To complete this step, examine the ideas on your list. Decide which ideas belong together in the same paragraph and group them accordingly. All the ideas that belong together in one body paragraph can be marked *A*. All the ideas that belong together in another body paragraph can be labeled *B* and so on. It is possible that you will have some ideas that do not group with other ideas. These ideas, at least for the time being, will be labeled individually to be treated in separate paragraphs.

Step 5. Cross Out and Add.   Once again, review your list of ideas. Cross out any you will not use after all (and if you still do not see a relationship

run the risk of allowing what you *meant* to write interfere with your perception of what you actually *did* write.

3. Be Aware of the Kinds of Mistakes You Typically Make. If, for example, you have a history of writing fragments, pay special attention to fragments when you proof. In fact, proofread one extra time, checking just for fragments.

4. Proofread More than Once. The first time you proof, look at everything. The next time or times through examine your work for the kinds of errors you have a tendency to make. How many times you proof is a decision only you can make. But base that decision on an honest judgment of just how likely you are to make errors.

There are several ways to proofread. Try them all and determine which method or combination of methods works best for you.

1. Place your finger, pen, or pencil below the first word of your theme. Examine that word for correctness and then move to the next word or piece of punctuation and examine that. Move in this fashion, one word or punctuation mark at a time, until you come to the end of the theme. This technique forces you to examine everything in the theme closely. It also minimizes the chance of mentally substituting or inserting material that isn't really there. It is important to go one word or punctuation mark at a time; otherwise, you will pick up too much speed to be accurate.

2. Place a ruler or other straight edge below one line of your theme and proof just that line one word or punctuation mark at a time. This method is a bit faster than the previous one, and for that reason it may not be quite as effective for you. You must judge for yourself.

3. Read your theme out loud very slowly, one word at a time. This method allows you to see and hear errors. Be sure you say *exactly* what you have written.

4. Slowly recite your theme into a tape recorder, being sure you say exactly what you have written. Then play back the tape, following along with your written theme as you listen. This method also allows you to see and hear errors.

A quick, casual reading through of your theme may bring some weaknesses to your attention, but it does not qualify as careful, efficient proofreading. Regardless of which technique or combination of techniques you use, remember that proofreading is time-consuming. However, the time spent proofing is time wisely spent because it is far better to find your own errors than to have someone else find them for you.

GRAMMAR AND USAGE

In this chapter, you will learn how to avoid run-on sentences, errors in subject-verb agreement, and errors in tense shift so you do not confuse your reader. Also, three more comma rules will be presented along with rules for the semicolon.

Run-on Sentences

As you recall from the previous chapter, use of the sentence is both conventional and a service to the reader. Yet sometimes, as the last chapter pointed out, writers believe they are writing sentences when, in fact, they are writing sentence fragments. Other times, writers think they are writing a single sentence when what they are writing should be two or more sentences. To write something as one sentence that should be more than one sentence is to write a run-on sentence. Consider the following example.

> Dr. Jones gave me a C on my final exam the grade is quite a disappointment and sure to hurt my average.

From the beginning to "exam," the words form a complete thought and hence have sentence status. From "the grade" to the end, a second complete thought is formed, and hence these words have sentence status. Two complete thoughts that run on into each other without the proper punctuation to separate them form a run-on sentence.

Run-on sentences are to be avoided for the same reason fragments are to be avoided: They can confuse, alienate, or lose a reader. In short, they interfere with effective communication. Furthermore, when complete thoughts are not separated properly and are permitted to run into each other, confusion can be created in the mind of both the reader *and* the writer. Since this chapter is about clearing away confusion, this is a good time to pause and discuss how to correct run-on sentences.

Correcting Run-On Sentences:
Using a Period and Capital Letter

The easiest way to correct a run-on sentence is to make each word group that has sentence status the sentence it should be by using periods and capital letters.

Run-on:　　　I searched the apartment thoroughly my chemistry book was nowhere to be found.

Correction:	I searched the apartment thoroughly. My chemistry book was nowhere to be found.
Explanation:	The word groups before and after the period each express a complete thought and therefore have sentence status.

EXERCISE:
Correcting Run-On Sentences

Correct the run-on sentences by using periods and capital letters.

Example:	In the checkout line the child cried for gum her mother refused to buy it for her.
Correction:	In the checkout line the child cried for gum. Her mother refused to buy it for her.

1. Janet called her supervisor to tell him she would not be in because she was sick later that night Mr. Pearson saw her entering a disco club.

_____

_____

2. In the middle of the night Mr. Dawson heard strange noises downstairs he called the police who arrested a cat burglar prowling behind the garage.

_____

_____

3. Under no circumstances should a student cheat it's far better to fail honestly and have self-respect.

_____

_____

4. A trip to Las Vegas is just what I need unfortunately I only have $65.00 in my savings account.

_____

_____

5. Jake hired a man to paint his apartment I told him I would do it for nothing I guess he just doesn't trust me to do a good job.

_____

_____

_____

Correcting Run-On Sentences:
Using a Semicolon

Think of a semicolon (;) as being formed by placing a period over a comma. It therefore signals a pause that is longer than that for a comma but shorter than that for a period. Semicolons can be used to separate complete thoughts.

Run-on:	By midnight we were so exhausted we couldn't stand up thus we all agreed to call it a night.
Correction:	By midnight we were so exhausted we couldn't stand up; thus we all agreed to call it a night.
Explanation:	The word group before and the word group after the semicolon each expresses a complete thought.

If both the semicolon and the period and capital can correct a run-on, you may well be wondering which correction to use in your own writing. As a writer, base your decision on the kind of relationship you want to demonstrate between your complete thoughts. Because a semicolon signals a pause shorter than that for a period, it is used to show a closer relationship between your ideas than a period does. Therefore, if you wish to signal a close relationship between your complete thoughts, use a semicolon. If you wish to signal more of a break between your complete thoughts, use a period and capital letter.

Note: When a semicolon is used, no capital letter is used after it.

EXERCISE:
Correcting Run-On Sentences

Correct the following run-ons by adding semicolons.

Example:	The team was fired up for the game unfortunately, its defense was weak, so it was behind after the first half.
Correction:	The team was fired up for the game; unfortunately, its defense was weak, so it was behind after the first half.

1. The prospect of leaving at 5:00 A.M. to go fishing did not please Jim however, no one would agree to a later departure, so he had to go along with the idea.

2. The minute Karen signed the lease she had misgivings she was, however, obligated to stay in the apartment for a year.

3. After the last guest left, I surveyed the living room and groaned it would take at least four hours to clean up the mess.

4. The moment Noreen opened the door, she realized something was wrong it was far too quiet, for one thing for another, the dog didn't run to greet her.

5. Grades are rarely an accurate index of what a student knows therefore, I believe we should do away with them.

Correcting Run-On Sentences:
Using a Comma and Coordinate Conjunction

A *conjunction* is a word that joins other words or word groups. A *coordinate conjunction* is a word that joins words or word groups of equal value or rank. The common coordinate conjunctions are:

and	nor
but	for
or	yet
	so

Example:	Please bring my hat *and* gloves.
Explanation:	The words *hat* and *gloves* are of equal value; they receive the same amount of emphasis in the sentence. The coordinate conjunction *and* can connect words of equal value.
Example:	I think I'll order the spaghetti special *or* the hamburger plate.
Explanation:	The word groups *the spaghetti special* and *the hamburger plate* are of equal value; they receive the same amount of emphasis in the sentence. The coordinate conjunction *or* can connect word groups of equal value.

Coordinate conjunctions can be used to correct run-ons because a run-on contains at least two equally ranked elements—complete thoughts (known in grammar terminology as *coordinate clauses*).

If you wish to correct a run-on by using a coordinate conjunction, be sure to place a comma *before* that coordinate conjunction.

Run-on:	I must get to work by 9:00 my boss will be angry for sure.
Correction:	I must get to work by 9:00, or my boss will be angry for sure.
Explanation:	The word group before and after the comma and coordinate conjunction each expresses a complete thought.

Notice that in the previous example only the coordinate conjunction *or* carries a meaning that makes sense in the corrected sentence. To correct a run-on, you cannot choose just any coordinate conjunction. Instead you must select one that makes for a sensible sentence. Also notice that when you correct a run-on with a comma and coordinate conjunction, you can demonstrate to your reader what the relationship between your two ideas is by virtue of the coordinate conjunction you choose. Notice, for example, the difference in meaning in the following two sentences.

> A. I would like to go outside, <u>but</u> the snow is quite high.
> B. I would like to go outside, <u>for</u> the snow is quite high.

Note: It is important to remember that a comma alone will *never* correct a run-on sentence. It is the comma and conjunction together that fills the bill.

EXERCISE:
Correcting Run-On Sentences

Correct the following run-on sentences by using commas and coordinate conjunctions.

Example: Joanne explained why she can't return to school next semester I think she is making a mistake.

Correction: Joanne explained why she can't return to school next semester, but I think she is making a mistake.

1. Ann Landers' column is the first thing I turn to in the newspaper it is filled with human interest.

_____

_____

2. Kevin certainly surprised his parents when he got a job he shocked them when he cut his hair.

_____

_____

3. Never before have I won anything you can imagine my disbelief when I realized I held the winning lottery ticket.

_____

_____

4. Everyone admits that the ability to write well is important to survival in college few people realize that writing can play an important role outside the classroom as well.

_____

_____

_____

5. I better study calculus at least three hours each night I will never pass the course and graduate on time.

_____

_____

Correcting Run-On Sentences:
Using a Subordinate Clause

A *clause* is a group of words with a subject and a verb. There are two kinds of clauses, the coordinate clause and the subordinate clause. The *coordinate clause* expresses a complete thought, whereas the *subordinate clause* does not.

Coordinate clause: the heavy rains lasted only thirty minutes

Subordinate clause: because the heavy rains lasted only thirty minutes

In both the above clauses, the subject is *rains,* and the verb is *lasted.* However, only the coordinate clause expresses a complete thought. Thus if a period and capital were added to the coordinate clause, it would stand as a sentence, but if they were added to the subordinate clause, it would still lack a complete thought and be only a sentence fragment.

A run-on sentence can be defined as two or more coordinate clauses that are not separated by a period and capital, by a semicolon, or by a comma and coordinate conjunction. So far we have discussed correcting run-ons by separating the coordinate clauses. There is, however, another way to make the correction. This way involves changing one of the coordinate clauses to a subordinate clause.

Run-on: The heavy rains lasted only thirty minutes it was possible to resume the baseball game.

Correction: Because the heavy rains lasted only thirty minutes, it was possible to resume the baseball game.

Explanation: The word group from the beginning of the sentence to the comma is a subordinate clause. The remaining words form a coordinate clause.

In the correction, notice that the coordinate clause carries the main idea of the sentence, while the subordinate clause conveys the less important idea.

To aid you in correcting run-ons by changing one of the coordinate clauses to a subordinate clause, here is a list of some common subordinate conjunctions that can be used to begin subordinate clauses.

after	as though	in order that	until
although	because	once	when
as	before	since	where
as if	even though	so long as	whereas
as long as	if	unless	while

Punctuation Note: If your subordinate clause comes at the beginning of the sentence, follow it with a comma. If it comes at the end of the sentence, precede it with a comma if it is not closely related to the coordinate clause.

Example: Although I was never good at math in high school, I got an A in college algebra.

Explanation: The introductory subordinate clause is followed by a comma.

Example: Janet cannot tolerate apartment living, whereas her husband hates the idea of home ownership.

Explanation: The comma precedes the subordinate clause because the subordinate clause shows some separation from the coordinate clause.

Example: I thought I would faint when Chuck arrived unshaven and dirty to meet my parents.

Explanation: The subordinate clause shows no separation from the coordinate clause, so no comma is used.

EXERCISE:
Correcting Run-On Sentences

Correct the following run-on sentences by changing one of the coordinate clauses to a subordinate clause (add a subordinate conjunction). Place the subordinate clause first. Then rewrite each sentence, placing the subordinate clause last. Be sure to use commas correctly.

Example: Halloween is my favorite holiday. I'm just a kid at heart.

Revision A: Because I'm just a kid at heart, Halloween is my favorite holiday.

Revision B: Halloween is my favorite holiday because I'm just a kid at heart.

1. I did not have my television repaired after it broke I have no interest in the programs now on the air.

    a. _____

    _____

    b. _____

    _____

2. I quickly pulled my car to the curb I heard a siren.

    a. _____

    _____

    b. _____

    _____

3. Mr. Jordan is qualified for the position I worry about the frequency with which he changes jobs.

    a. _____

    _____

    b. _____

    _____

4. I swam every day in the ocean I lived in Atlantic City.

    a. _____

    _____

    b. _____

    _____

5. Seafood was never appealing to me I spent a summer in Maine and grew to love it.

    a. _____

    _____

    b. _____

    _____

Proofreading for Run-Ons

If you have a tendency to write run-on sentences, proofread an extra time looking only for run-ons. Use the two-finger proofing method discussed for fragment finding (see p. 77). When you find a run-on in your writing, correct it by using one of the four methods described in this chapter.

A Word about Commas with Clauses

Included in the discussion of how to correct run-on sentences were three comma rules. Let's look at them once again.

1. Use a comma before a coordinate conjunction connecting coordinate clauses.
   Example: I really hate to leave so soon, but I promised Mom I'd be home for dinner.

2. Use a comma after an introductory subordinate clause.
   Example: Before I leave for vacation next week, I plan to have all my work done.

3. Use a comma before a subordinate clause that follows a coordinate clause, if the subordinate clause shows some separation from the coordinate clause.
   Example: I'd love to take you with me, although I'm not sure Claudette would like the idea.

Remember: In Chapter 2 you also learned to separate coordinate modifiers with a comma when *and* is not separating them.

EXERCISE:
Commas with Clauses

In the following sentences place commas where they are needed. Some of the sentences are correct.

 1. If you are seeking a job in advertising prepare yourself for a highly competitive sometimes disappointing career.

 2. My grandmother remembers the day when telephone calls from a pay station cost only a nickel.

 3. The sky was mostly cloudy and the weather forecast promised a high of only 65 but we decided to head out for the beach nonetheless.

 4. Pete was furious with Linda for standing him up although he said he would forgive her if she apologized.

5. Mom claims she did not wait up for me but I don't believe her because the coffee in her cup was still hot when I came in.

6. Since I cannot make the party you may borrow my red floor-length skirt and matching blouse.

7. After we looked at fifteen houses we decided to buy the two-story one in the country.

8. I hesitate to accept my uncle's job offer yet it may be the only one I get.

9. Mother and Dad made me promise to call them if I expected to be late.

10. Although most ten-year-olds are too young to baby-sit the one who lives next door is quite mature for her age and I believe she can handle my young son.

A Word about the Semicolon

In the discussion about correcting run-ons, you learned that a semicolon can be used to separate complete thoughts (coordinate clauses). You also learned that it is convenient to think of a semicolon as signaling a pause that is longer than a comma's but shorter than a period's. For this reason, you should separate complete thoughts with a period and capital letter to signal a long pause that indicates a complete break between the complete thoughts. Use a semicolon to indicate a shorter pause and hence a closer relationship between the complete thoughts. Use a comma and coordinate conjunction to signal the briefest pause and thus the closest relationship between the complete thoughts.

Example:	The temperature dropped ten degrees in one hour. It was clear the storm was rapidly approaching.
Example:	The temperature dropped ten degrees in one hour; it was clear the storm was rapidly approaching.
Example:	The temperature dropped ten degrees in one hour, so it was clear the storm was rapidly approaching.
Explanation:	In the first example the relationship signaled between the complete thoughts is the most distant; in the second example the relationship is closer; and in the third example the relationship between the complete thoughts is the closest.

Note: As a writer, you must decide how close a relationship you want to indicate between your complete thoughts. This will determine what punctuation you use.

There is also another time to use the semicolon: to separate items in a series when commas are used within the series.

Example: Several of my favorite people decided to join the travel group: Professor Caldwell, my sophomore history teacher; Janie Levy, my old roommate; Aunt Esther, my godmother; and Ivan Dickins, my boyfriend's best friend.

Explanation: The semicolons separate the items in the series because commas are used in the phrases. Hence the semicolons serve to avoid the confusion of too many commas.

EXERCISE:
The Semicolon

In the following sentences, place semicolons where they are needed. One sentence is correct.

1. Lauren refuses to take any more courses from Professor Higley however, I find him a fascinating lecturer.

2. As far as I'm concerned, you would be wise to minor in education in case you ever wanted to teach.

3. The four-dollar buffet is a real bargain because it includes two salads, one that is fruit and one that is vegetable three soups, all of them homemade a main course, which is always tasty and a choice of pies, some fruit and some cream.

4. At first I thought I could never pass organic chemistry now I know I can't.

5. By the time we reached Ft. Worth, everyone was exhausted the only thing to do was get some rooms for the night.

Subject-Verb Agreement

Subject-verb agreement means that when you use a singular subject (only one thing is referred to), you should also use a singular verb. Similarly, when you use a plural subject (more than one thing is referred to), you should use a plural verb. That is, your subject and verb should *agree* in number. Often this is not a problem for us. We don't write, "the dog are barking," because *dog* as singular (one) doesn't work with the plural (more than one) *are*.

In many cases, subject-verb agreement need not be a problem for us if we remember that most nouns have an *s* in the plural, and most verbs have an *s* in the singular. Thus subject-verb agreement is often easy to achieve if this simple hint is kept in mind: If the noun subject has a final *s*, the verb does not; if the noun subject lacks a final *s*, the verb adds one.

Example: An aged <u>parent</u> <u>deserves</u> special attention.

Example: Aged <u>parents</u> <u>deserve</u> special attention.

Explanation: In the first example, <u>parent</u>, which is singular, does not end with *s*. To achieve agreement, the singular verb <u>deserves</u> is used, which does end with *s*. In the second example, <u>parents</u>, which is plural, ends in *s*, but the plural verb <u>deserve</u> does not end in *s*.

There are many exceptions to this *s* rule (for example, *child* does not add an *s* in the plural), but it does work often enough with noun subjects to serve as a useful guide.

Sometimes the verbs *be, have, do,* and *go* cause agreement problems, especially when their subjects are pronouns rather than nouns. If these verbs present agreement problems for you, the best thing to do is to memorize the chart below.

	Singular	**Plural**
Be	I am	we are
	you are	you are
	he, she, it is	they are
	I was	we were
	you were	you were
	he, she, it was	they were
Have	I have	we have
	you have	you have
	he, she, it has	they have
Do	I do	we do
	you do	you do
	he, she, it does	they do
Go	I go	we go
	you go	you go
	he, she, it goes	they go

There are some other situations that give us pause because the subject-verb agreement may be just a bit tricky. It's worthwhile to note those occasions to avoid the confusion that can come from lack of agreement.

Compound Subjects Joined by And

1. When two subjects are joined by *and,* a plural verb is used if each subject is a separate unit.

   Example: Both my history professor and my English teacher agree that I should go on to graduate school.

   Explanation: the plural *agree* is used because the history professor and the English teacher are two separate individuals.

2. When the two structures in the subject joined by *and* are to be taken together as a single unit, a singular verb is used.

   Example: Toast and jelly is my favorite bedtime snack.

   Explanation: The singular *is* appears because toast and jelly is meant as a single food.

Compound Subjects Joined by Or, Nor, or Either–Or, Neither–Nor

1. If both subjects are singular, a singular verb is used.

   Example: Neither Jonathan nor his brother is able to be here to help.

   Example: The week before Christmas a card or package arrives each day.

2. If both subjects are plural, a plural verb is used.

   Example: Either the kids down the street or the neighbors across the street are responsible for that mess.

   Example: No vegetables or dairy products are allowed on this diet.

3. If one subject is singular while the other is plural, the verb agrees with the closer subject.

   Example: Neither the scouts nor their scoutmaster is willing to take on such a dangerous project.

   Example: My mother or my sisters are always available to help.

Subjects with Phrases

When the complete subject includes a phrase, disregard the phrase to determine subject–verb agreement.

Example: This stack of old books <u>has</u> been collecting dust for too long; let's move it.

Explanation: The complete subject, *this stack of old books,* contains the phrase *of old books,* which is disregarded when determining agreement. The singular *has* is therefore used to agree with the singular *stack.*

Example: A blend of rare spices <u>is</u> responsible for the meat's distinctive flavor.

Explanation: The complete subject, *a blend of rare spices,* includes the phrase *of rare spices.* The phrase is disregarded, and the singular *blend* remains. Thus the singular verb *is* appears.

Note: Phrases like those above are called *prepositional phrases.* To remember what a *preposition* is, think of a box and a ball. Any word that can describe the relationship of the ball to the box is a preposition. The ball can be on the box, in the box, or near the box, so *on, in,* and *near* are prepositions. Two exceptions to this guideline are *of* and *to.* It's hard to think of a ball being "of the box," or "to the box," but *of* and *to* are still prepositions. Below are some common prepositions.

against	away from	at	inside
around	beneath	in	beside
into	near	of	over
to	through	under	with

Indefinite Pronouns Used as Subjects

1. The following indefinite pronouns are singular and take singular verbs:

anyone	either/neither	no one	someone
anybody	everyone	nobody	somebody
each	everybody	one	

Example: Each of us <u>favors</u> a different vacation spot.

Note: Remember to disregard the phrase when determining agreement.

Example: One of the teams <u>is</u> sure to get a hit this inning.

Note: Remember to disregard the phrase when determining agreement.

Example: Anyone who comes to class so infrequently <u>deserves</u> to fail.

Example: Neither is the type to do such a thing.

Example: Everybody is certain the storm will pass by.

Note: A good way to remember this group of singular words is to notice how many of them end in the obviously singular forms *one* and *body*.

2. The following indefinite pronouns can be either singular or plural, depending on the meaning intended:

all   more   none
any   most   some

Example: Some of the theme is quite well written.

Example: Some of the boys are leaving at noon.

Example: All of the members agree that the by-laws must be revised.

Example: All of the apple pie remains to be enjoyed.

Note: You may have noticed that with this group of indefinite pronouns the prepositional phrase does determine the verb used. This, of course, is an exception to the rule about subjects with prepositional phrases. This exception exists because it is only by looking at the phrase that we can tell whether an indefinite pronoun from this special class is meant to be singular or plural.

Collective Noun Subjects

1. A *collective noun* is one that has a singular form but nonetheless refers to a group. Ordinarily, collective nouns use singular verbs. Some common collective nouns include:

army   choir   family   staff
audience committee faculty team
band   crowd   jury

Example: Today's army wants to join you.

Example: The budget committee reports that at last we are in the black.

Example: The office staff is preparing the holiday celebration.

2. Expressions of weights, measure, time, degree, and so on use singular verbs when the amount is to be taken as a single unit.

Example: Four cups of milk is all this recipe requires.

Example: Two weeks in this town is like a life sentence.

Explanation: In both cases above, the units of measure or time are meant as single units.

When more than one unit is meant, a plural verb is used.

Example: Seven gallons of milk <u>are</u> at the back door; surely the milkman made an error.

Example: At least ten of these pounds <u>have</u> to come off, or I'll never fit in that dress.

Explanation: The units of measure above are meant as more than one separate unit.

There Is, There Are

When you begin a sentence with *there is* or *there are,* the choice of singular or plural verb is made according to the subject that follows the expression.

Example: There <u>is</u> no agreement about who would make the best class president.

Explanation: The subject is the singular *agreement.*

Example: There <u>are</u> several ways to answer that question.

Explanation: The subject is the plural *ways.*

Inverted Order

Word order is said to be inverted when the verb comes before the subject. At such times be careful to make the verb agree with the subject and not just another nearby word.

Example: Staying with Mom last weekend <u>were</u> Uncle Ed and Aunt Jean.

Explanation: The subject is the compound *Uncle Ed and Aunt Jean.*

Example: Behind the cars <u>is</u> a little lost puppy.

Explanation: The subject is the singular *puppy.*

Relative Pronouns as Subjects

The relative pronouns used as subjects are:

who   which   that

A verb should always agree with the word to which the relative pronoun refers (the referent).

Example:	The chapters that <u>are</u> to be read for next time cover the Civil War.
Explanation:	*That* refers to *chapters,* so the plural *are* is used.
Example:	The student who <u>studies</u> every night keeps up with all assignments.
Explanation:	*Who* refers to *student,* so the singular *studies* is used.

EXERCISE:
Subject–Verb Agreement

Underline the appropriate verb in each sentence below.

1. One of the many children in the crowd (is, are) my niece.

2. Two hundred dollars (seems, seem) too much for that coat.

3. The English faculty (believes, believe) that all students should take at least one literature course.

4. Toast and coffee (is, are) not a very substantial breakfast, but bacon and eggs (is, are).

5. Of all the students in the class, there (was, were) only a few willing to do extra-credit work.

6. Neither my sister nor my parents (wants, want) me to go away to school.

7. Both the governor and his wife (hopes, hope) to attend the ground-breaking ceremonies.

8. Two weeks (is, are) a painfully long time to wait for final grades.

9. My sister or one of my brothers (plans, plan) to attend my commencement.

10. None of the excuses he supplied (is, are) a satisfactory explanation for missing class.

11. Either the play or the movie (sounds, sound) appealing.

12. Each of us (is, are) obligated to contribute some small sum to such a worthy charity.

13. Any person who (works, work) the way he does deserves a great deal of credit.

14. At the rear of the auditorium (was, were) the band waiting to perform, and just behind that group (was, were) the soloist and her parents.

15. Any of you (is, are) welcome to join me for lunch.

16. Everyone (needs, need) to be complimented from time to time.

17. His collection of old records (strikes, strike) me as being quite valuable.

18. Either a bed jacket or reading materials (makes, make) a suitable gift for a sick person.

19. What we hope for and what we get (is, are) often miles apart.

20. The parts of the movie that I enjoyed most (was, were) what most critics disliked.

Tense Shift

Verbs have various tenses (present, past, and future) to show different times. For the most part, a writer should be consistent in the use of tense throughout a piece of writing to avoid confusing the time scheme and thereby confusing the reader. This means that the writer should not move from one tense to another unless it is necessary to do so to pinpoint the time accurately. The following paragraph, which begins in the past tense, has several tense changes. The underlined shifts are inappropriate, but the bracketed ones are acceptable.

> When I awoke that December morning to the 5:00 A.M. news on my clock radio, I winced at the realization that it was yet again another Monday. "Blue Monday" [is] what Mom always [calls] it. Dutifully, I rolled from my bed and stumbled to the kitchen to start some tea water. I hear Jim in the apartment above beginning his morning ritual and remember how long it had been since I stopped to see him. Poor Jim—because he was laid off he [is] terribly depressed. I [guess] I should be grateful I [have] a job, even if it [means] rising so early each day. The shrill blast from the kettle jolts me from my thoughts of Jim. I poured my tea, sighed, and begin to prepare for my day as just another working stiff.

EXERCISE:
Tense Shift

In the paragraph above, the underlined verbs reflect inappropriate tense shifts. The bracketed verbs are ones that shifted tense for an acceptable reason. In the left column below, change the incorrect underlined verb to what it should have been in the paragraph. In the right column, explain why the bracketed verb represents an acceptable shift. Number 1 in each column is done for you as an example.

1. hear _____heard_____

2. remember _____

3. jolts _____

4. begin _____

1. [is] present tense because Mom still (in the present) calls the day Blue Monday

2. [calls] _____

3. [is] _____
_____

4. [guess] _____
_____

5. [have] _____
_____

6. [means] _____
_____

WRITING ASSIGNMENT I

The idea behind this chapter is that writing can help you sort through confusion and solve problems. So far, you have seen how freewriting can help you clear up some uncertainty and find the source of a problem. Also, you have written an exercise based on your goals to see how writing can help you clarify what you are after and establish the steps to achieve what you want. You have, in addition, studied ways to take the confusion out of the writing process, and you have learned some grammar and usage points that also can eliminate confusion in your writing. Now it is time to write a theme.

In "Life for My Child Is Simple, and Is Good," Gwendolyn Brooks writes of a fear many adults have—the fear of failure. If we have this fear, it is indeed a problem, because it keeps us from reaching out. It keeps us from trying the new, the adventurous, the risky—so it keeps us from experiencing life to the fullest.

Now, let's be honest. We all have our fears; we wouldn't be human if we didn't. And just as the fear described in Brooks' poem is a problem because it gets in the way, so, too, may our own fears be troublesome. So let's use writing to tackle one of our fears and solve a problem that way.

For this assignment, you are to select one fear you have or had. Mention what the fear is or was and why you have or had it (if you know this). Then explain the effect the fear has or had on you. If you still have the fear, try to discover a way you might overcome it. (Sometimes just getting the fear out in the open or down on paper goes a long way toward helping you deal with it.) If you no longer have the fear, discuss what you learned from it that you can apply to your present life.

A Sample Theme:
"Fear of Death"

The sample theme below illustrates writing assignment I. Read it carefully and answer the questions that follow it. Also, see p. 114 for questions to answer before submitting your theme.

Fear of Death

There was a time in my life not too long ago when reason failed me, and fear took over to dictate my actions. This began when a friend called to tell me that her child of five months had died. Crib death, the doctor had ruled it. Being a mother myself, the incident hit me hard.

My first reaction was one of disbelief. I felt numb to the reality and refused to believe it. I knew older children died. They drove their bikes down driveways and in front of cars; they swam in unsafe places; they fell out of trees. But infants didn't die. Infants were special gifts from God, innocent, pure, and specially protected.

Eventually, the disbelief passed, and I realized what had happened. I ached at the thought of the pain the parents had to be suffering, and I wanted to be a sympathetic friend. I knew I should go to the house to comfort them. I knew I should go to the funeral to mourn with them. I did neither. At the time, I was puzzled and concerned by my inability to do anything to help ease their suffering. Then it hit me: If death had visited the house once, it could still be lingering there. I was scared, scared to be in death's shadow.

It wasn't for me that I feared. It was for my son. If death was hunting babies, I had to protect mine. I had to stay away from death's shadow, lest it follow me home and claim my son. I worried that death would take him before he could enjoy life and before I could enjoy him. I knew I had to protect him.

My fear of Randy's death became an obsession. I started finding it hard to go to sleep, for I had to be awake to ward off the evil spirit. I would lie there in bed listening to the breathing of my son. Each time he moved, I would hurry in to check him. I felt I could fight death by watching for it. If I did go to sleep, I would wake with a start every few minutes. Each time I'd go to Randy's crib to check. As I stood there, I trembled, knowing that I'd slept and momentarily given up my vigil. As an extra precaution, I kept a light on by his crib, for death lurks in darkness.

As time progressed, the fear became stronger. I could no longer control it with light or frequent checks. Finally, I brought Randy in to sleep with me. I felt I could protect him by keeping him close. If he was in my arms, Randy could not be stolen away.

The fear had become all-consuming, yet somehow I realized I had to get a grip on myself. Perhaps it was the last, desperate gesture of an exhausted woman, but I turned to God. I began to pray. I knew on my own I wasn't strong enough to protect Randy, so I asked for help. At last I was strengthened, and I found peace of mind. I came to understand that if death did come, it was only as the messenger of God.

As terrible as that whole experience was, some good did come of it. I learned something. I learned that human beings are capable of handling only so much on their own. Once they have passed the point of being able to cope alone, people must look beyond themselves for the help they need. Since the death I have learned that when I need help I can seek spiritual guidance. My fear is gone now, but when problems come up and I can't handle them alone, I know where to turn.

Questions for Discussion:
"Fear of Death"

1. Did you enjoy this theme? Explain.

_____

_____

_____

2. What is the thesis?

_____

_____

3. What kind of lead-in is used?

_____

4. What are the topic sentences for each body paragraph?

_____

_____

_____

_____

_____

_____

5. Is each topic sentence relevant to the thesis?

_____

6. Check the supporting detail for each body paragraph. Is it relevant and adequate? Explain.

_____

_____

_____

7. What kind of conclusion is used?

_____

_____

8. Cite one example of coordinate clauses that are properly connected with a coordinate conjunction and explain the use of the comma.

_____

_____

_____

9. Cite one example of an introductory subordinate clause linked to a coordinate clause and explain the use of the comma.

_____

_____

_____

10. Cite a sentence that uses semicolons correctly and explain why the use is correct.

_____

_____

_____

_____

Questions to Answer before Submitting Your Theme

Before handing in your theme, be sure you can answer yes to the following questions:

1. Did you outline or use the twelve-step approach?
2. Is your diction precise, economical, and free of clichés?
3. Have you checked subject–verb agreement?
4. Have you checked for inappropriate tense shifts?
5. Have you used commas with coordinate modifiers? Before coordinate conjunctions connecting complete thoughts? After introductory subordinate clauses? Before final subordinate clauses that show separation from the rest of the sentence?
6. Have you used semicolons correctly?
7. Have you punctuated conversation correctly?
8. Have you used capitals for the titles of relatives used like names?
9. Have you checked for fragments and run-ons?
10. Does your introduction have a lead-in and narrow thesis?
11. Do your body paragraphs have relevant topic sentences and adequate, relevant supporting detail?
12. Is your conclusion effective?
13. Did you try to use new vocabulary words?
14. Have you proofread more than once, paying special attention to the kinds of mistakes you have a tendency to make? Did you check spellings?

WRITING ASSIGNMENT II

I was most impressed with the following letter, which appeared in Ann Landers' syndicated column.

Dear Ann Landers:

I'm a 26-year-old woman and I feel like a fool asking you this question, but—should I marry the guy or not? Jerry is 30, but sometimes he acts like 14. We have gone together nearly a year. He was married for three years but never talks about it. My parents haven't said anything either for or against him but I know deep down they don't like him much.

Jerry is a salesman and makes good money but he has lost his wallet three times since I've known him and I've had to help him meet the payments on his car.

The thing that bothers me most, I think, is that I have the feeling he doesn't trust me. After every date he telephones. He says it's to "say an extra goodnight" but I'm sure he is checking to see if I had a late date with someone else.

One night I was in the shower and I didn't hear the phone. He came over and sat on the porch all night. I found him asleep on the swing when I went to get the paper the next morning at 6:30 A.M. I had a hard time convincing him I had been in the house the whole time.

Now on the plus side: Jerry is very good-looking and appeals to me physically. Well—that does it. I have been sitting here with this pen in my hand for 15 minutes trying to think of something else good to say about him and nothing comes to mind.

Don't bother to answer this. You have helped me more than you will ever know.—Eyes Opened

It is clear that Eyes Opened used writing to solve a pressing problem and thereby ordered some confusion in her life. Why could she not solve her problem simply by thinking it through? Well, many of our problems can be solved that way. But others may be solved more easily by working them through on paper. This is true for two reasons. First, as was the case for Eyes Opened, the mere act of putting the problem on paper can clarify it to such an extent that the solution suddenly just suggests itself. Second, the act of writing can trigger logical thought and insightful thinking. As you know, writing demands we find a logical order to and relationship among our thoughts, whereas thinking without recording can often be less ordered. As a result, sometimes we can just take our thinking further when we record it.

Try it yourself to see. Select a problem or difficult decision you face. Write a letter to Ann Landers fully describing your difficulty. If the mere act of writing the letter does not lead to a solution, turn around and pretend you are Ann Landers and write a response to the letter as objectively as you can.

WRITING ASSIGNMENT III

Sometimes writing can aid problem-solving by formalizing a plan of attack. Try this approach once and see if it works for you. Identify some problem you have. It can be anything from "I need more money" to "I wish I had more friends."

At the top of a sheet, write the problem as precisely as you can. Below your statement of the problem, list every acceptable solution you can think of. (I say "acceptable solution" because if you need more money, I do not think bank robbery is a course of action for you to consider.) If you want more friends, your solution list might include some of the following:

Strike up more conversations with classmates

Join a church or synagogue group

Rush a university fraternity or sorority

Call some old acquaintances I no longer see

Throw a party for people I've met on campus

Arrange to study with some classmates

Go to popular bars on weekends

Offer to tutor a classmate whose grades are weak

Once you have exhausted the possible solutions to put on your list, number your solutions in the order you wish to try them. You may want to try the easiest solution first or the one that seems to stand the best chance of working. Next, work to put the first solution into effect. If after a reasonable time the problem still exists, move to try the second solution. Continue this way until your problem is solved or the situation is improved to your satisfaction. Obviously, for some problems this technique may fail altogether. But at least you have a way to order your efforts and work to overcome a problem. Many students tell me that this procedure has worked for them.

WRITING ASSIGNMENT IV

Early in this chapter I mentioned that as we get older our lives get more complex. Of course, this isn't necessarily bad, but on occasion our lives can become so complicated that we get confused and lose sight of those things that we really consider important. When this happens, we often feel the need to sort through the confusion by simplifying things and getting back in touch with our basic needs and desires.

To help you get in touch with the things you consider most important, try this assignment. Pretend that you only have three days to live. Write a theme telling how you would spend those days and explaining why you would do the things you write about. To benefit from this writing, you must be realistic. Thus you shouldn't say you would buy a Corvette if you only have fifty dollars in the bank. Because three days is not very much time, you will need to plan your activities carefully, choosing only those that mean the most to you. In turn, this careful planning will reveal to you what *really* matters in your life. This should help you identify your more basic wishes.

A FINAL WORD

We all have problems; we all become confused. This chapter has shown you ways writing can help when problems and confusion make their way into your life. Sometimes writing can help you identify the problem; sometimes writing can help you see things more clearly; and sometimes writing can lead you to find answers and solutions. So the next time you have trouble solving a problem or working through some confusion, sit down and do some writing.

The Bridge

Chapter **5**
Clarifying and Stimulating Thought:
Persuasive Writing

Have you ever tried to think something through, only to find that your thoughts don't go anywhere? Well, you're not alone; we've all had that experience. Sometimes we make no headway because our thinking wanders off into unrelated areas. Other times, our thinking takes a circular route and we don't develop any new insights. Instead we just keep returning to what we already know. Then there are times when we try our best, but we just can't clarify anything, and in the end our ideas are as fuzzy as they were when we started.

I'm not sure why our best efforts to think things through are sometimes troubled in these ways, but I do have a theory. I believe that at times we all lack a certain discipline to *force* our thoughts to move forward. Why this problem exists need not really concern us, because regardless of the cause, there is a solution. Yes, once again, writing can help.

In the last chapter, you learned ways to structure the writing process in order to reduce confusion (remember the twelve-step approach?). Well, when the writing process is structured and ordered, a degree of discipline is imposed on the writer. With definite steps to follow, the writer can move in an orderly fashion. This order can make the difference between productive and unproductive thinking.

When we think without writing, there are no definite steps to follow, so it's easier to go off into unrelated areas, travel in circles, and fail to clarify things. However, with steps to follow, we are driven to advance from one point on to the next, often with satisfying results. Please don't get me wrong, though. Thinking by itself is very useful. Even lack of order and digression can lead to a brainstorm. But there are those times when lack of order gets us nowhere. At these times, writing can help by structuring the thought process.

In addition, because a good piece of writing should be organized logically, even more discipline is imposed on us. We are forced to be sure ideas relate clearly and progress logically. This forces us to think things through even further to determine how our ideas relate to each other. Similarly, because good writing has adequate detail, we must continue thinking until we have enough ideas to back up our points. This means that when we write, we often follow our ideas further than we would otherwise—when a conclusion alone seems enough and we may not bother searching for material to support the validity of the conclusion.

Also, when our thoughts must end in a finished product—the theme—we are often better able to stimulate thought than when the results of our thinking are an unwritten conclusion. It is harder to say, "Ah, forget it; I'm not getting anywhere," for example, when the finished product must be handed in on Tuesday.

Finally, it seems that, for many people, seeing their thoughts written on a page objectifies them. As a result, these thoughts seem clearer and more easily pursued, so that new thoughts follow fast on their heels. Furthermore, a written idea is captured and more easily examined for validity. Unwritten thoughts are easily lost and less easily evaluated.

Actually, if the assignments in this book are successful, all the writing you are asked to do will help you clarify and stimulate your thought to achieve an insight where none existed before. Take a moment to reflect on the writing you have done so far to see that this is true. In this chapter, however, writing to clarify thought and stimulate insight will be the main focus, so you can see for yourself how writing helps in this area. Probably this function of writing is seen most clearly when you write persuasively. Therefore, it is persuasive writing—attempting to win a reader to your point of view, using logic and reason—that you will do in this chapter.

I have noted that persuasive writing can help you clarify your thought and stimulate ideas, but I have also said that the purpose of persuasive writing is to convince your reader of the wisdom of your point of view. In order to convince your reader, you must consider that person's possible point of view and reaction to your ideas. For this reason, some attention is given in this chapter to ways to consider your reader when you write.

READING SELECTION:
"How to Say Nothing in Five Hundred Words"

This chapter is about using writing to clarify your thoughts and stimulate insight; many kinds of writing can do this. Even the prewriting you have learned to do serves this purpose. However, at no time do we have to think more clearly and develop ideas more carefully than when we write to convince others of something—that is, when we write persuasively. This is why persuasive writing is what you will study in this chapter.

As a first step toward learning about persuasion, you will read three persuasive pieces. This first writing is a portion of a longer essay by Paul Roberts. In his delightful essay Roberts includes a very weak piece of persuasive writing supposedly written by a student. Roberts intends the mock (pretend) theme to be bad in order to make a point. We, too, shall use that weak "student" theme to make some points—about persuasive writing.

How to Say Nothing in Five Hundred Words
Paul Roberts

It's Friday afternoon, and you have almost survived another week of classes. You are just looking forward dreamily to the weekend when the English instructor says: "For Monday you will turn in a five-hundred-word composition on college football."

Well, that puts a good hole in the weekend. You don't have any strong views on college football one way or the other. You get rather excited during the season and go to all the home games and find it rather more fun than not. On the other hand, the class has been reading Robert Hutchins in the anthology and perhaps Shaw's "Eighty-Yard Run," and from the class discussion you have got the idea that the instructor thinks college football is for the birds. You are no fool. You can figure out what side to take.

After dinner you get out the portable typewriter that you got for high school graduation. You might as well get it over with and enjoy Saturday and Sunday. Five hundred words is about two double-spaced pages with normal margins. You put in a sheet of paper, think up a title, and you're off:

WHY COLLEGE FOOTBALL SHOULD BE ABOLISHED

College football should be abolished because it's bad for the school and also bad for the players. The players are so busy practicing that they don't have any time for their studies.

This, you feel, is a mighty good start. The only trouble is that it's only thirty-two words. You still have four hundred and sixty-eight to go, and you've pretty well exhausted the subject. It comes to you that you do your best thinking in the morning, so you put away the typewriter and go to the movies. But the next morning you have to do your washing and some math problems, and in the afternoon you go to the game. The English instructor turns up too, and you wonder if you've taken the right side after all. Saturday night you have a date, and Sunday morning you have to go to church. (You can't let English assignments interfere with your religion.) What with one thing and another, it's ten o'clock Sunday night before you get out the typewriter again. You make a pot of coffee and start to fill out your views on college football. Put a little meat on the bones.

WHY COLLEGE FOOTBALL SHOULD BE ABOLISHED

In my opinion, it seems to me that college football should be abolished. The reason why I think this to be true is because I feel that football is bad for the colleges in nearly every respect. As Robert Hutchins says in his article in our anthology in which he discusses college football, it would be better if the colleges had race horses and had races with one another, because then the horses would not have to attend classes. I firmly agree with Mr. Hutchins on this point, and I am sure that many other students would agree too.

One reason why it seems to me that college football is bad is that it has become too commercial. In the olden times when people played football just for the fun of it, maybe college football was all right, but they do not play football just for the fun of it now as they used to in the old days. Nowadays college football is what you might call a big business. Maybe this is not true at all schools, and I don't think it is especially true here at State, but certainly this is the case at most colleges and universities in America nowadays, as Mr. Hutchins points out in his very interesting article. Actually the coaches and alumni go around to the high schools and offer the high school stars large salaries to come to their colleges and play football for them. There was one case where a high school star was offered a convertible if he would play football for a certain college.

Another reason for abolishing college football is that it is bad for the players. They do not have time to get a college education, because they are so busy playing football. A football player has to practice every afternoon from three to six and then he is so tired that he can't concentrate on his studies. He just feels like dropping off to sleep after dinner, and then the next day he goes to his classes without having studied and maybe he fails the test.

(Good ripe stuff so far, but you're still a hundred and fifty-one words from home. One more push.)

Also I think college football is bad for the colleges and the universities because not very many students get to participate in it. Out of a college of ten thousand students only seventy-five or a hundred play football, if that many. Football is what you might call a spectator sport. That means that most people go to watch it but do not play it themselves.

(Four hundred and fifteen. Well, you still have the conclusion, and when you retype it, you can make the margins a little wider.)

These are the reasons why I agree with Mr. Hutchins that college football should be abolished in American colleges and universities.

Vocabulary List:
"How to Say Nothing in Five Hundred Words"

In the spaces below, write the words you are unsure of that you came across in the Roberts essay. Then next to each word write briefly the definition that fits the way the word was used in the selection. Pick one word you wish to include in your vocabulary and add it along with its definition to your vocabulary list in Appendix A. Remember, you should be reviewing the words on your list each day and working to use them in your speech and writing.

_____   _____

_____   _____

_____   _____

Questions for Discussion:
"How to Say Nothing in Five Hundred Words"

   1. Explain what is wrong with the "student's" method of approaching a writing assignment.

_____

_____

_____

   2. What advice could you give the "student" for a better approach to writing?

_____

_____

_____

   3. What is the thesis of "Why College Football Should Be Abolished"?

_____

_____

   4. What three points are meant to support the thesis?

_____

_____

_____

   5. Is the support for each body paragraph satisfactory? Why or why not?

_____

_____

_____

   6. Overall, is the diction economical? Cite three examples to support your view.

_____

_____

_____

7. How do you react to the conclusion of "Why College Football Should Be Abolished"? Why do you react this way?

_____

_____

_____

8. Do you feel convinced that college football should be abolished after reading the "student" theme? Why or why not?

_____

_____

_____

9. How, then, does the student writer manage to say nothing in 500 words?

_____

_____

_____

READING SELECTION:
"Strike Out Little League"

The next selection, by former Philadelphia Phillies pitcher Robin Roberts, is a far better piece of persuasion than the mock (pretend) student theme you read previously. As you read, try to discover what Roberts does to be so convincing.

Strike Out Little League
Robin Roberts

In 1939, Little League baseball was organized by Bert and George Bebble and Carl Stotz of Williamsport, Pa. What they had in mind in organizing this kids' baseball program, I'll never know. But I'm sure they never visualized the monster it would grow into.

At least 25,000 teams, in about 5,000 leagues, compete for a chance to go to the Little League World Series in Willamsport each summer. These leagues are in more than fifteen countries, although recently the Little League organization has voted to restrict the competition to teams in the United States. If you judge the success of a program by the number of participants, it would appear that Little League has been a tremendous success. More than 600,000 boys from 8 to 12 are involved. But I say Little League is wrong—and I'll try to explain why.

If I told you and your family that I want you to help me with a project from the middle of May until the end of July, one that would totally disrupt your dinner schedule and pay nothing, you would probably tell me to get lost. That's what Little League does. Mothers or fathers or both spend four or five nights a week taking children to Little League, watching the game, coming home around 8 or 8:30 and sitting down to a late dinner.

These games are played at this hour because the adults are running the programs and this is the only time they have available. These same adults are in most cases unqualified as instructors and do not have the emotional stability to work with children of this age. The dedication and sincerity of these instructors cannot be questioned, but the purpose of this dedication should be. Youngsters eligible for Little League are of the age when their concentration lasts, at most, for five seconds—and without sustained concentration organized athletic programs are a farce.

Most instructors will never understand this. As a result there is a lot of pressure on these young people to do something that is unnatural for their age—so there will always be hollering and tremendous disappointment for most of these players. For acting their age, they are made to feel incompetent. This is a basic fault of Little League.

If you watch a Little League game, in most cases the pitchers are the most mature. They throw harder, and if they throw strikes very few batters can hit the ball. Consequently, it makes good baseball sense for most hitters to take the pitch. Don't swing.

Hope for a walk. That could be a player's instruction for four years. The fun is in hitting the ball; the coach says don't swing. That may be sound baseball, but it does nothing to help a young player develop his hitting. What would seem like a basic training ground for baseball often turns out to be a program of negative thoughts that only retards a young player.

I believe more good young athletes are turned off by the pressure of organized Little League than are helped. Little Leagues have no value as a training ground for baseball fundamentals. The instruction at that age, under the pressure of an organized league program, creates more doubt and eliminates the naturalness that is most important.

If I'm going to criticize such a popular program as Little League, I'd better have some thoughts on what changes I would like to see.

First of all, I wouldn't start any programs until the school year is over. Any young student has enough of a schedule during the school year to keep busy.

These programs should be played in the afternoon—with a softball. Kids have a natural fear of a baseball; it hurts when it hits you. A softball is bigger, easier to see and easier to hit. You get to run the bases more and there isn't as much danger of injury if one gets hit with the ball. Boys and girls could play together. Different teams would be chosen every day. The instructors would be young adults home from college, or high-school graduates. The instructor could be the pitcher and the umpire at the same time. These programs could be run on public playgrounds or in schoolyards.

I guarantee that their dinner would be at the same time every night. The fathers could come home after work and relax; most of all, the kids would have a good time playing ball in a program in which hitting the ball and running the bases are the big things.

When you start talking about young people playing baseball at 13 to 15, you may have something. Organize them a little, but be careful; they are still young. But from 16 and on, work them really hard. Discipline them, organize the leagues, strive to win championships, travel all over. Give this age all the time and attention you can.

I believe Little League has done just the opposite. We've worked hard with the 8- to 12-year-olds. We overorganize them, put them under pressure they can't handle and make playing baseball seem important. When our young people reach 16 they would appreciate the attention and help from the parents, and that's when our present programs almost stop.

The whole idea of Little League baseball is wrong. There are alternatives available for more sensible programs. With the same dedication that has made the Little League such a major part of many of our lives, I'm sure we'll find the answer.

I still don't know what those three gentlemen in Williamsport had in mind when they organized Little League baseball. I'm sure they didn't want parents arguing with their children about kids' games. I'm sure they didn't want to have family meals disrupted for three months every year. I'm sure they didn't want young athletes hurting their arms pitching under pressure at such a young age. I'm sure they didn't want young boys who don't have much athletic ability made to feel that something is wrong with them because they can't play baseball. I'm sure they didn't want a group of coaches drafting the players each year for different teams. I'm sure they didn't want unqualified men working with the young players. I'm sure they didn't realize how normal it is for an 8-year-old boy to be scared of a thrown or batted baseball.

For the life of me, I can't figure out what they had in mind.

Vocabulary List:
"Strike Out Little League"

Record below the words from "Strike Out Little League" that you are unsure of. Also write a brief definition from a dictionary that fits the way the word was used in the essay. Finally, pick one word to add to your list in Appendix A for daily study.

_____   _____

_____   _____

_____

Questions for Discussion:
"Strike Out Little League"

1. According to the thesis, what idea will the essay develop?

_____

2. Does Roberts have some convincing reasons to support his view? Cite examples to defend your stand.

_____

_____

_____

_____

3. Are these reasons developed with adequate detail? Cite two examples to defend your stand.

_____

_____

_____

_____

4. Roberts takes some time to suggest how Little League should be changed. Is this effective? Explain why you feel as you do.

_____

_____

_____

_____

5. What is the main reason Robin Roberts is more convincing than the "student" in the previous selection?

_____

_____

_____

6. What is the effect of the second to the last paragraph?

_____

_____

_____

_____

7. In what way is Robin Roberts' conclusion similar to the one in "Why College Football Should Be Abolished"? (**Hint:** Roberts' conclusion is in the last two paragraphs.)

_____

_____

8. In what way is Robin Roberts' conclusion different from the one in "Why College Football Should Be Abolished"?

_____

_____

9. Which is the more effective conclusion? Why?

_____

_____

READING SELECTION:
"Away with Big-Time Athletics"

The following selection by Roger M. Williams is an impressive piece of persuasive writing. As you read, try to discover what makes it so good.

Away with Big-Time Athletics
Roger M. Williams

At their mid-January annual meeting, members of the National Collegiate Athletic Association were locked in anguished discussion over twin threats to big-time college athletic programs: rapidly rising costs and federal regulations forcing the allocation of some funds to women's competition. The members ignored, as they always have, the basic issue concerning intercollegiate athletics. That is the need to overhaul the entire bloated, hypocritical athletic system and return athletics to a sensible place in the educational process.

A complete overhaul of the athletic programs, not the fiscal repair now being attempted by the NCAA, is what is necessary. For decades now big-time football, and to a lesser degree basketball, have commanded absurdly high priorities at our colleges and universities. Football stands at the center of the big-time system, both symbolically and financially; the income from football has long supported other, less glamorous sports.

Many American universities are known more for the teams they field than for the education they impart. Each year they pour hundreds of thousands of dollars apiece into athletic programs whose success is measured in games won and dollars earned—standards that bear no relation to the business of education and offer nothing to the vast majority of students.

The waste of resources is not the only lamentable result of the overemphasis of intercollegiate athletics. The skewing of values is at least as damaging. Everyone involved in the big-time system—players, coaches, alumni and other boosters, school officials, trustees, even legislators—is persuaded that a good football team is a mark of the real worth of an educational institution. Some of the most successful coaches elevate that bizarre notion to a sort of philosophy. Woody Hayes of Ohio State has said that the most important part of a young man's college education is the football he plays. Jim Kehoe, athletic director at the University of Maryland, has said of the games played by Maryland: "You do anything to win. I believe completely, totally, and absolutely in winning."

Anyone doubtful of the broad psychic satisfaction provided by winning teams need only observe who it is that shouts, "We're number one!" It is seldom the players and only sometimes other students. The hard core of team boosters is composed of middle-aged men—mainly alumni but also legions of lawyers, doctors, and businessmen with no tangible connection to the school.

In the South, where football mania rides at a shrill and steady peak, winning seems to offer a special reward: an opportunity to claim the parity with other regions that has been so conspicuously lacking in more important areas of endeavor. In Alabama in the late Sixties, when Coach Bear Bryant was fielding the first of his remarkable series of national championship teams, both Bear and team were the objects of outright public adulation: that is, *white* public adulation. White Alabamians, reacting to the assaults on George Wallace and other bastions of segregation, took a grim, almost vengeful pride in "their" team. During those years, when I covered the South as a reporter, one could

hardly meet a white Alabamian who didn't talk football or display, on an office or den wall, a picture of Bryant and the Crimson Tide squad.

The disease of bigtime-ism seems to run rampant in provincial places where there is little else to do or cheer for: Tuscaloosa and Knoxville, Columbus and Lincoln, Norman and Fayetteville. But everywhere, always, it feeds on a need to win—not just win a fair share of games but win almost all of them, and surely all of the "big" ones.

At the University of Tennessee last fall, coach Bill Battle nearly lost his job because the Volunteers won a mere 7 of their 12 games. Never mind that Battle's Tennessee teams had previously amassed a five-year record of 46 victories, 12 defeats, and 2 ties and had been to a bowl in each of those years. Although Battle was eventually rehired, he received no public support from a university administration which seemed to agree with the fanatics that, outstanding as his record was, it was not good enough.

Everyone knows something about the excess of recruiting high-school players and something about the other trappings of the big-time system: the athletic dormitory and training table, where the "jocks" or "animals" are segregated in the interests of conformity and control, the "brain coaches" hired to keep athletes from flunking out of school; the full scholarships ("grants in aid"), worth several thousand dollars apiece, that big-time schools can give to 243 athletes each year. (Conference regulations restrict the size of football traveling squads to about 60, while the NCAA permits 95 players to be on football scholarships. This means that some three dozen football players at each big-time school are getting what's called a full ride without earning it.)

What few people realize is that these are only the visible workings of a system that feeds on higher education and diverts it from its true purposes. The solution, therefore, is not to deliver slaps on the wrist to the most zealous recruiters, as the NCAA often does, or to make modest reductions in the permissible number of athletic scholarships, as it did last year. The solution is to banish big-time athletics from American colleges and universities.

Specifically, we should:

(1) Eliminate all scholarships awarded on the basis of athletic ability *and* those given to athletes in financial need. Every school should form its teams from a student body drawn there to pursue academic interests.

(2) Eliminate athletic dormitories and training tables, which keep athletes out of the mainstream of college life and further their image as hired guns. Also eliminate special tutoring, which is a preferential treatment of athletes, and "red shirting," the practice of keeping players in school an additional year in the hope that they'll improve enough to make the varsity.

(3) Cut drastically the size and the cost of coaching staffs. Football staffs at Division I schools typically number 12 or 14, so that they are larger than those employed by professional teams. With practice squads numbering 80 or 50, the present staff size creates a "teacher–pupil" ratio that permits far more individualized instruction on the playing field than in the classroom. The salaries paid to assistant coaches should be spent to hire additional faculty members. The salaries of head coaches, who in some states earn more than the governor, should be reduced to a point where no head coach is paid more than a full professor.

(4) Work to eliminate all recruiting of high-school athletes. It has produced horrendous cases of misrepresentation, illegal payments, and trauma for the young man involved.

The worst of the abuses is the athletic scholarship, because it is central to all the others. If members of a college team are not principally athletes, there is no need to lure them to the school by offering special treatment and platoons of coaches. They should be students to whom football or basketball is the season's major extracurricular activity.

What will happen if these changes are made? The games will go on. In fact, they may well be more like real games than the present clashes between hired, supertrained, and sometimes brutalized gladiators. Will the caliber of play suffer? Of course, but every school will be producing the same lower caliber. Given a certain proficiency, which the best of any random selection of student-athletes always possesses, the games will be as competitive and as exciting for spectators as they are today. Is a 70-yard run by a non-scholarship halfback less exciting than the same run by Bear Bryant's best pro prospect? For spectators who crave top athletic performance, it is available from a myriad of professional teams. We need not demand it of students.

Certainly, the counter-argument runs, alumni and other influential supporters would not stand for such changes. There would indeed be ill feeling among—and diminished contributions from—old grads who think of their alma mater primarily as a football team. Let them stew in their own pot of distorted values. Those legislators whose goodwill toward a state university depends on winning seasons and free tickets can stew with them. A serious institution is well rid of such "supporters." They may discover the pleasures of a game played enthusiastically by moderately skilled students who are not in effect paid performers.

Will athletic-program revenues drop? They undoubtedly will, at least for a while; not many people will pay seven dollars to see games of admittedly lower quality, nor will the TV networks pay fancy fees for the right to televise them. The fans and the networks will eventually return, because these will be the only college games available. And think of the financial savings, as the costs of the typical big-time athletic program drop by hundreds of thousands of dollars a year. If a revenue gap persists, let it be made up out of general funds. The glee club, the intramural athletic program, and innumerable other student activities do not pay for themselves. Why should intercollegiate athletics have to do so?

Supporters of big-time programs often say piously that, thanks to those programs, many young men get a college education who otherwise would have no chance for one. That is true. But there are even more young men, of academic rather than athletic promise, who deserve whatever scholarship money is available. If somebody has to pay an athlete's way to college, let it be the professional teams that need the training that college competition provides.

The president of a good Southern university once told me privately that he would like to hire outright a football team to represent his school and let the educational process proceed. George Hanford of the College Entrance Examination Board, who has made a study of intercollegiate athletics, would keep the present system but legitimize the preparation of players for professional sports. Hanford would have a college teach athletes such skills as selecting a business agent and would permit student-athletes to play now and return later to do the academic work required for a degree.

While Hanford's suggested changes would remove the mask of hypocrisy from big-time college athletic programs, they would not solve the fundamental problem: the intrusions the programs make on the legitimate functions and goals of an educational institution. For institutions with a conscience, this problem has been persistently vexing. Vanderbilt University football coach Art Guepe summed it up years ago, when he characterized Vanderbilt's dilemma as "trying to be Harvard five days a week and Alabama on Saturday."

Because of pressures from alumni and others who exalt the role of football, Vanderbilt is still attempting to resolve this dilemma; and it is still failing. Now it is time for all the Vanderbilts and all the Alabamas to try to be Harvard whenever they can and Small-Time State on Saturday.

Vocabulary List:
"Away with Big-Time Athletics"

Record below the words from "Away with Big-Time Athletics" that you are unsure of, along with brief dictionary definitions for these words. Select one word to write in your vocabulary list in Appendix A.

_____   _____

_____   _____

_____   _____

_____   _____

Questions for Discussion:
"Away with Big-Time Athletics"

1. What does the thesis state is the main idea of this essay?

   _____

   _____

2. State three reasons Williams gives for his view.

   _____

   _____

   _____

3. Are these reasons developed with adequate supporting detail? Explain.

   _____

   _____

   _____

4. Like Robin Roberts, Williams suggests the changes that should be made. What are these four suggestions?

   _____

   _____

   _____

   _____

5. Is suggesting what should be done an effective persuasive technique? Why?

   _____

   _____

   _____

6. Williams goes on to discuss what might happen if the changes he suggests are made. Does this make his stand more convincing? Why or why not?

   _____

   _____

   _____

7. Williams also takes some time to discuss what people who disagree with him might say. He also answers these people and tries to prove them wrong. Cite one example of this.

_____

_____

_____

8. When Williams mentions what people who disagree think, and when he then answers these people to prove them wrong, he is doing what is called *countering objections*. How does countering objections add to the persuasiveness of the piece?

_____

_____

_____

GETTING READY: GATHERING SUPPORT

Any issue that can be debated—that has two sides—can be the subject for a persuasive theme. You do not need to stick with the traditional "burning issues" such as abortion, capital punishment, legalizing marijuana, or mercy killing. Suitable persuasive topics can be found in issues that strike closer to home: coed dorms, campus cafeteria food, campus parking, course requirements, registration, grading systems, conditions where you work, dating practices. Although writing on such topics will not shed light on pressing universal concerns, it will still exercise your powers of logical reasoning and show you how writing can clarify thought and stimulate insight.

As a prewriting exercise, pick some debatable issue that you have an opinion about. This time, avoid the larger, "burning issues" and select something related to school, work, or some other aspect of your life. For example, you might want to argue for a longer lunch break at work, for better parking facilities at school, or for eliminating required courses. Or perhaps there is a local controversial issue you are interested in, such as an upcoming school levy vote.

Once you have settled on an issue, you may discover that you know how you feel about that issue, but you can't really say *why* you believe the way you do. Or perhaps you can mention one or two reasons for your belief, but you somehow feel there must be more to support your view—and you can't think of what that might be just yet. Well, we all have that experience at times. We've all been in discussions with people and offered an opinion. Then when asked why we hold that opinion, we have found ourselves struggling a bit to come up with some convincing reasons. That just indicates the need we all have from time to time to clarify our thinking and stimulate our thought. This prewriting exercise is meant to help you do just that.

At the top of a sheet of paper, state the issue and stand you are taking. Then list down the left side of the page every reason you can think of to support your stand. Once you have exhausted your ideas for support, turn the tables and down the middle of the page, write every reason you can think of for opposing your stand.

When everyone has finished a list, break into groups of four or five. A first person in the group begins by reading the statement of his or her stand. That person then reads the items of support. The other group members have the responsibility of evaluating the reader's support. They should mention possible objections to the reader's support, suggest support the reader did not think of, discuss which support is the strongest and which the weakest, and mention which objections are the most compelling and which the least compelling.

While the other group members are offering these comments, the reader should make notes to the right of the second list. Once discussion of the first reader's stand and support is complete, a second reader should take over and have his or her stand and list discussed. This procedure should continue until everyone in the group has the benefit of the group's input.

TIPS FOR HANDLING THE PERSUASIVE THEME

When you write persuasively, your purpose is to convince your reader of the wisdom of your stand in order to win that person over to your point of view. Keep this in mind as you examine the following tips.

1. Pick an Issue That Can Be Argued.   An appropriate persuasive topic must be controversial; it must have two sides. To argue that children need attention, for example, is foolish because no one would disagree with you. Also, matters of taste are not debatable and not really suitable for persuasive treatment. To argue that today's fashions are more attractive than those of a generation ago is really quite pointless.

2. Rely on Reason and Logic.   A reasonable reader will be turned off by a passionate plea that neglects reason for emotional appeals. No matter how strongly you feel about an issue, you must never lose control. Instead, you must use your powers of reason and logic to move the reader's intellect, not inflame the reader's emotions. Otherwise, you will alienate the thoughtful reader who resents an emotional appeal such as "Anyone who votes for Jones is unpatriotic."

3. Use Convincing Support.   Instead of using emotional appeals, make your support convincing by drawing on facts and evidence at hand. These may include examples from your experience or the experience of someone you know. Or convincing support may come from information you have learned in the classroom, from your reading, from your television viewing, or from your observations. Clearly identify the source of your evidence with a few words. For example, if you are writing against mothers working, some of the following might appear in your theme (the source of information is underlined only for the purpose of example).

> A. In a sociology class I took recently, the teacher said that some working mothers suffer more guilt than their nonworking counterparts.
>
> B. My own mother, who worked while I was young, tells me that she now regrets not having had more time with me.
>
> C. Some working mothers I know report that their children view their babysitter as more of a mother than they are.
>
> D. It seems to me that working mothers are deprived of the joy of watching their children grow.

However, to say something like "Working mothers do not love their children as much as nonworking mothers" is an emotional appeal and a sweeping generalization with no evidence to support it. Such a statement has no place in a persuasive theme. If you reread "Why College Football Should Be Abolished," you will see it is the lack of convincing support that makes the persuasion so weak. By the same token, if you reread the other two persuasive pieces at the beginning of this chapter, you will see that they succeed because of the use of convincing support.

4. Avoid Personal Attacks.   Although it often is fair to criticize a person's actions, it is in very poor form to advance an argument by attacking an individual personally. Thus, there is no room in a persuasive theme for a statement such as "The mayor's indecision on the school issue shows he is an insecure person who fears making enemies." One can fairly say, though, something like "The mayor's indecision on the school issue causes me to doubt his ability to lead."

5. Argue Only One Issue.   It is a mistake to attempt to argue too much. Stick to one issue only. For example, a paper with the thesis "We need stricter gun control laws and larger police forces to enforce those laws" is arguing one point too many. Also, do not try to argue both sides of an issue, but stick with your stand. Thus, if you are writing in favor of gun control, you do not want to give all the reasons against gun control.

6. State the Issue and Your Stand in the Thesis.   You will weaken your position significantly if your reader cannot tell early what the issue is and where you stand on it. One useful technique is to write a lead-in that traces briefly what has caused the issue or sketches the history of the issue. Then follow the lead-in with a thesis that gives your stand.

7. Mention Possible Positions.   It is sometimes effective to state all the possible positions on an issue or all the possible solutions to a problem and then logically disqualify all but the position you are in favor of.

8. Acknowledge Objections to Your Argument and Counter Them.   No matter what reasonable stand you take on a controversial issue, there will be plenty of clear-thinking people who will disagree with you. When writing persuasively, it is important to recognize this fact and deal with it by acknowledging objections to your stand and dealing with them.

This is important mainly for two reasons. First, when you acknowledge opposing views, you demonstrate to your reader that you have considered all sides of the issue. This shows the reader you are aware of other points of view and demonstrates that your stand is the result of a careful weighing of all points. Second, it reveals your sense of fair play by demonstrating that you are not neglecting opposing views to make your own look better. In short, acknowledging and countering objections strengthens your argument and gives it credibility by showing it to be competent and unbiased. The reader is thus led to trust your intentions and content.

There are three effective ways to acknowledge and counter objections:

1. You can state an opposition view and disprove it.

2. You can state that an opposition point is a good one, but your point is better.

3. You can state that an opposition point is true, but your point is also true.

Below are three examples of acknowledging and countering objections that might appear in a theme arguing a case for working mothers. Which of the above techniques does each illustrate?

1. There are those who claim that children of working mothers suffer from neglect. However, with today's licensed day-care facilities staffed by trained professionals, children of working mothers often receive more and superior attention than they would if their mothers were home with them. After all, these trained staff members do nothing but care for their charges, whereas full-time mothers divide their time among tending the children, housekeeping, cooking, running errands, and sewing.

2. Although it is true that working mothers spend less time with their children, child psychologists have long agreed that the amount of time mothers spend with their young is not as important as the quality of that time.

3. It is argued that working mothers are too tired at day's end to enjoy their children. Indeed, a working mother comes home tired, but she also comes home feeling gratified and thus returns to her children in a positive frame of mind.

There are four ways to organize the acknowledgment and countering of objections within your theme:

1. You can raise and counter all objections in your lead-in.
2. You can raise and counter all objections in your conclusion.
3. You can raise and counter all objections in the last body paragraph.
4. You can raise and counter various objections at the appropriate points within your body paragraphs.

How you handle this depends upon your topic, your style, and the number and seriousness of the objections, but it is usually easiest and most effective to raise and counter the objections at the appropriate points in your body paragraphs. However, choose the method you believe will most enhance your theme's persuasiveness.

9. Consider What Will Happen If Your View Is Adopted. Like Roger M. Williams does in his article, you may want to explain what effects the adoption of your view will have. This technique is not useful for all persuasive topics, but for some it is highly effective. As the writer, you must decide whether this technique is effective persuasion for your particular topic.

EXERCISE:
Tips for Handling the Persuasive Theme

Before answering the following questions, review the tips for handling the persuasive theme. Also review the three sample persuasive writings at the beginning of this chapter.

1. Circle the thesis sentences that are acceptable for a persuasive theme.
   a. Everyone can benefit from a vacation.
   b. Something must be done about the poverty in our country.
   c. A two-year degree program should be available at all state colleges.
   d. It would be a mistake to defeat the police tax levy.
   e. Professional sports are too violent and the players are overpaid.

2. Circle the statements that do not belong in a persuasive theme because they do not rely on reason and logic.
   a. Students who disrupt classes are nothing but troublemakers who couldn't care less about getting an education.
   b. The student who disrupts a class interferes with the right of others to get an education.
   c. A two-year degree program at state colleges would attract students away from vocational schools to provide more money for universities.
   d. Anyone who favors a two-year degree program at a college does not know what a college education is all about.
   e. Professional athletes are eager to cause a fight during a game.

3. Suggest at least two pieces of support that could be added to "Why College Football Should Be Abolished" to make the piece more convincing.

_____

_____

4. Circle the statements below that should not be in a persuasive theme because they are personal attacks.
   a. Senator Collantone's history of voting against the ERA makes me doubt his commitment to human rights.
   b. Senator Collantone is a bigot.
   c. President Harper's decision to raise tuition will create a hardship for many students.
   d. President Harper's decision to raise tuition shows he is a money-hungry man who doesn't care about students.
   e. The mayor's budget cuts are sure to lead to widespread city layoffs.

5. Is the thesis for "Why College Football Should Be Abolished" effective? Why or why not?

_____

_____

6. Write a suitable thesis for "Why College Football Should Be Abolished."

_____

_____

7. List three objections that Williams acknowledges and counters in "Away with Big-Time Athletics."

_____

_____

_____

8. Robin Roberts does not acknowledge and counter objections in "Strike Out Little League." If he had, what two objections might he have raised? What could the counter arguments have been?

Objection: _____

Counter: _____

Objection: _____

Counter: _____

9. Which author considers what will happen if his view is adopted? How many paragraphs does this discussion run?

_____

WRITING STRATEGIES

The "student" who wrote "Why College Football Should Be Abolished" really didn't approach his writing project very well. Unfortunately, many people do pretty much what that fictional writer did, and the results are often just as unsatisfying. Sometimes people approach their writing in such a poor manner because they really don't know any other way to go about it. Fortunately, you won't face this problem if you follow the procedures I have been suggesting when you write. The discussions of such aids as prewriting, the twelve-step approach, outlining procedures, and proofreading techniques are all meant to help you approach your writing in an organized fashion.

Still, even armed with a sound way to approach their writing, writers can run into problems. I would be dishonest if I said that once you master certain procedures everything will be easy. Nothing as worthwhile as writing comes easily all the time. So let's discuss what you can do when you run into a writing problem.

There are certain "tricks of the trade"—strategies you can try when you write—that just might ease you over the rough spots that can be a normal part of the composing process. Whether you are an experienced writer or new to the game, from time to time you might hit a snag. If you do, you have two choices: You can throw up your hands in despair and frustration, which won't be productive. Or you can recognize that some stumbling blocks are inevitable and deal with them in a productive way—one that will help you over the obstacles and allow you to go forward.

It's important to keep in mind that all writers, including professional ones, can hit snags when they write. Sometimes ideas don't come just because they're needed; sometimes a phrase can't be shaped just right despite the greatest effort; and sometimes ideas resist logical organization no matter how often they are rearranged. Yet so often student writers think they alone are struggling with the writing process. This just isn't so; we all stumble and sweat on occasion.

Once you recognize that any writer can face difficulties when composing, you can come to accept the fact that because writing isn't always easy, you too may have a problem from time to time. This is not something that should cause you undue concern. When you face writing problems, avoid becoming tense, discouraged, or frustrated. Instead, rely on some of the little "tricks" writers use to get around their difficulties or to avoid them altogether. Below is a list of some of these strategies. Try them and incorporate the ones that work for you into your composing routine.

1. Set Short-Term Goals for Yourself.   Try not to attempt too much at once when you sit down to write. Instead, break any writing project up into smaller tasks and handle just one or two of these tasks at a time. For example, tell yourself that today you will only list your ideas and settle on a preliminary thesis. Then tomorrow you will construct an outline, the next day you will write the first draft, and so on. The psychological advantage of this approach is great, for it allows you to focus on each step of the composing process and feel satisfaction as each is completed. If you don't move in this fashion, you may feel overwhelmed and discouraged by the size of the project looming ahead of you, and negative feelings such as these can interfere with your progress and the quality of your work.

2. Always Have a Plan.   Whether it is the twelve-step approach described in Chapter 4 or another procedure you have worked out for yourself, you should have a set procedure to follow when you write. Such a routine will give you direction and a logical plan of attack. The routine alone is reassuring, because you know what steps you will take and thus avoid the anxiety that comes from uncertainty. Also, having a plan helps to ensure efficiency. Too often writers jump in and then try to fight their way out of a writing task. The result is usually wasted time and wasted energy—and often unnecessary frustration.

3. Write What You Know.   Perhaps it is too obvious to state, but if you don't know anything about a subject, you cannot write about that subject. Similarly, you can't write a 1000-word theme on a subject if you only have 500 words worth of ideas. You must choose your writing topic carefully so that you know your subject well enough to have something to say about it. If you are forced to write on a subject you know little about, you must first become knowledgeable by reading and/or talking to people.

4. Discover What Your Ideas Are Before You Try to Write a Draft.   Sometimes you have good ideas right there at the front of your brain waiting to spill onto the page. Other times those ideas are lurking in the far corners of your mind, and they have to be coaxed forward. Regardless, it is always wise to discover just what ideas you do have by prewriting. Once you have your ideas on paper, you can examine them objectively and decide what to do with them.

5. Don't Try to Do Everything at Once When You Write Your First Draft.   All too often writers make the mistake of thinking that a first draft should be perfect, or close to it. As a result, they spend far too much time and energy agonizing over every aspect of the draft: They won't go on to a new sentence until the previous one is completely satisfactory; they spend a great deal of time shaping every phrase and finding the perfect word; they worry about the placement of each comma; and so it goes.

Typically, this is not the way to advance. Remember, another name for a first draft is a *rough* draft. This first draft is rough because this is not the time for editing your work for mechanics and usage. It is the time to go from start to finish in order to get your ideas down so you can examine them and determine what shaping, rearranging, adding, and subtracting you have to do. It is the time to get your thoughts down so you can examine them and their organization. Only later do you clean up your work by editing and revising.

So when you write your first draft, don't worry about mechanics and don't spend a great deal of time striving for the best expression of your thoughts. Instead, settle for the less perfect—whatever comes to mind. Then go back and deal with all the changes. If you insist on perfection the first time through, you are only building in unnecessary frustration and defeat. So be good to yourself and allow your first draft to be what it should be— rough.

6. If You Hit a Snag, Don't Panic.   I've tried to reassure you that every writer gets stuck now and then. If you have a problem, know that you are not alone. Also know that becoming tense or panicking is not the appropriate response to a writing problem; such feelings will only get in the way of clear thinking. Instead, if you have a problem along the way, relax and walk away from your work for a while. Do something else—listen to music, clean a drawer, or play some racquetball. While you are engaged in other activities, a part of your brain will be working to solve the problem, so that when you return to your work, you may well find the answer you seek.

Personally, I take a walk when I'm stuck. The exercise is stimulating both physically and mentally. You might try it yourself. Another useful strategy when you have trouble writing something is to imagine yourself explaining what you mean to a friend. Then write the explanation just as you would say the words. Afterward you can go back and make the necessary changes to make the material more suitable for the written format.

7. Distance Yourself from Your Work to Regain Your Objectivity.   It is probably inevitable that you will get so close to your writing that you will have a hard time viewing it objectively and evaluating it critically. That's because writers have in mind what they mean to say and tend to see that on the page whether it's there or not. That is why we often overlook our own mistakes. We have the correct form in mind, so we tend to think it's on the page. Also, we have a tendency to fill in gaps in detail mentally, and we fail to see where more explanation may be necessary. To overcome this tendency, writers must get away from their work to clear their heads and restore objectivity. At two points in the writing process it is critical to leave your work for a time—before you revise and edit your first draft and before you proofread. Distancing yourself for a time will allow you to revise, edit, and proof objectively and critically. Each time you distance yourself, it should be for at least several hours; a day is better. Of course, the longer you can stay away, the more objective you can be when you return.

8. Try Writing Your Introduction Last.   It's not unusual for writers to spend more time on an introduction than on any other single part of an essay. Sometimes it's just very hard to get started, and despite our best efforts, the wastebasket fills with crumpled sheets as we begin again and again. Yet it is not productive to keep traveling the same road if it doesn't lead anywhere, so if you can't get through that introduction, skip it for the time being. Go on and write your body paragraphs and conclusion, and then return to write the first paragraph. With the rest of your theme complete, you may well find that writing the introduction is easier. There is one caution that goes along with this strategy, however: Formulate a preliminary thesis before you skip your introduction so you have a clear statement of what your theme is about. Otherwise, you run the risk of creating a relevance problem.

9. After You Have Written Your First Draft, Type It.   There's something about seeing your work in type that lends a fresh view and objectivity. Suddenly you can see things you never noticed before. Mistakes, faulty organization, sketchy detail all seem apparent in type, even when they went unnoticed in your handwritten manuscript.

10. Outline Your First Draft After You Write It.   Books on writing and teachers of writing frequently mention the wisdom of outlining a theme *before* writing the first draft, and indeed this is a good idea. However, it is often valuable to outline a first draft *after* it is written to double-check the organization and relevance of the supporting detail. After writing the draft, outline all your material (see p. 86). If you notice detail that doesn't fit logically into your outline, you have identified a relevance problem. Try shifting the idea to another paragraph to see if it works there. If there is no suitable spot in the outline for the idea, you must omit it or adjust your thesis or a topic sentence to allow for it.

11. Find Out What Successful Writers Do and Try It Yourself.   Talk to classmates, teachers, and anyone else you know who writes well and ask what procedures they follow and what little tricks they use successfully. Then try some of these things yourself to see if they work for you.

12. Allow Plenty of Time to Complete a Writing Assignment.   Let's be honest—we all put things off on occasion. Some people even make a habit of putting things off until the last minute. They may even justify this by claiming that they perform better under pressure. But when it comes to writing, you need time. Aside from the obvious fact that you cannot do well when you're rushed, there are other reasons for giving yourself a comfortable amount of time to complete a writing project. If you are going to follow the suggestions listed here, you must have time to do so—time to work toward short-term goals, time to discover your ideas, time to edit and revise, time to take a walk if you hit a snag, time to distance yourself from your work, and time to type your first draft and/or outline it. So when you first learn that you have a writing task, begin at once in order to have as much time available as possible.

13. Think about Your Writing Project While You Are Doing Other Things.   Ideas don't occur only when you are bent over a page. While driving to work or shopping for a sweater, you might think of the perfect organizational strategy or a brilliant approach to your conclusion. Even when you are away from your work, you should have a corner of your brain working on it. You'll be surprised at the times you get a flash of insight. One student even confided in me that he got his best ideas in the shower.

14. Don't Rely on Inspiration.   It's true that on occasion a stroke of brilliance hits, and it's a good feeling when it does. Unfortunately, inspiration is a sometime thing, and not anything to depend on. So don't sit around waiting to be inspired, because it may never happen. Instead, take charge yourself and work through your writing assignment. Remember, in the absence of *inspiration,* you can always rely on *determination.*

15. Settle for Less Than the Ideal.   You cannot afford to be a perfectionist. If you never turned in a piece of writing until you were 100 percent satisfied with it, I doubt that you would turn in very much. If you have tried in vain to come up with ideas that please you completely, then do the best you can with the ideas you *do* have. If you have written your introduction twenty times and still feel it lacks that certain something, then all you can do is content yourself with using the best one of the twenty, or perhaps you could combine the best features of several of the twenty. Regardless, you are only human, and once you have done your best, you cannot expect more. When necessary, accept your best efforts—even if they are not perfect—and go forward.

16. When You Discover a Strategy That Works for You, Stay with It.   There's an expression in the sports world that you may have heard: "Never change a winning game." This idea applies to your writing procedures as well. Once you've hit upon a technique that works for you, hang on to it. Don't change a successful routine just for the sake of change. Of course, if you want to try something new because you believe it might be better or more efficient than what you've been doing, fine. But if the new technique fails you, go back to the old, reliable method.

17. Read a Little Bit Everyday.   Reading can help improve your writing in at least three ways. First, after repeated exposure to good, fluent sentence structures, you will come to incorporate these structures in your writing. Second, while reading you will no doubt come across unfamiliar words. If you check these in a dictionary and work to include them in your vocabulary, you can expand the storehouse of words you draw on when you write. Finally, reading will expose you to ideas—lots of them—and these ideas may well make their way into your writings or serve as a springboard for other thoughts you can include in your work.

Despite the joys and usefulness of reading, students often say they just can't find the time to read. Of course I understand the tight schedule students keep, but there is a way: Keep some reading material (perhaps a weekly news magazine) on your bedtable. Each night, read for just fifteen minutes before sleep. This practice has the added bonus of helping you relax before dozing off.

18. Be Aware of Your Weaknesses.   When you know the kinds of mistakes you have a tendency to make, you can work to guard against them. If run-ons are a problem, proof carefully for them; if organization is your weakness, pay special attention to your outline; if precise diction hangs you up, use a dictionary and thesaurus. Whatever your particular weakness (and we all have at least one), be aware of it so you can work to avoid it.

GRAMMAR AND USAGE

In this section we will look at transitional words and word groups as another way to show relationships among your ideas. Also, another comma rule will be presented.

Transitional Words and Word Groups

When we talked about sentence fragments and run-ons, we noted that the writer tries to make the reader's job as easy as possible by expressing ideas in sentences. Another service the writer performs for the reader is to indicate just what the relationships are between ideas. To do this, a writer often decides on the techniques of coordination (see p. 96) and subordination (see p. 98).

When you establish what the relationship between ideas is, you are helping your reader, but you are also clarifying thought. A string of ideas without a connection is one thing. But these ideas take on added significance when you determine how they relate to each other. Seeing the relationship between ideas can stimulate thinking. Once you determine how idea A relates to idea B, you find idea C coming to you more quickly.

In addition to using the techniques of subordination and coordination, there is another way to demonstrate relationships among ideas: by using transitional words and word groups. Actually, transitional words and word groups serve two important functions. They show the relationships among ideas, and they make for smoothly flowing writing. Consider the following two sentences:

I left the house in plenty of time to meet Joan. The traffic was heavy, so I was ten minutes late.

By adding one word to the second sentence, we can demonstrate clearly the relationship between the ideas and achieve a smoother flow.

> I left the house in plenty of time to meet Joan. However, the traffic was heavy, so I was ten minutes late.

Notice that the word *however* signals to the reader that the idea to follow is somehow in contrast to or the opposite of the one that came before. Also notice that the two sentences read more smoothly with the transition added.

Transitions do not always have to come at the beginning of a sentence, although many times they work best there. Look at the following:

> I enjoy pizza. However, my husband hates it.
>
> I enjoy pizza. My husband hates it, however.
>
> I enjoy pizza. My husband, however, hates it.

Transitions can also connect two ideas in the same sentence. In this case, one of the coordinate or subordinate conjunctions functions transitionally. In the following examples, the transitions are underlined.

> Baseball has been called the favorite sport of Americans, but I believe football is more popular.
>
> The game was called in the fifth inning since the rain showed no sign of letting up.

Note: As these examples show, coordinate and subordinate conjunctions often function as transitions.

Below is a list of commonly used transitions and the relationships they show.

Relationship	**Transitional Words and Word Groups**
Addition:	also, and, and then, another, too, in addition, furthermore, further, on top of that, first, second, third, . . . , moreover
Example:	During my vacation I slept each day until noon. Also, I took a nap each day before dinner.
Time:	now, then, earlier, before, after, afterward, after that, later, years ago, immediately, soon, next, in a few days, meanwhile, often, suddenly, finally, previously, before, next, once

Example:	I <u>now</u> no longer worry about meeting new people. <u>Earlier</u>, I was painfully shy.
Space:	near, beside, far, far from, close by, in front of, in the rear of, beyond, above, below, inside, outside, to the right, to the left, over, around, on one side, alongside, there, behind, next to, away from, near the back
Example:	As you enter the room, a huge, overstuffed sofa catches your eye. <u>To the right of it</u> are a matching chair and ottoman.
Comparison:	likewise, just like, just as, in the same way, in like manner, similarly
Example:	Math has always been difficult for me. <u>Similarly</u>, science has not come easily, and I've had to work hard to learn it.
Contrast:	but, still, yet, on the other hand, conversely, on the contrary, nevertheless, despite, however, in spite of, in contrast
Example:	<u>In spite of</u> his fear of heights, Mike went on a mountain climbing expedition.
Cause and effect:	so, since, therefore, consequently, as a result, because, if . . . then, accordingly, thus, hence
Example:	Kathy studied all night for the exam. <u>As a result,</u> the next day she was too tired to concentrate and got a low mark.
Purpose:	so that this may occur, in order for, for this purpose, for this reason
Example:	Sue plans to fit into her bikini by June. <u>For this reason</u>, she exercises twice a day.
Emphasis:	in fact, to repeat, undoubtedly, surely, without any doubt, in any event, truly, indeed, certainly, to be sure, again
Example:	I am confident that I will do well on my sociology final. <u>In fact</u>, I expect to get an A.
Illustration:	for example, for instance, as an illustration, specifically, to be specific, as proof
Example:	The cost of housing today is outrageous. Even a small house, <u>for example</u>, can cost as much as $70,000.

Summary or clarification:	in summary, in conclusion, as I have shown, as has been stated, in other words, in brief, to sum up, in short, all in all, that is
Example:	<u>As I have shown</u>, transitions are very useful.
Admitting a point:	although, while this may be true, granted, even though
Example:	<u>Although</u> the working mother is under a great deal of pressure, she learns to handle the demands of home and work.

Transitions can connect ideas within sentences, and they can connect ideas between sentences. However, transitions can also connect ideas between paragraphs. Using transitions in this way is useful for improving the flow of your writing from one paragraph to the next. To see that this is true, turn back to p. 146 and look at the third paragraph in the discussion of transitions. This paragraph begins with "In addition." These two words act as a transition. They indicate that the first idea in the paragraph appears in addition to the ideas in the paragraph before. Thus, this transition connects the ideas in two paragraphs and in that way aids the flow from the one paragraph to the next.

Remember to think of transitional words and word groups as a service to the reader. That is, by using transitions you allow your reader to go smoothly from idea to idea, ever aware of the connection between thoughts. Furthermore, transitions make for smoothly flowing sentences and paragraphs.

EXERCISE:
Transitions

1. Examine the previous paragraph. Note that I used two transitions: *that is* and *furthermore*. Notice that the instant you read *that is,* you were clued to expect clarification. Thus, my first transition points the reader in the direction I am taking. Now look at *furthermore*. What does it clue the reader to expect?

_____

2. Examine the language of the first exercise above. What transitions have I used? The instant they are read, what does the reader perceive will follow?

_____

_____

3. Supply transitions in the following pairs of sentences. To do this, first determine the relationship between the sentences (example, contrast, space, time, and so on) and then supply an appropriate transition. Try placing some transitions at the

beginning of a sentence, some in the middle, and some at the end. If you wish, you can turn two sentences into one.

Example: Food prices in this town are quite high. Gasoline is fairly reasonable.

Revision with transition: Food prices in this town are quite high. On the other hand, gasoline is fairly reasonable.

a. We went to the movies. We ate at an expensive restaurant.

_____

_____

b. Learning to ski is difficult. It's worth the effort.

_____

_____

c. Class was cancelled Thursday. We went outside and sat on the grass.

_____

_____

d. Jane is so lazy. Last week she cut classes three times.

_____

_____

e. By 10:00 it was storming. The picnic was postponed a week.

_____

_____

f. These days the cost of a college education is outrageous. There are many scholarships available at most schools.

_____

_____

g. Dr. Jones told me I had written the best paper in the class. I got only a B−.

_____

_____

h. He finished all his work by noon. He felt no guilt about taking off for the beach.

_____

_____

i. Unless you change your ways, you will never amount to much. I suggest you turn yourself around immediately.

_____   _____

_____

j. My roommate missed two weeks of classes because of illness. Her midterm grades were quite low.

_____

_____

4. Read "Give Me the Home Life" on p. 153. Two of the body paragraphs have topic sentences that contain transitions to link the ideas in different paragraphs and improve the flow between these paragraphs. What are these transitions?

_____

A Word about Commas with Interrupters

Commas are used to set off interrupters. *Interrupters* are words or word groups not part of the main idea of the sentence that break up the flow or movement of the sentence. Interrupters can come at the beginning, middle, or end of a sentence. Examine the following three examples that contain the interrupter, *incidentally*.

Jane, incidentally, refused to serve on the nominating committee.

Incidentally, Jane refused to serve on the nominating committee.

Jane refused to serve on the nominating committee, incidentally.

Note: In all three cases above, the interrupter is set off by commas. Notice that when the interrupter comes in the middle of a sentence, a comma is placed before and after it, as in the first example.

Here is a list of some common interrupters:

after all	incidentally
as a matter of fact	in any event
as a result	in fact
at any rate	in general
by the way	in the same way
for example	nevertheless
for the most part	of course
however	on the other hand
I believe	on the whole
I hope	therefore
I think	to be sure
in my opinion	to tell the truth

Some of the words in the above list can function as interrupters at some times and necessary parts of a sentence at other times. If a word or word group is an interrupter, it can be eliminated from a sentence, and the remaining words will still form a complete thought.

Interrupter: Joanne, I believe, is a strong candidate for student council president.

Noninterrupter: I believe in the power of suggestion.

Explanation: Take out I believe in the first sentence and you still have a complete thought. Take out I believe in the second sentence and you are left with a fragment.

The transitional words and word groups frequently function as interrupters and are set off with commas.

Example: Indeed, the hardest freshman course is geology.

Example: Mike, for example, mentioned that he would be an hour late.

Example: Going to college is not easy, but it can be fun, to be sure.

Explanation: The underlined phrases are transitions that also act as interrupters. Take them out, and a complete thought remains.

People disagree about whether to use commas with very short transitions and interrupters, so you may use commas or not as you prefer. Just be sure to base your decision on whether to use or omit the comma on the kind of reading you want your sentence to have.

Example with comma: Nevertheless, I will always think highly of Mr. Markham.

Example without comma: Thus few people came to view the governor as a strong candidate for the senate.

EXERCISE:
Commas with Interrupters

Place commas where they are needed in the following sentences. Decide whether you wish to set off short interrupters according to the reading you desire.

1. Believe it or not Dr. Kantick agreed to postpone the exam.

2. Inga and Jim were late for the party as usual.

3. His idea seemed popular; at any rate it was voted in by a wide margin.

4. Someone I am sure will forget to bring a pencil or pen to the exam.

5. In fact someone will probably have forgotten that today is test day.

6. Nevertheless the exam will procede as scheduled.

7. Without a doubt the exam was not as difficult as I thought it would be.

8. Dr. Johnson is the best professor on campus to be sure.

9. On the other hand Mark has a good point.

10. I doubt however that we can reach Myrtle Beach by noon.

WRITING ASSIGNMENT I

For your first writing assignment in this chapter, use the information in the list made as part of the Getting Ready exercise as support for a persuasive theme. Remember, you picked a topic "close to home," made a list of support and objections, and added support and objections offered by group members. Before you write, look again at the tips for writing a persuasive theme. Then read the sample theme below and answer the questions. Before handing in your work, be sure you can answer yes to the Questions to Answer before Submitting Your Theme (p. 156).

A Sample Theme:
"Give Me the Home Life"

The persuasive theme below was written by a freshman student. As you read, try to decide what the writer does to be convincing. Then answer the questions that follow the piece.

Give Me the Home Life

"I can't stand living with my parents one more day; they are always telling me what to do and when to do it." That was the irate statement I overheard one of my classmates make last week. Then he went on to complain about all the perils of living with his parents. Although he had some good points to make, my experience has shown that living at home while attending college has many advantages.

For one thing, I don't have to worry about money because I live at home. In the afternoon after classes, I work as a stockboy in a small hardware store. I don't make much money, but then I don't put in many hours either. This means I have plenty of time left during the week to hit the books. Of course, it's possible for me to get by on a small paycheck because I live at home, so my expenses don't amount to much. I don't have to worry about rent or dorm fees. What? Me—buy food? No, Mom does the grocery shopping. Buying gum and candy bars is about the extent of my food shopping.

Sure, my folks ask questions; sometimes they even tell me what to do and when to do it. But that's a small price to pay for the ease and comfort of home life. I don't have to cook; Mom takes care of that, and the food's great. I don't have to sit in a dorm cafeteria with a hundred other guys eating rubbery meat and powdered eggs either. My clothes are washed for me once a week, and just as often clean sheets appear on my bed. You can't say that when you're living on your own. I'd say that's worth answering a couple of questions or being told what to do once in a while.

Then there's the car. If I lived away from home I couldn't afford the gas, let alone the monthly payments. But living with my parents means I can borrow the family car for dates and bumming around with the guys. All it costs me is an occasional fill-up.

Some people say that when you live at home, you don't get to meet many new people, but I haven't found this to be true at all. This is only my third quarter in school, and already I've become close to a half-dozen guys I've met in my classes. Also, I'm dating two girls I met in the Spanish Club.

Probably the biggest advantage to living at home is the support and encouragement I get from my parents. When I'm studying for an exam, Mom always comes to me and whispers, "Luis, is there any way I can help you?" When I look up at her, I see a woman who wishes she could take the exam for me. That's enough motivation to keep me studying for the rest of the night. Then there's my father. He's the one who proudly passes around my composition and boasts, "My son wrote this all alone; I know I can't write anything like this—can you?" Even though I get a little embarrassed, I know he is proud of me so I work all the harder to keep him proud. Of course, it's not just when I'm doing well that Mom and Dad help me. If I get a bad grade, they're concerned and supportive. They tell me that if I've done my best, they're satisfied. Even though I don't think my best is enough to repay them for their support, they do. What more could a struggling freshman ask for?

Getting through college is a tough job. With studying, writing, and testing to be concerned about, I'm glad I don't have to worry about money, meals, a car, or clean clothes. But most of all I'm glad that two people I love are there when I need them. Indeed, living at home has its advantages.

Questions for Discussion:
"Give Me the Home Life"

1. What kind of lead-in is used?

_____

2. What is the thesis?

_____

3. Examine the topic sentence of each body paragraph; what points do they indicate will be made to support the thesis?

_____

_____

_____

_____

4. What kind of conclusion is used?

_____

5. Cite two examples of acknowledging and countering objections.

_____

_____

6. Does the author rely more on reason or on emotional appeal?

_____

7. Is the support for the thesis convincing? Explain. (Is there enough support? Is it persuasive? Is it relevant? Should anything have been added?)

_____

_____

_____

_____

8. Cite four examples of effective use of transitions.

_____

_____

_____

_____

9. Cite one example of a comma setting off an interrupter.

_____

10. A semicolon is used in the first sentence of paragraph 3. Why?

_____

11. A comma is used in the thesis. Why?

_____

12. A comma is used in the third sentence of paragraph 2. Why?

_____

Questions to Answer before Submitting Your Theme

Before handing in your theme, be sure you can answer yes to the following questions.

1. Have you organized carefully and checked your introduction, thesis, topic sentences, and conclusion?

2. Is your support adequate, relevant, and convincing? Have you acknowledged and countered objections?

3. Have you followed the tips for handling the persuasive theme?

4. Is your diction precise, economical, and free of clichés?

5. Have you checked comma usage? Remember, commas are used:
   a. Between coordinate modifiers
   b. Before conjunctions connecting coordinate clauses
   c. After introductory subordinate clauses
   d. Before final subordinate clauses that show separation from the coordinate clause
   e. To set off interrupters

6. Have you avoided fragments and run-ons? Do your subjects and verbs agree? Have you avoided improper tense shifts?

7. Did you punctuate conversation correctly if you used it?

8. Did you capitalize titles of relatives used like names?

9. Did you show the relationships among your ideas with coordination, subordination, and transitions?

10. Did you proofread carefully more than once? Did you check spellings?

WRITING ASSIGNMENT II

For another opportunity to write persuasively in order to see how writing can clarify thought and stimulate insight, try this. Write a persuasive theme on the same subject you did for the previous writing assignment. Only this time let your thesis present the *opposite* point of view. Thus, the student who wrote the sample theme on the advantages of living at home would write on its disadvantages. Or he could write about the advantages of living away from home.

Because now you will be writing to support a point of view you don't really hold, you will probably not have as many ideas at first to back up your stand. Nonetheless, I am sure you can complete this assignment. And when you have, I believe you will discover two things. First, when you write to support a view you don't agree with, it's possible to come up with many ideas you hadn't considered before. Second, these new ideas may well clarify your thinking on a subject and lead you to a fresh point of view—or perhaps new reasons for keeping your old point of view. Either way, ideas will be stimulated, and your thinking will be clearer.

WRITING ASSIGNMENT III

When you studied descriptive writing in Chapter 2, you learned that sometimes things become so familiar that we stop noticing them. Of course, the cure I suggested for that was to do some descriptive writing. Interestingly, persuasive writing can also be a help in this area. Persuasive writing can help because it forces us to form an opinion and decide on supportive evidence. It causes us to look hard at something we might have been numb to and rather ignored.

Take, for example, television commercials. They are so much a part of our lives that many of us have stopped being aware of them. Yet these commercials do have a significant impact, and we should be more aware of them for this reason. For this assignment, you will write a persuasive essay about the way people are presented in television commercials. To come up with your topic, select one of the sentences below and fill in the blank.

Mothers in television commercials are presented as _____.

Housewives in television commercials are presented as _____.

Career women in television commercials are presented as _____.

Blacks in television commercials are presented as _____.

Fathers in television commercials are presented as _____.

Husbands in television commercials are presented as _____.

Businessmen in television commercials are presented as _____.

Children in television commercials are presented as _____.

Teenagers in television commercials are presented as _____.

Your completed sentence will represent the point of view you will take in your theme. You should form your thesis from this sentence. Your support will be examples of commercials that have the portrayal given in your thesis. Also, you might want to argue what effect the commercial portrayal has on how people are viewed and treated.

As a result of this writing, you should have new ideas and clearer thoughts on a subject to which you may not have turned your full attention in the past, even though it affects you and your world, and is therefore worth considering.

A FINAL WORD

Whether you are writing persuasively or not, writing is an excellent way to clarify thought and stimulate ideas. Keep this in mind as you do all the writing assignments in this book.

Chapter 6

Working Against the Clock:
Writing Essay Examination Answers and In-Class Themes

As students, from time to time you are asked to show what you know by answering essay questions. This can be tricky business because to be successful you must be able to do three things. You must be able to read the question and understand what is expected of you; you must know the material you are being tested on; and you must be able to convince your instructor that you know the material by writing solid, clear, well-organized answers.

Many students become overly nervous about essay exams, so they cope with them by jumping right in and writing as much as they can—in any way they can—before time runs out. Unfortunately, this isn't a wise idea. Aside from creating additional tension, this practice usually does not produce the best results. But here's good news: There are ways to deal with essay exams that can reduce pressure and improve results. And since essay exams are a frequent, important part of your life as a student, learning how to deal with them effectively will promote your academic well-being.

READING SELECTION:
"Rah! Rah! SELL! SELL!"

The following article is from *Time*, May 4, 1981. It is interesting for its content and also for the fact that it packs in quite a bit of information—just as your textbooks do. The selection will be the basis for your early practice with the essay exam in this chapter.

Rah! Rah! SELL! SELL!
Kenneth M. Pierce

Why had student applications leveled off at Minnesota's small but academically topnotch Carleton College? Research by college officials revealed that high school seniors from warmer climes were shivering over the thought of Minnesota's winters. Prospects from the East Coast worried whether Carleton was prestigious enough; laid-back Westerners, on the other hand, figured the campus might be too formal. So Carleton changed its admissions pitch. Into a shiny, new brochure went a photo of skiing on campus. Those effete Eastern intellectual snobs got a letter filled with information about faculty achievement. Westerners were told about nearby hiking trails and canoe trips. Result: annual applications rose 44%, from about 1,400 to 2,010.

Carleton is just one of hundreds of schools that have begun to lure students with market research techniques like those used by soap and cigarette companies. Reason: tuition costs are skyrocketing and the nation's pool of 18-year-olds is shrinking (from 4.2 million in 1975 to an estimated 3.6 million by 1985).

Schools sometimes advertise on roadside billboards. More make their pitch on radio and in newspapers. But the sales aids that really hit home are the unsolicited recruitment letters that jam mailboxes of high school seniors.

As Vidur Mahadeva, 17, a top-scoring scholar from Wisconsin's Oshkosh North High School, puts it: "I get an awful lot of mail, especially from the little colleges—Beloit, St. Olaf and the rest." Fully 75% of four-year private colleges and 61% of state colleges and universities now buy mailing lists to send brochures to prospects. Lists of the

1.3 million juniors and seniors who take college entrance exams each year are sold to schools at roughly 12¢ a name—provided the students have authorized test sponsors to release their names (80% do).

When the College Entrance Examination Board introduced its computerized Student Search Service in 1971–72, about 120 schools purchased 6 million names for recruitment mailings. Last year, 880 schools purchased 22.5 million names. Some schools favor a buckshot approach. At the University of Miami, for example, where two-thirds of undergraduates come from out of state, recruiters have sent as many as 265,000 brochures at a single mailing. Most schools prefer mailings of 12,000 or so. Computers allow colleges to select student names for promotional mailings by zip code, ethnic group and family income—as well as class rank, test scores, anticipated college major and planned career. There is a "Bible college" list, a list of students interested in West Point or Annapolis, even a list of Missouri women who hope to become engineers. The student most often sought, though, according to the College Board's Darrell Morris, "is likely to be from the Northeast, in the upper third of his high school class, with verbal scores on the Scholastic Aptitude Test between 400 and 600, intending to major in the liberal arts."

Like commercial mail-order marketers, college recruiters constantly ask which types of mailings produce the best response. According to College Board researchers, four-color booklets get a 50% better response (in the form of college applications or follow-up inquiries) than booklets printed in black and white. Letters personalized by computers ("Dear Adam") pull better than the impersonal "Dear Student." Students say they dislike letters that virtually "assured them of admission if they applied."

When colleges hire marketing experts, they learn that in a competitive situation they must sharpen their identities vis-à-vis other schools, just as cerealmakers strive to convince buyers of the differences among brands. In commerce this is known as "positioning," and the term is now being applied on campus. In Cambridge, Mass., for example, Lesley College, which specializes in teacher education, is trying to become known for a special new program designed to help its graduates teach economics at the grade school level. Lest applicants think that Sweet Briar College for women, near Lynchburg, Va., is some antebellum finishing school for Southern belles, the full-color photo introducing the school's brochure features three alumnae, employed in New York's financial industry, standing before the urban, limestone hulk of the American Stock Exchange. The new Sweet Briar selling motto: "An education for reality."

Most students apply to several colleges.

To increase the number of those who actually enroll after being accepted—known to admissions officers as the "yield rate"—many schools sponsor spring get-togethers, known as "yield parties," for accepted students and their parents. Explains Fred Neuberger, admissions director of Vermont's Middlebury College: "If Princeton and Middlebury both accept a student and then Princeton invites him to a gathering but Middlebury doesn't, we've lost out." At Triton College in River Grove, Ill., anyone who gets in touch with the school admissions office is assigned to one of twelve full-time advisers. They offer personal counsel and coordinate financial-aid requests during the application process. Before the program was begun two years ago, only 53% of those who contacted Triton eventually enrolled. Now, a solid 70% do.

Is all this competitive hype dangerous? Not at all, says College Marketing Consultant Tommi Thornbury of Kansas City, Mo., happily reconciling Socrates and the hard sell: "Positioning means to know thyself." And then go out and merchandise like mad.

Vocabulary List:
"Rah! Rah! SELL! SELL!"

As you are now in the habit of doing, record below the words from the reading selection that you are not sure you know the meaning of. Then next to each word write a brief dictionary definition that reflects how the word was used in the article. Finally, select two words to study and work into your vocabulary. Record these in Appendix A.

I have mentioned before the importance of vocabulary building. However, I'd like to call to your attention how very important it is that you look up unfamiliar words when you are studying your textbooks. If you do not, you may well find you do not understand all the material—the very material you will be tested on.

_____   _____

_____   _____

_____   _____

GETTING READY: PRETEND YOU ARE THE INSTRUCTOR

Have you ever put yourself in an instructor's place and tried to determine what that person is seeking from students? Instructors are generally reasonable people, you know, with reasonable expectations for students. And it is really not very hard to figure out just what instructors look for in your essay examination answers. Pretend for a while that you are a marketing instructor who is testing students' knowledge of "Rah! Rah! SELL! SELL!" by asking them the essay question: "Describe what lengths some colleges go to in order to recruit students."

As the marketing instructor who requests this essay on an exam, make a list of everything that should be apparent in a complete, correct answer. Include in your list all the facts that must be present (such as buying mailing lists) and the writing skills that should be present (such as the correct spelling of key words and strict relevance). Then list those things that would annoy you (such as unnecessary information and unreadable handwriting). When everyone in the class has finished a list, return to your role of student. As a class, discuss the items on the lists. Your classroom instructor will record on the board those items that the class agrees should appear in the essay as well as those annoying elements that should not. When the discussion is complete, you will have on the board a fairly accurate list of dos and don'ts for a well-formed essay examination answer.

TIPS FOR HANDLING THE ESSAY EXAMINATION

The first thing you must do in order to cope with the essay exam is to consider your attitude. So often, students dread and fear these exams; they view them as a large obstacle to get over in order to get through a course. Let me suggest a healthier, more productive point of view. Look at the essay exam as an opportunity—a chance to display your knowledge and be rewarded for it. Also, think of the essay exam as a chance to do some insightful thinking (writing for insight was discussed in Chapter 5).

Sure, an essay exam will often require you to recall facts. But often the exam will also call on you to understand those facts, interpret them, and see relationships among them. In short, the essay examination requires you to see the significance and meaning of information. For this reason, the essay exam can be more than a test; it can be a valuable learning experience.

Once you acquire the necessary test-taking skills, you will come to welcome the essay exam as an opportunity both to "strut your stuff" and to learn even more. Truly, this is an exciting prospect. So be positive and pleased that you have the opportunity to participate in such a learning experience. And be grateful when you have an instructor who presents you with this chance. After all, it's much harder and more time-consuming for the teacher to read essays than to score an objective test.

The essay exam draws upon your knowledge of the material *and* your writing skills. Keep this in mind as you study the following tips for writing essay examinations.

1. Study the Material.   There is no substitute for preparing by studying the material carefully. Different students have different styles and hence like to study in different ways. When studying for an essay exam, you might try reading the material four times. The first time through, read to get an overview—an awareness of the general topics treated. The second time through, pay special attention to major points and try to remember as many of them as you can. The third time, make a list of questions you might ask if you were the teacher. After you complete the third reading, write the answers to these questions and then consult the text to check their accuracy and completeness. Save your fourth reading for the night before the exam. This reading should serve as a refresher. Also as a refresher, review the answers to the questions you constructed.

Some essay examinations are open-book tests, allowing you to consult text and notes while taking them. Some students think this means they can get away with less studying. This is not true; if you are not well prepared for an open-book exam, you will spend so much time hunting facts, you will not have enough time to write good answers. Furthermore, many open-book exam questions test your ability to relate facts in ways not given in the text or notes. Unless you know these facts, you will be unable to answer the questions in the given time.

It is also a good idea to ask students who are doing well how they study. Then you can try some of their methods.

2. Wear a Watch.   Working efficiently against the clock is impossible if you cannot keep track of the time.

3. Be Relaxed and Confident.   When you enter the classroom to take the exam, be relaxed and confident. If you have studied, you have every reason to expect to do well. A negative attitude is self-defeating. If you expect to fail, you probably will. On the other hand, if you expect to do your best and are confident that you know a fair amount of the material, your performance will be satisfactory. Above all, do not panic. A cool head makes for clear thinking; a panicked head makes for confusion. However, if you are feeling a bit nervous, don't be concerned. A little tension is good because it keeps you sharp. If you are too relaxed, you probably aren't keyed up enough to perform as well as you would with a bit of an edge on. The trick is to be keen but not so nervous that you cannot function.

4. Understand What You Are to Do.   When you get your copy of the exam, read it through to be sure you understand what is expected of you. If you are unsure about any question or direction, ask your instructor for help. Most essay questions contain key terms that direct the approach your answer should take. Below is a list of some of these terms. Be certain you note them in the questions and gear your answers accordingly.

Agree; disagree:	State your position and support it with facts (take one side only).
Comment on; evaluate:	State your position and support it with facts (you may treat two sides of an issue).
Analyze:	Break down into all its parts or divisions.
Compare:	Show similarities.
Contrast:	Show differences.
Define:	Provide and explain precise meaning.
Describe; discuss:	Examine in detail.
Explain:	Tell why something happened.
Illustrate:	Give examples and relate them to the statement in the question.
Interpret:	Explain the significance or meaning of something.
Prove; defend:	Demonstrate why something is true.
List; state:	Make a list of points or facts.
Summarize:	Hit the high points.

5. Plan Your Strategy.   After reading through the exam, form a strategy (plan of attack). If you have a choice of questions, select the ones you know the most about. If some questions are worth more points or require longer answers, plan to spend more time on these. If you know more about some questions than others, answer the ones you know the most about first. This will build your confidence. Also, while you are answering these, a part of your brain will be working on the others, so you may end up surprised to discover how much you know when you get to the questions you thought would give you the most trouble.

6. Skip Troublesome Questions.   If there are questions you cannot answer, go on to the ones you can. Return to the troublesome questions after completing the others. If you are still uncertain, guess. You may get lucky and get some credit.

7. Outline Your Answers.   On your test sheet or scratch paper, take a moment before writing to jot down the points you want to include in your answer. This emptying of the head is very important because it minimizes the chance of forgetting ideas you want to include. Also, take a moment to number the ideas in the order you wish to handle them. This step is important because it helps ensure a well-organized answer.

8. Organize Simply.   Because time is a factor, you should organize your essay answers quite simply. One way to do this is to skip the lead-in and make the first sentence of paragraph 1 your thesis. Try to repeat the language of the question in your thesis. For example, if the question is "Explain the function of DNA," begin your answer, "The function of DNA is. . . ." However, be careful not to refer to the question as though it were already a part of your essay. That is, if the question is "Discuss the function of DNA," do not begin, "It is . . ." or "Its function is. . . ." After your thesis, state and develop your first main point. You may leave out a formal conclusion or write a simple one-sentence closing.

9. Be Clear and Direct.   Keep two things in mind as you work on the essay: You do not have unlimited time to write it, and your instructor does not have unlimited time to read it. Therefore, be clear and direct. The length of your answer is not a key factor; putting the right facts together in a well-organized fashion is. Above all, never pad your answer with unnecessary information, repeat yourself, or provide more than you are asked to. The first two can annoy a busy instructor. The last will not earn you any extra points and will cut into your writing time.

10. Number Your Answers to Correspond with the Exam Questions.   This is particularly important when you are given a choice of questions to answer, and the order of your answers is not the same as the order of questions on the exam sheet.

11. Proofread.   Always save at least five to ten minutes to proofread your answers. Proofreading in an exam situation serves three purposes. First, it gives you an opportunity to catch and correct errors in content. Second, it gives you a chance to add material that may have occurred to you after writing the answer. Third, it gives you a chance to correct or refine your grammar and organization—areas that can shape an instructor's view of your competence. Should it be necessary to cross out, add, or change, do so as neatly as possible. Your instructor realizes you are writing what amounts to a first draft and will not be put off by a few changes as long as they are reasonably neat and clear.

EXERCISE:
Two Essay Exam Answers to Study

Below are two essay examination answers. Each is a response to the question "Describe what lengths some colleges will go to in order to recruit students." The first answer is a good one, but the second is weak. Review the article, "Rah! Rah! SELL! SELL!" on p. 162 and then read each answer and answer the questions that follow. You might want to review the Tips for Handling the Essay Exam on p. 164 before answering the questions.

Answer 1.   In order to recruit students, some colleges are using marketing techniques. Carleton College, for example, sends out brochures with a skiing picture in them to attract students. It also sends letters geared to appeal to specific groups: Westerners are told of the outdoor life; Easterners are told of the excellent instructors. Most schools also buy mailing lists so they can send material to large numbers of high school juniors and seniors. They can even get lists that contain names of select groups, like people interested in Bible colleges. But colleges don't stop there. They also try to discover what kinds of mailings work the best. For instance, they have learned that color brochures are better than black-and-white ones. Further, schools advertise on billboards, radio, and television to attract students. They also hire marketing experts to tell them what image they should project. In addition, many colleges have admissions officers who advise people who show an interest in their school and help with requests for financial aid. As if all that weren't enough, some schools even throw parties for those who apply.

1. Does this answer "describe" as the question requires? Explain.

_____

_____

2. Why is the one-paragraph format satisfactory?

_____

_____

_____

3. Explain why the topic sentence is a good one.

_____

_____

4. Is the supporting detail adequate? (Are any major points left out? Are points developed enough?) Cite one well-developed point.

_____

_____

_____

_____

5. Is all the support relevant?

_____

6. What makes the support in this answer so good? (**Hint:** Refer to the answers to numbers 4 and 5.)

_____

_____

7. Comment on the clarity and directness of the answer. (**Hint:** Consider whether everything is understandable, relevant, economical, precise, and well organized.)

_____

_____

_____

8. Cite three transitions used in the answer. What purpose do these transitions serve? How do they improve the quality of the answer?

_____

_____

_____

9. Evaluate the grammar and usage of the answer.

_____

_____

10. In your opinion, what are the three chief strengths of the answer?

_____

_____

_____

Answer 2.   They'll do pretty much anything. They advertize on television and radio, and they mail letters and brochures to pretty much everyone they can. Colleges will entertain kids at parties and help them get finnancial aid. It seems to me that these schools are being ridiculous they really shouldn't do so much. All the money they spend on advertising should go into getting better teachers, buildings etc. One thing schools do that is really bad is send different letters to different people. They also advertise on billboards. The parties they throw for students are what get me the most though. Schools also send different letters to diferent people.

1. Does answer 2 describe, as the topic requires? Explain.

_____

_____

2. What is the chief weakness of the topic sentence?

_____

_____

3. Is the supporting detail adequate? (Are any major points left out? Are the points developed enough?)

_____

_____

4. Is all the support relevant? Explain.

_____

_____

5. Cite two weaknesses in the way the detail is organized.

_____

_____

6. What makes the support in this answer so weak? (**Hint:** Refer to answers to numbers 3, 4, and 5.)

_____

_____

7. Comment on the clarity and directness of answer 2. (**Hint:** Consider whether everything is understandable, relevant, economical, precise, and well organized.)

_____

_____

_____

8. Evaluate the grammar and usage of answer 2.

_____

_____

_____

9. What do you think would be an instructor's view of the competence of the student who wrote answer 2? Why?

_____

_____

BECOMING PROFICIENT AT WRITING ESSAY EXAMINATION ANSWERS

As with most everything else, you will find writing essay examination answers easier as you get more practice. However, it is not necessary to get all your experience in actual test situations. You can conduct some dress rehearsals at home. Practice by forming questions of your own to answer. Remember the Tips for Handling the Essay Examination and allow yourself about fifteen minutes to write each answer. Soon you will gain skill at writing clear, correct, well-organized answers in a limited time. This will build your confidence so that writing essays in the classroom will be a manageable task for you. Also, if you write questions about information you will be tested on at some later time, these practice sessions will have the added advantage of helping you learn the material.

EIGHT STEPS FOR WRITING THE IN-CLASS THEME

Very often in composition and other English classes, you are asked to write a theme in class. This situation is similar to that with the essay exam because you are asked to complete your writing in a limited time. In addition, writing in-class themes causes some students to feel the same kind of tension they feel when they take exams. This tension often exists because students don't know the best way to handle in-class writing. But once they learn a strategy—a plan of attack—they find themselves coping much better with this kind of timed writing.

Some of the tips for handling the essay examination also hold true for the in-class theme. You should wear a watch, be relaxed and confident, understand what you are to do, outline your writing, and proofread. In addition, there are procedures you can follow when writing in class. This section presents one of the procedures you can follow when you find yourself writing a theme against the clock. It is meant to be a plan of attack to reduce tension and improve results.

Before you look at the steps for writing an in-class theme, I'd like to call one important point to your attention: It is unlikely that you can write something against the clock and have a finished product as good as the one you would have if you wrote it at home with far more time. Your instructor knows this, too. Thus, don't expect your in-class themes to be as good as the ones you write at home. I mention this to ease your mind by giving you a realistic picture of what you can expect of yourself when you write against the clock.

Step 1. Think.   When you learn what your topic is, take a moment to think about it and be sure you understand the topic and what is expected of you. If you have any questions, speak to your instructor. This step is important because you cannot give your instructor what he or she wants if you do not know what that is.

Step 2. Empty Your Head.   You are familiar with this step; you learned it with the twelve-step procedure (see p. 89). After you are sure you understand the topic, list on scratch paper all the ideas that occur to you. Do not stop to decide if the ideas are good or not—just get them down before you forget them.

Step 3. Cross Out and Add.   Examine your list of ideas. Cross out the ones you decide shouldn't be in your theme and add any new ones you would like to include.

Step 4. Form Your Thesis.   Write a thesis that will allow you to discuss the ideas on your list. If you cannot construct a thesis that allows you to discuss everything on your list, cross out the ideas that don't relate to the thesis to avoid a relevance problem.

Step 5. Group and Number Your Ideas.   Decide which ideas relate to each other; these related ideas should be handled in the same paragraph. For example, the first and fourth ideas in your list may be related; label both of these *A*. Perhaps three other ideas are related; you can label these *B*, and so on. If you have some ideas that don't relate to other ideas, decide whether to cross these out or treat each one separately in its own paragraph. Now you know what ideas will appear in each of your paragraphs. Each letter represents a different body paragraph.

Next, decide on the order of your body paragraphs. Do this by giving each letter group a number. If you will discuss the ideas you labeled *B* first, place a *1* next to the *B* ideas to get *1-B*. These *1-B* ideas will be in the first body paragraph. Continue until you have a letter and a number next to every idea on your list. After this labeling, you will know what main ideas you will be including and in what order you will write those ideas.

Step 6. Write Your Theme.   Now you know pretty much what you will say and at what point you will say it, so you are ready to write your theme. Using your list of numbered ideas as a guide, write your theme. Now here's the important part: *Do not* write a rough draft on scratch paper and expect to copy it over later. The draft you write should be the one you hand in. When you are writing against the clock, you generally do not have enough time to write two drafts. It's much wiser to use the time you *do* have revising and editing on your original draft. Furthermore, if you copy over when you are writing against the clock, you run the risk of making careless errors, leaving things out, and so forth. So don't spend your limited time copying over; make your first draft the best it can be, and then revise and edit directly on the original copy.

Step 7.   Revise and Edit.   After writing your theme, go back over it. First check your content and organization. Add detail if necessary, cross out if need be, indicate a new paragraph if you like, and so forth. Then check your grammar and usage. Insert omitted words, correct spellings, correct mistakes in grammar, cross out unnecessary words, and so forth.

I'm sure you're thinking that the paper won't be very neat—and in many cases you will be right. However, instructors don't expect perfectly neat papers when you are writing in a limited time. But they do expect your theme to be readable and clear. So when you make your revision and editing changes, do so in such a way that your instructor can still read your work easily. Otherwise, don't worry about neatness.

Step 8. Proofread.   When you are writing against the clock, careful proofreading is extremely important. All human beings tend to make mistakes when they are rushed, so you can appreciate that errors are likely to occur when you are writing in a limited time. That's why it is absolutely a must for you to save time to proof your work.

Practicing the In-Class Theme

Having a plan of attack is one way you can reduce tension and improve the quality of your in-class writing. Also, as you get more practice writing against the clock you will find yourself improving. This improvement will help you become more comfortable with timed writing.

There is another reason practice with the in-class theme is helpful. You need practice to figure out how much time you should spend on each of the eight steps. You see, I can't tell you this because it will differ from writer to writer. Instead, you must discover for yourself how much time to spend on each step.

But why wait for actual in-class writings to get this valuable experience? Why not practice at home and be ahead of the game? If you wish to practice at home, try this. Provide yourself with a topic by filling in the blanks in some variation of this sentence: _____ is the most _____ I know. The possibilities are endless: Uncle Jeb is the most selfish man I know. Registration is the biggest hassle I know. My brother is the biggest slob I know. Williamsburg is the most interesting vacation spot I know. Then give yourself an hour and write your theme, following the eight steps. After several practices (each time using a different topic), you will be aware of how to budget your time. You will also feel more confident and capable.

GRAMMAR AND USAGE

Because essay examinations frequently require you to show the relationships among various facts, this a good point to pause and consider two techniques for showing the relationship between ideas: coordination and subordination. (A reminder: Transitions also show the relationship between ideas.) Also, to continue the practice of learning comma rules gradually, two new rules for the comma will be presented, along with some information about the colon, dash, and parentheses.

Coordination

You probably recall from the discussion of how to correct run-ons that a *coordinate clause* is a group of words with a subject and verb that conveys a complete thought. You probably also recall that coordinate clauses are connected in a single sentence by one of the coordinate conjunctions *and, but, or, nor, for, so,* or *yet.* The technique of connecting coordinate clauses with coordinate conjunctions is called *coordination.* When a writer wishes to express that two or more ideas in a sentence have equal weight or value, he or she relies on coordination.

Example: President Kennedy's actions following the Bay of Pigs were courageous, but they were certainly risky and could have led to war.

Explanation: The complete thoughts on either side of the coordinate conjunction <u>but</u> are of equal importance.

Whenever you wish to express that two coordinate clauses are of equal importance, coordination will serve. However, the specific relationship between the clauses will be indicated by your choice of coordinate conjunction. The different meanings of the coordinate conjunctions are explained below.

and	The information in the second coordinate clause functions in addition to the information in the first.
Example:	Mental health centers exist in all major cities, and their services are often inexpensive.
but; yet	The information in the second coordinate clause functions in contrast to the information in the first.
Example:	Psychological treatment takes time, but (yet) many people expect quick cures.
or	The information in the second coordinate clause functions as an alternative to the information in the first.
Example:	A troubled person can seek help from a community mental health center, or he or she can look for help from a trusted family doctor.
nor	The information in the second coordinate clause functions as a negative idea in addition to a negative idea in the first.
Example:	Hypnosis is not a cure-all, nor is it the right therapy for every patient.
for	The information in the second coordinate clause functions to tell why the information in the first happened or should happen.
Example:	Many people resist seeing a psychiatrist, for they believe mental illness is a sign of inferiority.
so	The information in the second coordinate clause functions as a result of the information in the first.
Example:	Many famous people have admitted to seeing a psychiatrist, so now fewer people feel embarrassed about psychological problems.

Note: The semicolon can also be used as a coordinator. When it is, frequently no coordinate conjunction is used.

Example:	Behavior modification is becoming increasingly popular; it does, however, have its share of opponents.
Also acceptable:	Behavior modification is becoming increasingly popular; but it does, however, have its share of opponents.

EXERCISE:
Coordination

Write eight sentences using coordination and let each sentence have a different coordinator. Remember to use a comma before the coordinate conjunction separating complete thoughts. Topics for each of your sentences are suggested, but if you like you may choose your own subjects. The first one is done for you as an example.

1. exams *I was very nervous about finals last semester, but I got much higher grades than I ever expected.*

2. in-class themes

3. horror movies

4. football

5. television commercials

6. summer school

7. inflation

8. blind dates

Subordination

You probably recall from the discussion of how to correct run-ons that a *subordinate clause* is a word group containing a subject and verb but lacking a complete thought. When a subordinate clause appears in a sentence with a coordinate clause, the coordinate clause conveys the main point, while the subordinate clause conveys the less stressed point. Thus when you want to connect ideas so that one is stressed more than another, use *subordination*.

Example:	Whenever the temperature drops below 60 degrees, Janet complains of a chill.
Explanation:	The stressed idea is conveyed in the coordinate clause, Janet complains of a chill. Because it is an incomplete thought, whenever the temperature drops below 60 degrees gets less stress.

Subordinate clauses can appear either before or after coordinate clauses. Regardless of their position in the sentence, they are introduced by one of the subordinate conjunctions. There are many subordinate conjunctions, and some were listed for you when subordination was discussed as a way to correct run-ons (see p. 99). It is possible to group subordinate conjunctions according to the relationship the writer wishes to demonstrate between the ideas in the subordinate and coordinate clauses.

since	to show why the idea in the coordinate clause occurred
because	or occurs
in order that	
so [that]	

Examples:	Since we tend to view our own ways as the best, cultural tolerance is not easy to achieve.
	Peace in the Middle East is not likely to come soon because hostility and resentment run high between Arabs and Israelis.

after	to show when the idea in the coordinate clause occurred
as	or occurs
whenever	
while	
until	
when	
before	

Examples:	When news of Franklin Roosevelt's death reached the people, an entire nation mourned.
	There can be no real equality until every person is guaranteed a job.

where	to show where the idea in the coordinate clause occurred
wherever	or occurs

Examples:	Where poverty is widespread, the crime rate will be high.
	A Democratic candidate will be popular wherever he campaigns in this state.
as if as though	to show how the idea in the coordinate clause occurred or occurs
Examples:	As if he could not believe his own words, Nixon delivered his resignation speech.
	Reagan campaigned across the country as though victory were certain.
although if though unless provided once	to show under what condition the idea in the coordinate clause occurred *or* occurs. to admit a point
Examples:	If public education is to survive in this state, a new tax support system must be found.
	Women have made great strides, although they have sacrificed some things to gain others.
	Although your argument is convincing, I must follow my conscience.

EXERCISE:
Subordination

Write ten sentences using subordination, two for each relationship that can exist between the ideas in the subordinate and coordinate clauses. For each relationship construct one sentence with the subordinate clause at the beginning and one with the subordinate clause at the end. Topics are suggested for you, but you may choose your own if you prefer. Also, remember your comma rules: An introductory subordinate clause is set off by a comma. A subordinate clause at the end of a sentence is set off if it shows some separation from the coordinate clause. Number 1 is done for you as an example.

1. exams

   a. *Because Jake must pass algebra to stay on the soccer team, he hired a tutor to help him prepare for next week's test.*

   b. *Dr. Welles gave us an extra week to prepare for the next exam, since we were all having trouble understanding the material.*

2. in-class themes

a. _____

_____

b. _____

_____

3. horror movies

a. _____

_____

b. _____

_____

4. football

a. _____

_____

b. _____

_____

5. television commercials

a. _____

_____

b. _____

_____

Relative Clauses

Relative clauses are clauses beginning with one of the following relative pronouns: *who, whose, which,* or *that.* Relative clauses can function to subordinate (give less stress to) a description of something in the coordinate clause.

Example: John F. Kennedy, who was one of our favorite presidents, was a brilliant political campaigner.

Explanation: The relative clause, *who was one of our favorite presidents,* describes *John F. Kennedy.*

Example: The Vietnam conflict, which did much to arouse American sentiments, is now almost forgotten.

Explanation: The relative clause, *which did much to arouse American sentiments,* describes *the Vietnam War.*

A Word about Commas and Relative Clauses

Relative clauses are of two types: essential and nonessential. The *essential clause* is one that is required for specific identification of something in the coordinate clause. The *nonessential clause* is one that is not required for specific identification of something in the coordinate clause. Nonessential clauses are set off with commas, but essential clauses are not.

Essential clause: The book that I borrowed from Dr. Kaplan was chewed by my dog.

Explanation: The relative clause is necessary to identify which book was chewed, so no commas are used.

Nonessential clause: *Catch 22,* which is one of my favorite books, is not read as much as it once was.

Explanation: The relative clause is not necessary for identification because *Catch 22* is precise, so commas are used.

EXERCISE:
Commas and Relative Clauses

Every sentence below contains a relative clause. First, underline the clause. Then decide if the clause is essential or nonessential. If it is nonessential, set off the clause with commas.

1. The instructor who teaches urban sociology is well known for her interesting lectures and class projects.

2. Jesse Norris whose father is a city cop told our sociology class that armed robbery is up 30 percent in our city.

3. The president of the city council who has always prided himself on his good attendance record has missed the last three council meetings.

4. The textbooks that I bought used were so marked up I could barely read them.

5. The lake which is on the edge of town is now so polluted I refuse to swim there anymore.

6. The lake on the edge of town which was always a favorite of mine is now so polluted I refuse to swim there anymore.

7. Three of the kittens that my cat just had have already been given away.

8. My roommate whose parents are wealthy drives a Jaguar XKE.

A Word about Commas and Introductory Phrases

You have already learned one rule governing comma use after an introductory element: Use a comma after an introductory subordinate clause. There is also a rule for comma use after an introductory phrase (a *phrase* is a group of words that does not have both a subject and a verb). You should use a comma after a long introductory phrase (usually one that contains more than four words). If the introductory phrase does not have more than four words, use a comma only if the phrase shows some separation from the rest of the sentence.

Example:	By the end of the sixth inning, neither team had scored a run.
Explanation:	The introductory phrase, *by the end of the sixth inning*, has more than four words, so a comma is used.
Example:	To regain his strength, Jeff exercised twice a day.
Explanation:	The introductory phrase, *to regain his strength*, is fewer than five words but shows separation from the rest of the sentence, so the comma is used.
Example;	Under the bed Rags whimpered with fear.
Explanation:	The introductory phrase, *under the bed*, is fewer than five words, and no separation is shown, so no comma is used.

EXERCISE:
Commas with Introductory Phrases
and Relative Clauses

Place commas where they are needed in the following sentences. Some of the sentences are correct and need no commas.

1. Upon learning the truth about Peter Diane decided to break the engagement.

2. Anyone who hopes to make a great deal of money should not become a teacher.

3. Noticing the menacing sky the lifeguards quickly cleared the pool and sent everyone home.

4. At the party last night Diane who clearly had drunk too much made everyone most uncomfortable.

5. Until recently I admired Carl as a man who knows his own mind.

6. Before leaving the house Mother reminded the younger children who were left alone for the first time not to answer the door.

7. My brother decided to postpone college to accept a construction job that would pay him $8,000 a year.

8. Staring intently at the raindrops sliding down the window pane the child stroked his teddy bear.

9. At noon Michael left to pick up his mother who was returning from California.

10. Over a mile from here there is a lake that is stocked with catfish.

A Word about the Colon, Dash, and Parentheses

The colon (:) is a punctuation mark that can indicate how something relates to something else in a sentence. For this reason, you will learn about the colon in this chapter, where you have learned about two other techniques for showing the relationship between ideas (coordination and subordination).

The dash (—) and parentheses are punctuation marks that can signal how much stress an idea is to get. You will learn about these marks in this chapter because the amount of stress an idea gets is a clue to how it relates to other ideas. Thus, all three of these punctuation marks can help you show relationships among your ideas, something valuable in essay exam writing— and all writing.

The Colon

1. Use a colon (:) after a coordinate clause to signal that a list will follow.

   Example: There were three qualities Maria sought in a man: wealth, honesty, and ambition.

   Note: Do not use a colon between a verb and an object or complement.

   Incorrect: The leaders of the campus cleanup drive are: Jean Jefferson, Carla Sanchez, and Ruth Goldstein.

   Correct: The leaders of the campus cleanup drive are Jean Jefferson, Carla Sanchez, and Ruth Goldstein.

2. Use a colon to signal that what comes after the colon will explain, clarify, or illustrate what comes before the colon.

   Example: I had been to Las Vegas twice before, so I was aware of what I could expect: fast action, glitter, great entertainment, and excitement.

   Example: My beliefs are simply this: We are all responsible for our own actions; we are capable of improving ourselves; and we are all able to bring happiness to others.

   Example: To refuse aid to the poor is to deny one simple fact: Everyone deserves to have the basic essentials of life.

   Note: When a sentence follows a colon, you may capitalize the first word or not, as you prefer. However, be consistent.

The Dash

1. A dash (—) is used to signal a pause longer than that of a comma. Usually a dash is used for emphasis or dramatic effect.

   Example: The new housing legislation—which has been long overdue—will establish ample public housing in our state.

   Explanation: The dashes set off *which has been long overdue* to emphasize that clause.

   Example: I can't believe that Harold Grange—a convicted felon—has the nerve to run for public office.

   Explanation: The dashes, which set off *a convicted felon,* provide dramatic effect.

2. A dash can be used to set off a list that appears at the beginning, middle, or end of a sentence.

   Example: Old clothes, repairable toys, used furniture, old magazines—these are "hot sellers" at flea markets.

   Example: It is true that your candidate is many things—forceful, diplomatic, personable, and well informed—but he is still too inexperienced in foreign affairs to make a good president.

   Example: Only three things can stop us now—a storm, car trouble, or lack of funds.

   Note: You may have noticed that in the example sentences for number 1 above, commas could have been used instead of the dashes. Similarly, in the third example sentence for number 2 above, a colon could have been used instead of the dash. Which punctuation you use depends upon what you want to signal to your reader.

Parentheses

1. Use parentheses to enclose material that you want to be taken as an aside or as a bit of an afterthought.

   Example: Colleen (who happens to be the mayor's daughter) has always been queen of the St. Patrick's Day parade.

2. Use parentheses to enclose details and examples that are incidental or unimportant.

   Example: This year's Campus Art Award winner (Jerry Morris) is the first freshman to win the award.

   Note: In the example sentences above, commas or dashes could have been used instead of the parentheses. Which punctuation you use depends upon what you want to signal to your reader.

EXERCISE:
Commas, Semicolons, Colons, Dashes, and Parentheses

In the following sentences place commas, semicolons, dashes, parentheses, and colons where they are needed. At times more than one punctuation mark is possible, and you will have to make your decision according to what you want to signal to your reader.

1. The most appealing places for our vacation are Miami, New York, Nashville, and Denver unfortunately we can't all seem to agree on which of these cities to visit.

2. Dr. Helsinki said he liked the insight, originality, and depth of my paper and then he gave me a B+.

3. The president's belief and I happen to agree is that we must trim the waste from big government even if it means layoffs.

4. The following issues were raised at Thursday's student council meeting tuition hikes are inevitable the parking decks are not as safe as they could be and the homecoming celebration may run over budget.

5. The mayor's reaction to the city council's road repair plan was clear forget it we don't have the money.

6. Senior citizens, veterans, the unemployed these seem to be the candidate's biggest supporters.

7. Not everyone believes as you do that this tax hike will cure the city's problems the mayor, for one, feels the hike is inflationary the president of the city council is on record as saying the hike isn't big enough and I am afraid that the revenue will be mishandled of course I never judge these things very well.

8. Anita the woman Jim is engaged to told me that she is planning a St. Patrick's Day party and she's not even Irish.

9. In composition class this semester we wrote one each of the following kinds of themes description, narration, comparison, and cause and effect the description was the hardest for me.

10. Somebody I can't remember who just now mentioned at the meeting that the membership drive should begin in April that strikes me as a bit early.

READING SELECTION:
"How TV Violence Damages Your Children"

To help you become more experienced in writing essay examination answers, you will be asked to take an essay test. First, read and study "How TV Violence Damages Your Children," which follows. After the reading selection, there is an essay examination for you to take. The test is open book, so you may refer to the reading when you answer the questions. The questions will give you experience recalling facts and achieving insight. To get the maximum benefit from the assignment, do not look at the questions before taking the exam. I know you will be tempted to do so—anyone would be—but why weaken an assignment that can help you so much in the future? Also, don't forget the tips you learned for handling the essay exam.

How TV Violence Damages Your Children
Victor B. Cline

ITEM: Shortly after a Boston TV station showed a movie depicting a group of youths dousing a derelict with gasoline and setting him afire for "kicks," a woman was burned to death in that city—turned into a human torch under almost identical circumstances.

ITEM: Several months ago, NBC-TV presented in early-evening, prime viewing time a made-for-TV film, *Born Innocent,* which showed in explicit fashion the sexual violation of a young girl with a broom handle wielded by female inmates in a juvenile detention home. Later a California mother sued NBC and San Francisco TV station KRON for $11,000,000, charging that this show had inspired three girls, ages 10 to 15, to commit a similar attack on her 9-year-old daughter and an 8-year-old friend three days after the film was aired.

ITEM: A 14-year-old boy, after watching rock star Alice Cooper engage in a mock hanging on TV, attempted to reproduce the stunt and killed himself in the process.

ITEM: Another boy laced the family dinner with ground glass after seeing it done on a television crime show.

ITEM: A British youngster died while imitating his TV hero, Batman. The boy was hanged while leaping from a cabinet in a garden shed. His neck became caught in a nylon loop hanging from the roof. His father blamed the TV show for his death—and for encouraging children to attempt the impossible.

These are just a sampling of many well-documented instances of how TV violence can cause antisocial behavior—instances that are proving that TV violence is hazardous to your child's health.

TV broadcasters can no longer plead that they are unaware of the potential adverse effects of such programs as *Born Innocent.* During the last decade, two national violence commissions and an overwhelming number of scientific studies have continually come to one conclusion: televised and filmed violence can powerfully teach, suggest—even legitimatize—extreme antisocial behavior, and can in some viewers trigger specific aggressive or violent behavior. The research of many behavioral scientists has shown that a definite cause–effect relationship exists beteen violence on TV and violent behavior in real life.

When U.S. Surgeon General Jesse Steinfeld appeared before the U.S. Senate subcommittee reviewing two years of scientific research on the issue, he bluntly concluded, "The overwhelming consensus and the unanimous Scientific Advisory Committee's report indicate that televised violence, indeed, does have an adverse effect on certain members of our society. . . . It is clear to me that the causal relationship between televised violence and antisocial behavior is sufficient to warrant appropriate and immediate remedial action. . . . There comes a time when the data are sufficient to justify action. That time has come."

The Federal Communications Commission was ordered by Congress to come up with a report by Dec. 31, 1974, on how children can be protected from televised violence (and sex). Hopefully, some concrete proposals will develop.

The television moguls have repeatedly paraded before various Congressional subcommittees over the last ten years, solemnly promising to reduce the overall amount of violence programmed, especially in time slots that had large numbers of child viewers. However, if we look at the data compiled throughout the 1960's and early 1970's, we find very little change in the average number of violent episodes per program broadcast by all three networks. In one study, the staff of U.S. Congressman John M. Murphy of New York found NBC leading the pack with violent sequences in 71 percent of its prime-time shows, followed by ABC with 67 percent and CBS with 57 percent.

With more and more mega-violent films coming to TV from the commercial theater market, as well as the increasing violence injected into made-for-TV movies, we find that the promise of television has been shamelessly ignored. In too many TV films, we see a glorification of violence that makes heroes of killers. The primary motivation for all of this is money and the fierce scramble for ratings. Thus the television industry's "repentence" for past wrongs, occurring after major national tragedies such as the assassination of the Kennedy brothers and Martin Luther King, Jr., with the transient public outrage and demand for change, has been all ritual with little substance.

We are a great free society with the power to shape our destiny and create almost any social–cultural environment we wish, but as the late President John F. Kennedy put it, "We have the power to make this the best generation in the history of mankind, or the last." If one looks at crime statistics, we find that we are by far the most violent of all the great Western nations. Our homicide rate is about ten times greater than, say, the Scandinavian countries', or four times greater than Scotland's or Australia's. There are more murders per year on the island of Manhattan or in the city of Philadelphia than in the entire United Kingdom, with its nearly 60,000,000 people. Violent crime has been increasing at six to 10 times the rate of population growth in this country. And interestingly, if one analyzes the content of TV programs in England, we find that their rate of televised violence is half that of ours; in the Scandinavian countries it is much less even than that.

Thus one of the major social–cultural differences between the United States with its high homicide and violence rates and those countries with low violence rates is the amount of violence screened on public television.

"Monkey See, Monkey Do"

Much of the research that has led to the conclusion that TV and movie violence could cause aggressive behavior in some children has stemmed from work in the area of imitative learning or modeling which, reduced to its simplest expression, might be termed, "monkey see, monkey do." Research by Stanford psychologist Albert Bandura has shown that even brief exposure to novel aggressive behavior *on a one-time basis* can be repeated in free play by as high as 88 percent of the young children seeing it on TV. Dr. Bandura also demonstrated that even a single viewing of a novel aggressive act could be recalled and produced by children six months later, without any intervening exposure. Earlier studies have estimated that the average child between the ages of five and 15 will witness, during this 10-year period, the violent destruction of more than 13,400 fellow humans. This means that through several hours of TV watching, a child may see more violence than the average adult experiences in a lifetime. Killing is as common as taking a walk, a gun more natural than an umbrella. Children are thus taught to take pride in force and violence and to feel ashamed of ordinary sympathy.

According to the Nielson Television Index, preschoolers watch television an average of 54 hours a week. During one year, children of school age spend more time in front of a TV set than they do in front of a teacher; in fact, they spend more time watching TV than any other type of waking activity in their lives.

So we might legitimately ask, What are the major lessons, values and attitudes that television teaches our children? Content analyses of large numbers of programs broadcast during children's viewing hours suggest that the major message taught in TV entertainment is that violence is the way to get what you want.

Who Are the "Good Guys"?

Another major theme that many TV studies have shown to occur repeatedly is that violence is acceptable if the victim "deserved" it. This, of course, is a very dangerous and insidious philosophy. It suggests that aggression, while reprehensible in criminals, is acceptable for the "good guys" who have right on their side. But, of course, nearly every person feels that he or she is "right." And often the "good guys" are criminals whom the film happens to depict sympathetically, as in *The Godfather*. Who is "good" and who is "bad" merely depends on whose side you're on.

Studies by McLeod and Associates of boys and girls in junior and senior high school found that the more the youngster watched violent television fare, the more aggressive he or she was likely to be. Other studies revealed that the amount of television violence watched by children (especially boys)

at age 9 influenced the degree to which they were aggressive 10 years later, at age 19.

The problem becomes increasingly serious because, even if your child is not exposed to a lot of media violence, the youngster still could become the *victim or target* of aggression by a child who is stimulated by the violence that he or she sees on TV.

And criminals are too frequently shown on TV as daring heroes. In the eyes of many young viewers, these criminals possess all that's worth having in life—fast cars, beautiful, admiring women, super-potent guns, modish clothes, etc. In the end they die like heroes—almost as martyrs—but then only to appease the "old folks" who insist on "crime-does-not-pay" endings.

The argument that you can't get high ratings for your show unless it is hyped up with violence is, of course, not true—as 20 years of *I Love Lucy* and, more recently, *All in the Family, Sanford and Son, The Waltons* and scores of other shows have demonstrated. Action shows featuring themes of human conflict frequently have appeal, yet even they needn't pander to the antisocial side of man's nature or legitimatize evil.

The hard scientific evidence clearly demonstrates that watching television violence, sometimes for only a few hours, and in some studies even for a few minutes, can and often does instigate aggressive behavior that would not otherwise occur. If only 1 percent of the possibly 40,000,000 people who saw *The Godfather* on TV were stimulated to commit an aggressive act, this would involve 400,000 people. Or if it were only one in 10,000, it would involve 4,000 people—plus their victims.

Some parents believe that if their children are suitably loved, properly brought up and emotionally well balanced, they will not be affected by TV violence. However, psychiatrist Fredric Wertham responds to this by noting that all children are impressionable and therefore susceptible. We flatter ourselves if we think that our social conditions, our family life, our education and our entertainment are so far above reproach that only emotionally sick children can get into trouble. As Dr. Wertham points out, if we believe that harm can come only to the predisposed child, this leads to a contradictory and irresponsible attitude on the part of adults. Constructive TV programs are praised for giving children constructive ideas, but we deny that destructive scenes give children destructive ideas.

It should also be noted that the "catharsis theory" in vogue a few years ago, which suggested that seeing violence is good for children because it allows them vicariously to discharge their hostile feelings, has been convincingly discarded. Just the opposite has been found to be true. Seeing violence stimulates children aggressively; it also shows them how to commit aggressive acts.

The author of this article has conducted research studying the "desensitization" of children to TV violence and its potential effects.

In our University of Utah laboratories, we set up two six-channel physiographs which had the capacity to measure emotional responsiveness in children while they watched violent TV shows. When most of our subjects saw violent films, those instruments measuring heart action, respiration, perspiration, etc., all hooked up to the autonomic nervous system, did indeed record strong emotional arousal. We studied 120 boys between the ages of 5 and 14. Half had seen little or no TV in the previous two years (hence had seen little media violence), and the other half had seen an average of 42 hours of TV a week for the past two years (hence a lot of violence). As our violent film, we chose an eight-minute sequence from the Kirk Douglas prizefighting film, *The Champion*, which had been shown many times on TV reruns but which none of the boys tested had ever seen. We considered other, more violent films, but they were too brutal, we felt, to be shown to children—even for experimental purposes. The boxing match seemed like a good compromise. Nobody was killed or seriously injured. Nothing illegal occurred. Yet the fight did depict very graphically human aggression that was emotionally arousing.

These two groups of boys watched our film while we recorded their emotional responses on the physiograph. The results showed that the boys with a history of heavy violence watching were significantly less aroused emotionally by what they saw—they had become habituated or "desensitized" to violence. To put it another way, our findings suggested that the heavy TV watchers appeared to be somewhat desensitized or "turned off" to violence, suggesting the possibility of an emotional blunting or less "conscience and concern" in the presence of witnessed violence. This means that they had developed a tolerance for it, and possibly an indifference toward human life and suffering. They were no longer shocked or horrified by it. It suggested to us the many instances of "bystander apathy," in which citizens in large urban areas have witnessed others being assaulted, yet did not come to their rescue or try to secure aid or help. Or incidents such as the My Lai massacre, in which American soldiers killed Vietnamese civilians. This suggests an unfeeling, indifferent, noncaring, dehumanized response to suffering or distress.

In any event, our research has presented the first empirical evidence that children who are exposed to a lot of TV violence do to some extent become blunted emotionally or desensitized to it.

Since our children are an important national resource, these findings suggest that we should teach them wisely. The kinds of fantasies to which we expose them may make a great deal of difference as to what kind of adults they become, and whether we will survive as a society.

The author, who is a psychotherapist and who treats many damaged children and families, was then faced with the problem of what to do about his own TV set and his own children, who regularly watched TV and had their favorite programs. The evidence had been stacking up in my laboratory—so what should I do about it at home? The thing that finally turned me from being the permissive, tolerant, "good-guy" dad to the concerned parent was the realization that whenever my children looked at TV for any lengthy period, especially violent action shows, they became frequently touchy, cross and irritable. Instead of playing outside, even on beautiful days, discharging tensions in healthy interaction with others, they sat passive for hours, too often hypnotized by whatever appeared on the tube. Frequently, homework didn't get done, chores were neglected, etc. One Saturday morning I was shocked to find my bright, 15-year-old son watching cartoons for four straight hours, having let all chores and other responsibilities go. It was then that we finally decided to turn off the TV set on a relatively permanent basis.

"No TV" Is a Turn-On

When we announced this decision, we found ourselves faced with a family revolt. There was much wailing and gnashing of teeth. It was as if the alcholic had been deprived of his bottle, or as if we had suddenly announced that no more food would be served at our table.

However, the "storm" lasted only one week. Interestingly, during that week, the children went outside and played with each other and the neighbors much more, a lot more good books got read, homework was done on time, chores got finished, and the children got along with each other better.

And very interestingly, the complaints about "no TV" suddenly stopped at the end of that week. Now, several years later, we do occasionally look at TV—some sports specials, a good movie, something required for school, even a mystery. But it's almost never on school nights—and it is no longer an issue in our home. Nobody feels deprived. It's now just not a major part of our lifestyle.

It should be stated, in all fairness, that television has the potential for great good—to teach children pro-social values and behavior, such as sharing with others, controlling one's impulses, solving problems through reason and discussion, being kind and thoughtful. Such programs as *The Waltons* suggest to me that such content can have wide popular appeal and be commercially marketable—if done with talent, care and commitment. In other words, television could be used for far more constructive programming than we have seen in the past. For the time being, parents should, in my judgment, be very cautious about what they expose their children to on television (as well as in movies). If something particularly objectionable is broadcast during children's prime-time hours, there are three things that can be done: 1) turn the television set off; 2) phone your local station expressing your concern; 3) write to the program's sponsor, indicating your objections (the firm's address will be found on the label of his merchandise).

The evidence is clear: a child's mind can be polluted and corrupted just as easily as his body can be poisoned by contaminants in the environment. Children are essentially powerless to deal with such problems. This means that the responsibility for effecting change rests with every adult citizen. Meaning you. Meaning me. Meaning us.

WRITING ASSIGNMENT I

Directions: Below is an essay examination on "How TV Violence Damages Your Children." You have one hour to complete the exam. Be sure you answer three questions according to the guidelines given. You may refer to the selection while taking the exam. Also be sure to look at the Questions to Answer before Submitting an Essay Exam on p. 190 before handing in your work.

30 points: Answer either number 1 or number 2.

1. Explain what Cline means by "monkey see, monkey do." How does this idea explain the effect violent television has on some children?

2. Define "catharsis theory." Does it hold true today? Why or why not?

30 points: Answer either number 3 or number 4.

3. Discuss the effects that violent television can have on how children act and think.

4. Explain why it is not always clear who the good guys on television are. How does this fact affect children?

40 points: Answer either number 5 or number 6.

5. Agree or disagree with Cline's decision to turn off the TV in his house.

6. Comment on what, if anything, you think television networks should do about violence on television.

Questions to Answer before Submitting an Essay Exam

1. Did you provide the kind of information each question called for? That is, did you *describe, compare, explain,* and so on according to the directions of each question?

2. Are your answers simply, yet clearly and logically, organized? Does each thesis restate the language of the question, and do your topic sentences note the main point of each paragraph?

3. Are your answers clear and direct, without padding and unnecessary information?

4. Did you use subordination, coordination, transitions, colons, dashes, and parentheses to show how your ideas relate to each other?

5. Are your answers numbered to correspond to the questions?

6. Have you proofread to check content and correct errors?

WRITING ASSIGNMENT II

Go through some of your textbooks and select a chapter that is not highly technical and can be understood without knowledge that does not appear in the chapter. (Perhaps an introductory chapter will qualify.) Read this chapter carefully and then construct a three- or four-question open-book essay exam that can be completed in one hour. Bring to class a Xeroxed copy of the chapter, and trade chapter copies with a classmate. Take the chapter you receive home to read and study. The next day bring the test you devised and give it to the person who read the chapter it is based on. Also bring the reading selection you studied.

Everyone should then take the exam he or she gets and return it when completed to the person who constructed the test. The person who constructed the test should then take the completed exam home to evaluate for content, organization, and important mechanics. At the next class everyone should be given back his or her evaluated exam. Time should be allotted so that each test evaluator can discuss the grading with the person who took the test. Areas of disagreement should be resolved, using the classroom instructor as mediator if necessary.

Hint: If it's possible, contact an instructor who knows the subject area you are constructing the exam in. Ask that person to read your questions, evaluate them, and make suggestions. Also ask the instructor to help you evaluate the answers you receive from the person who takes the test.

A FINAL WORD

You can develop skill at taking essay examinations with practice. By becoming experienced you will welcome the essay test as both a learning experience and a chance to let your instructor know you have studied, considered, and learned the material. Of course, questions will come up from time to time that you flat-out cannot answer. But for the most part, you can reach the point where fear of writing does not interfere with your ability to communicate your knowledge to your instructor. Similarly, with practice you can become skilled at writing in-class themes. Good luck to you with all your exams and in-class writings.

Chapter **7**
Communicating Effectively:
Writing for Your Audience

Without some form of communication, human beings could not come together to live in a society. To recognize this fact, we need only pause for a moment to consider the confusion of life without some means of communication. Yet despite the fact that language—our most frequent form of communication—is what enables us to come together and interact smoothly, all too often we do not use that tool effectively.

Often misunderstandings occur, and you find yourself saying something like, "No, that's not what I mean." And how often have you found yourself struggling for the right words to express what you mean, only to throw up your hands and say, "I know what I mean, but I can't explain it"? Perhaps you have had the experience of writing something—say, a letter—and you had to start over several times because you could not achieve the tone, impact, or clarity you were after.

Well, these are communication problems. And they can be very frustrating, particularly when what you want to say is important to you. Solving these problems and others like them comes under the heading of learning to improve your communication skills. Everything you have learned so far in this book has helped you improve your ability to communicate. That's important for any person, but it's especially important for you, the college student. After all, the ability to communicate effectively is one mark of the educated person.

Interestingly, as you improve your written communication, you will no doubt find that your ability to communicate in speech is also getting better. That's a nice bonus. No charge.

Finally, as your communication skills improve, in many ways your day-to-day living will become easier and better. For example, your ability to communicate effectively while taking an essay examination will make your life as a student easier. Your ability to reason and come up with sound persuasive support will make you a person whose views are respected and even sought out.

In this chapter we will look at other ways writing can improve communication—and ways written communication can improve your life.

READING SELECTION:
From *The Autobiography of Malcolm X*

Malcolm X was a Black Muslim leader assassinated in 1965. The following selection from *The Autobiography of Malcolm X* is a moving account of the man's discovery of the importance of effective communication skills. It is also a description of his efforts to acquire those skills.

The Autobiography of Malcolm X
Malcolm X, with the assistance of Alex Haley

I've never been one for inaction. Everything I've ever felt strongly about, I've done something about. I guess that's why, unable to do anything else, I soon began writing to people I had known in the hustling world, such as Sammy the Pimp, John Hughes, the gambling house owner, the thief Jumpsteady, and several dope peddlers. I wrote them all about Allah and Islam and Mr. Elijah Muhammad. I had no idea where most of them lived. I addressed their letters in care of the Harlem or Roxbury bars and clubs where I'd known them.

I never got a single reply. The average hustler and criminal was too uneducated to write a letter. I have known many slick, sharp-looking hustlers, who would have you think they had an interest in Wall Street; privately, they would get someone else to read a letter if they received one. Besides, neither would I have replied to anyone writing me something as wild as "the white man is the devil."

What certainly went on the Harlem and Roxbury wires was that Detroit Red was going crazy in stir, or else he was trying some hype to shake up the warden's office.

During the years that I stayed in the Norfolk Prison Colony, never did any official directly say anything to me about those letters, although, of course, they all passed though the prison censorship. I'm sure, however, they monitored what I wrote to add to the files which every state and federal prison keeps on the conversion of Negro inmates by the teachings of Mr. Elijah Muhammad.

But at that time, I felt that the real reason was that the white man knew that he was the devil.

Later on, I even wrote to the Mayor of Boston, to the Governor of Massachusetts, and to Harry S. Truman. They never answered; they probably never even saw my letters. I handscratched to them how the white man's society was responsible for the black man's condition in this wilderness of North America.

It was because of my letters that I happened to stumble upon starting to acquire some kind of a homemade education.

I became increasingly frustrated at not being able to express what I wanted to convey in letters that I wrote, especially those to Mr. Elijah Muhammad. In the street, I had been the most articulate hustler out there—I had commanded attention when I said something. But now, trying to write simple English, I not only wasn't articulate, I wasn't even functional. How would I sound writing in slang, the way I would *say* it, something such as, "Look, daddy, let me pull your coat about a cat, Elijah Muhammad—"

Many who today hear me somewhere in person, or on television, or those who read something I've said, will think I went to school far beyond the eighth grade. This impression is due entirely to my prison studies.

It had really begun back in the Charlestown Prison, when Bimbi first made me feel envy of his stock of knowledge. Bimbi had always taken charge of any conversation he was in, and I had tried to emulate him. But every book I picked up had few sentences which didn't contain anywhere from one to nearly all of the words that might as well have been in Chinese. When I just skipped those words, of course, I really ended up with little idea of what the book said. So I had come to the Norfolk Prison Colony still going through only book-reading motions. Pretty soon, I would have quit even these motions, unless I had received the motivation that I did.

I saw that the best thing I could do was get hold of a dictionary—to study, to learn some words. I was lucky enough to reason also that I should try to improve my penmanship. It was sad. I couldn't even write in a straight line. It was both ideas together that moved me to request a dictionary along with some tablets and pencils from the Norfolk Prison Colony school.

I spent two days just riffling uncertainly through the dictionary's pages. I'd never realized so many words existed! I didn't know *which* words I needed to learn. Finally, just to start some kind of action, I began copying.

In my slow, painstaking, ragged handwriting, I copied into my tablet everything printed on that first page, down to the punctuation marks.

I believe it took me a day. Then, aloud, I read back, to myself, everything I'd written on the tablet. Over and over, aloud, to myself, I read my own handwriting.

I woke up the next morning, thinking about those words—immensely proud to realize that not only had I written so much at one time, but I'd written words that I never knew were in the world. Moreover, with a little effort, I also could remember what many of these words meant. I reviewed the words whose meanings I didn't remember. Funny thing, from the dictionary first page right now, that "aardvark" springs to my mind. The dictionary had a picture of it, a long-tailed, long-eared, burrowing African mammal, which lives off termites caught by sticking out its tongue as an anteater does for ants.

I was so fascinated that I went on—I

copied the dictionary's next page. And the same experience came when I studied that. With every succeeding page, I also learned of people and places and events from history. Actually the dictionary is like a miniature encyclopedia. Finally the dictionary's A section had filled a whole tablet—and I went on into the B's. That was the way I started copying what eventually became the entire dictionary. It went a lot faster after so much practice helped me to pick up handwriting speed. Between what I wrote in my tablet, and writing letters, during the rest of my time in prison I would guess I wrote a million words.

I suppose it was inevitable that as my word-base broadened, I could for the first time pick up a book and read and now begin to understand what the book was saying. Anyone who has read a great deal can imagine the new world that opened. Let me tell you something: from then until I left that prison, in every free moment I had, if I was not reading in the library, I was reading on my bunk. You couldn't have gotten me out of books with a wedge. Between Mr. Muhammad's teachings, my correspondence, my visitors—usually Ella and Reginald—and my reading of books, months passed without my even thinking about being imprisoned. In fact, up to then, I never had been so truly free in my life.

Vocabulary List:
From *The Autobiography of Malcolm X*

Malcolm X came to understand the need for an adequate vocabulary. I'm sure you, too, are becoming more and more aware of the value of building your own word storehouse. So continue your vocabulary building in the usual way. Record below the words you are unsure of from the reading selection. Check a dictionary and write brief definitions that correspond to the way the words were used in the piece. Then add two of the words to your vocabulary list in Appendix A. Like Malcolm X, study your words each day so you can become familiar enough with them to use them in your speech and writing.

_____   _____

_____   _____

_____   _____

Questions for Discussion:
From *The Autobiography of Malcolm X*

1. When Malcolm X wrote to Sammy the Pimp, the thief Jumpsteady, and some dope peddlers, he got no reply. Part of the reason for this, says Malcolm X, is that he was writing things "as wild as 'the white man is the devil.'" Malcolm X reasons that those who got his letters

probably thought he "was going crazy in stir [prison]." This brings up a point about something a writer must consider. What is that point?

_____

_____

_____

2. Why do you suppose the mayor of Boston, the governor of Massachusetts, and Harry S. Truman never answered Malcolm X's letters? Consider the content of the letters and the way they were written.

_____

_____

_____

3. Malcolm X writes, "I became increasingly frustrated at not being able to express what I wanted to convey in letters that I wrote. . . ." Are you familiar with this frustration? What causes it and why is it so uncomfortable?

_____

_____

_____

4. Malcolm X says, "In the street, I had been the most articulate hustler out there—I had commanded attention when I said something." How is it that Malcolm X could communicate so effectively in one situation (speaking on the street) but have so much trouble in another (writing letters)?

_____

_____

_____

5. Are there some situations in which *you* find it difficult to communicate effectively? What are they? Or was there one specific time when you found it hard to communicate?

_____

_____

6. Malcolm X began his self-education by studying a dictionary. Why was this "the best thing" he could do?

_____

_____

7. How is vocabulary related to effective communication?

_____

_____

8. How can it be that Malcolm X enjoyed more freedom in jail than at any previous time?

_____

_____

GETTING READY: IMPROVING COMMUNICATION IN ONE SITUATION

I think we all have moments when we find it hard to communicate as effectively as we would like. Below is a list of situations that can cause some people communication difficulties.

Job interviews

Writing résumés

Talking or writing to people who scare, or annoy, or bother us

Taking essay exams

Having conferences with instructors

Writing letters home

Writing sympathy notes

Writing thank-you notes

Writing letters to the editor

Saying no to salespeople

Perhaps one or more of the situations in the above list cause some communication problems for you. Or perhaps it's a different situation that causes difficulty. Well, let's follow Malcolm X's example and meet the problem head-on and work to solve it. And let's use list writing to do it.

To do this, pick one situation that raises communication problems for you. Write that situation at the top of a sheet of paper. Also explain why you think you have trouble in this situation. Then list all the things you can do to overcome the difficulties. To get ideas for overcoming the problem, there are several things you can do. First, check this book's index. There are listings for résumés, essay exams, and perhaps other situations that may be on your sheet. Any useful suggestions you find, put on your list. Also, seek out experts and ask their advice. Counselors on campus, speech instructors, business instructors, your classroom teacher—all these may have tips for you to put on your list. In addition, speak to those you know who seem to communicate well in those situations where you have trouble. Ask them for advice and tips to add to your list. Finally, give the problem some careful thought yourself; you may well come up with some strategies on your own, just as Malcolm X did.

When your list of what to do is complete, begin working immediately on putting the suggestions to work. You may soon find yourself communicating effectively when you weren't before. Just remember, this may take time and practice, but it will be worth it.

GETTING READY: IMPROVING COMMUNICATION WITH THOSE CLOSEST TO US

It is sad but true that often we do not engage in enough meaningful communication with the people we care the most about. Sometimes we just do not take the time to share what is in our hearts and minds. Often habit leads us to keep repeating the same interactions without ever opening new areas for communication. We even believe at times that there are some things we cannot share with our loved ones, and this interferes with our communication.

Yet it is with the people we care the most about that we should be communicating the most extensively and the most effectively. Try this exercise to improve communication with someone you care about—someone you have not been communicating with as well as or as frequently as you would like.

You and the person you choose to improve communication with should begin keeping separate journals. In these journals each of you should record each day those things that somehow impress you, disturb you, excite you, depress you, or in any other way move you. A good way to handle this is to spend a half hour or so before bed making entries in your journal. An even better way is to keep a notebook with you throughout the day to record your thoughts, observations, and feelings.

Either way, be sure to date each entry, describe the occurrence, and note its effect on you and any thoughts or feelings the occurrence inspires. Once a week trade journals with the other person. Read each other's entries and discuss the most interesting ones. I believe you will discover your awareness, understanding, and appreciation for each other will be greatly improved as a result of this communication.

AUDIENCE

Your *audience* is who you are writing for. That audience will determine to a great extent the shape your writing will take. Your audience must be taken into consideration if you are to communicate effectively in writing. For example, if your audience is a group of your fellow students, you can use a more casual, informal vocabulary and style than you could if you were writing for one of your professors. Similarly, if you were writing about the dangers of nuclear waste disposal for an audience that knew little about the complexities of physics, chemistry, and ecology, your content would be less technical than if you were writing for a group of scientists who readily understood such things. Clearly, then, your style, vocabulary, approach, and choice of detail will be determined in part by just who will read what you write. In fact, if you do not take your audience into consideration, you run the risk of missing your mark. If this happens, you are not communicating.

When Malcolm X wrote to a pimp, a thief, and some dope peddlers, he missed his mark. He wrote "something as wild as 'the white man is the devil.' " His audience was not receptive to that idea expressed in that way, and hence Malcolm X did not communicate effectively. Again, when he wrote to a mayor, a governor, and a former United States president, Malcolm X failed to consider his audience; he "handscratched" a very hostile message. So once more, he did not communicate effectively. As a writer, you must gear your vocabulary, style, tone, and detail to your reader.

Sample Paragraphs:
"Never Ride with Strangers"

Read the two paragraphs below. The first was written for a class of third-graders to warn them against accepting rides with strangers. The second was written to caution teenagers against hitchhiking. After you have read the paragraphs, answer the questions that follow.

Never Ride with Strangers
In school and at home you learn many safety rules. You learn to look both ways before you cross the street. You learn not to touch a hot stove. You learn to be careful on your bike. What other safety rules do you know? The safety rules

teach you how to be safe. You follow the rules so you will not get hurt. One important safety rule is never ride with a stranger. A stranger is a person you do not know. If a stranger asks you to get in a car, you should run away. Run to your mom or dad or to the grown-up who is taking care of you. If a person you do not know asks you to take a ride, you should run away. Never get in a car with a stranger. Some strangers are bad. Some people you do not know may want to hurt you. Even if a person looks nice or acts nice, do not get in the car. If you are playing outside and a stranger asks you to get in a car and go for ice cream, what will you do?

Never Ride with Strangers

Karla's parents sat in the police station, their gaze frozen on the worn floorboards at their feet. The fear they had known the past days that Karla had been missing now peaked to a paralyzing numbness as they waited for the patrolman who would escort them to the morgue. There they would face the horror of identifying the body of their only daughter. Three days earlier Karla was hitchhiking on Route 82. She thought she was being careful. Already she had refused two rides because the drivers looked seedy. The third man who stopped, though, was a clean-cut type, a salesman in his early thirties in a late-model Chevy. A state policeman found Karla in a gully beside Highway 82. She had been brutally beaten. She was left to die out there by the side of the road. No, there's no way to be careful when hitching a ride. There are no clues in a person's face or actions to indicate who it's safe to ride with. And it doesn't matter if you're a guy or a gal. If you're thumbing a ride, you're risking your life. It's sad to say, but it's just not a safe world. Robbery, assault, abduction, murder—that's what the hitchhiker risks. That's not a free ride!

Questions for Discussion:
"Never Ride with Strangers"

Both paragraphs above warn not to ride with strangers. However, the pieces are very different because they are intended for different audiences. The questions here point out the difference audience can make in the content, vocabulary, style, and tone of writing.

1. How is the vocabulary of the two paragraphs different because of the different audiences? Cite two examples to support your view.

_____

_____

_____

2. How is the sentence structure of the two paragraphs different because of the different audiences? Cite two examples to support your view.

_____

_____

_____

3. Explain the different approach each paragraph has because of the different audiences.

_____

_____

_____

4. How does audience affect the opening of each paragraph?

_____

_____

_____

5. How is the detail selection different for each paragraph because of the different audiences?

_____

_____

_____

6. How does audience affect the closing of each paragraph?

_____

_____

_____

EXERCISE:
The Message Sent and the Message Received

You just learned how important it is for you to consider your audience when you write. You learned that you must gear your approach, vocabulary, sentence structure, and content to your reader so that person will get your message. So often, however, a writer focuses so hard on his or her end of the communication process that the reader's needs are overlooked. Therefore, it's a good idea for you to find out whether the message and impression you want to send your reader really are the same message and impression that person receives.

To do this, write a theme explaining how you feel about some aspect of college life. You could express your feelings about grades, exams, required courses, having to pay your own tuition, registration, a particular course, studying, your roommate, or any other part of your life as a student. You could, for example, discuss how hard it is to work while attending school. Or you could explain how much satisfaction you get from doing well on an exam.

The audience for this theme will be one of your classmates. Thus, as you write, consider the things you should do to get your message across to this kind of reader. After writing your theme, trade papers with one of your classmates. Read that person's theme and then answer the questions below.

1. What aspect of college life is discussed?

_____

2. How does the writer feel about this aspect?

_____

_____

3. What points does the writer make to support his or her view?

_____

_____

_____

4. Are there any details that should *not* have been included? If so, what are they and why should they have been left out?

_____

_____

_____

_____

5. Are there any details that should have been added? If so, what are they and why should they have been added?

_____

_____

_____

_____

6. Is the introduction interesting? Why or why not?

_____

_____

_____

7. Is the conclusion satisfying? Why or why not?

_____

_____

_____

8. Are there any words you would like to see changed? Which ones? What would you change them to? Why?

_____

_____

_____

_____

9. Are there any sentences you would like to see changed? Which ones? What would you change them to? Why?

_____

_____

_____

_____

_____

10. How do the grammar and usage affect your overall reaction to the theme?

_____

_____

_____

11. Does the theme hold your interest? Why or why not?

_____

_____

_____

_____

12. In about three sentences, summarize the message the writer is sending.

_____

_____

_____

_____

_____

13. Is there anything in the theme that you do not understand? If so, what is it?

_____

_____

_____

_____

After answering the questions, return the theme and your answers to your classmate. Also get from that person your theme and the answers he or she wrote. Reread your theme and study the comments. You should get an idea of how one person reacted to the content and structure of your writing. Was the message you wanted to send the one that was received? If not, you must decide whether the fault is yours or the reader's. Perhaps the reader's careless reading or lack of skill is responsible for your missing your mark. But if the fault is yours, learn from your mistakes. If you cannot decide whether the feedback you got from your reader is reliable, ask your instructor to help you decide.

GRAMMAR AND USAGE

In this grammar and usage section, you will learn several ways to improve your ability to communicate effectively. You will learn techniques for improving your vocabulary, for avoiding problems between pronouns and the words they refer to, and for avoiding dangling and misplaced modifiers. In addition, you will learn how to use the apostrophe and how to improve your style with sentence variety.

Building Your Vocabulary

When Malcolm X wanted to improve his ability to communicate, he turned first to the dictionary. He recognized that without an adequate vocabulary, he could not express himself well. But you have been working to build your vocabulary since Chapter 2; you realize that your ability to communicate is limited in part by the number of words you know.

But did you realize that the extent of your vocabulary can also determine the range of your thoughts? After all, we think using language. Unless we are thinking about mathematical problems, architectural blueprints, and the like, our ideas are most often symbolized in language. Hence, if we do not have a word to express an idea, it is questionable that we can have that idea at all. Once you realize this, you can appreciate even more the importance of having a broad vocabulary—it helps us express our ideas with precision, and it aids in the very formation of those ideas!

There are several steps you can take to continue improving your vocabulary.

1. Each time you see or hear a new word, look it up in the dictionary. Check carefully its meaning, spelling, and pronunciation. Notice its part of speech and what endings are used to change it to other parts of speech. Record all this information in a notebook or on index cards. Or continue to use the vocabulary list in Appendix A.

2. Study just a few of these words each day for several days. It is far easier to learn words this way than to attempt learning long vocabulary lists in a short time. Before you begin studying new words, go back and review the words you studied earlier.

3. Learn the difference between a word's connotation and denotation. The *denotation* is the actual dictionary definition of a word. The *connotation* refers to the feelings and associations a word arouses. For example, *lie* and *fib* both denote telling untruths. However, *fib* connotes a less serious offense than *lie*.

4. Make up sentences using new words. Try to use each word in more than one sentence as a different part of speech.

5. Begin using new words in your speech and writing often. This will make you more comfortable with them and speed your learning.

6. Try learning new words with friends or family members. Trade words, try to stump each other, use your new words with these people. Make it a game as much as a learning experience.

7. Subscribe to one of the weekly newsmagazines and read it each week from cover to cover. This will help you build your vocabulary because as you come across new words, you can look them up. This practice will have the added bonus of helping you become more informed.

While reading the entire sentence that contains the new word and recognizing smaller parts of a larger word may provide useful clues to a word's meaning, the only reliable way to determine meaning is to consult a dictionary.

Agreement of Pronouns and Referents in Number

1. To communicate effectively, you must be as clear as possible at all times. However, sometimes writers have trouble choosing correct pronouns, and they become unclear as a result. *Pronouns,* you probably know, are words that take the place of nouns. The nouns that pronouns refer to are called *referents* (from the word *refer*). Pronouns must always agree with their referents in number. This means that if you have a singular noun, the pronoun taking its place must also be singular. Similarly, if you have a plural noun, the pronoun taking its place must also be plural. The singular pronouns are:

I	me	my, mine
you	him	your, yours
he	her	his
she		hers
it		its

The plural pronouns are:

we	us	our, ours
you	them	your, yours
they		their, theirs

Note: You, your, and yours can be singular or plural.

Example: After the boys washed the car, they cleaned the yard.

Explanation: the plural pronoun they is used because its noun referent boys is plural.

In sentences like the above example, few people have difficulty choosing the correct pronoun. However, in sentences like those below, the choice of pronoun isn't always as easily handled.

Incorrect: Every student should pick up their registration materials by Thursday.

Correct: Every student should pick up his registration materials by Thursday.

Incorrect: If a person desires to travel abroad inexpensively, they can do so by planning carefully.

Correct: If a person desires to travel abroad inexpensively, he can do so by planning carefully.

Mistakes in sentences like those above are common because even though the noun referents such as student and person are singular in form, the writer is thinking of people in general. Despite this fact, when a singular referent is used, the pronoun should also be singular. It is true, however, that the "incorrect" examples above are acceptable in speech that is informal. Still, it is a good idea to get in the habit of always following the form shown in the "correct" examples.

Note: Many people today try to avoid sexist language. If you wish to avoid the use of his, he, or him when women are also involved, you have two choices. You can use a form such as his/her, he/she, or him/her, or write out or in place of the slash to get he or she, and so on. If you prefer, you can rework your sentence, when possible, to avoid the singular form. For the above examples, you could write: "All students should pick up their registration materials by Thursday" or "If people desire to travel abroad inexpensively, they can do so by planning carefully."

2. There is also a group of pronouns—the indefinite pronouns—that can cause agreement problems. *Indefinite pronouns* can function as referents and are so called because they do not refer to specific people or things. Some indefinite pronouns are almost always singular. Therefore, when they are referents, they require singular pronouns. Below is a list of singular indefinite pronouns.

anybody	each one	everyone	somebody
anyone	either	everything	someone
anything	neither	no one	something
each	everybody	nothing	nobody

Example: Anybody interested in attending summer school should report to room 232 with his or her registration materials.

Example: Each of the children should bring his or her lunch to the picnic.

Example: Either of those alternatives has its disadvantages.

Note: Sometimes a plural pronoun must be used to refer to a singular indefinite pronoun, but this is not usual.

Example: Everybody enjoyed the party, and they vowed to have another soon. (He or she simply does not work here.)

EXERCISE:
Choosing Pronouns

In the following sentences, circle the correct pronoun.

1. Either Phillip or George will bring (his, their) van so we can move the rest of the furniture.

2. If a person wants to be a physical therapist, (he or she, they) must have a great deal of patience and a genuine desire to help people.

3. Anyone who drives alone at night should keep (their, his or her) car doors locked.

4. In fact, people who drive in the daytime should keep (their, his or her) doors locked too, because all crimes do not occur at night.

5. Everybody who plans to graduate this spring should see (his or her, their) adviser for instructions.

6. Each of us should try to do (his or her, their) best at all times.

7. Each of the women decided to quit (their, her) job in order to return to school.

8. Both of the men agreed that without (their, his) wives' income, financial security would be impossible.

9. Some of the younger children brought (his or her, their) parents along, but one of the boys came with (his or her, his, their) grandfather.

10. If someone calls after I leave, tell (them, him or her) that I will be back in an hour.

Agreement of Pronouns and Referents in Person

Not only do pronouns have number (they are either singular or plural), but they also can be grouped according to person. There are first-person, second-person, and third-person pronouns in both singular and plural, as charted below.

Singular		**Plural**	
First person:	I, me, my, mine	First person:	we, us, our, ours
Second person:	you, your, yours	Second person:	you, your, yours
Third person:	he, she, it, him, her, his hers, its	Third person:	they, them, their, theirs

Note: The indefinite pronouns are always third person.

Very often people weaken the effectiveness of their written communication because they fail to make their pronouns and referents agree in person. Yet there is an easy way to avoid this problem: Remember that nouns are always in the third person. Thus, pronouns that refer to nouns will have to be in the third person as well.

Incorrect: Many students worry so much about examinations, they become too worked up to perform well. Therefore, you should relax as much as possible while taking a test.

Correct: Many students worry so much about examinations, they become too worked up to perform well. Therefore, <u>they</u> should relax as much as possible while taking a test.

Explanation: The noun <u>you</u> refers to is <u>students</u>. Since the referent is plural and <u>all</u> nouns are <u>third</u> person, the third-person plural <u>they</u> is required—not the second-person <u>you</u>.

When you fail to make your pronouns and referents agree in person, you have made a mistake called a *shift in person*. Shifts in person can annoy or confuse a reader and thereby weaken the effectiveness of your communication. Not only should you avoid such shifts within a single sentence, but you should also generally be sure your entire essay is written in the same person.

EXERCISE:
Choosing Pronouns

In the following sentences, some pronouns are incorrect because they do not agree in number and/or person with their referents. Correct any pronoun errors you find by crossing out and writing the correct form above the incorrect one. In some cases, a change in the pronoun will make a change in the verb necessary.

1. When a student buys his texts used, they shouldn't expect them to be in good condition.

2. Not a single person turned in their term paper on time.

3. It always seems as though the harder a person tries, the more mistakes they make.

4. Children are expected to help out around the house. You have no right to be lazy all the time.

5. Actually, anyone can learn to bowl. All you need is some coordination and the right equipment.

6. If everyone brought their own liquor, the party wouldn't cost us very much.

7. Many people give up bridge because it takes so long to learn, but you should realize that all good things take time.

8. A nurse works extremely hard and does not get paid as well as they might.

9. A professional football player often earns a high salary, but they do not hold the job very long.

10. Someone who scares easily should not canoe down these rapids. You could easily kill us all by not staying in control.

Other Pronoun Problems:
Ambiguous Reference, Remote Reference, and Implied Reference

1. Be careful when you use pronouns not to have an ambiguous reference, or your communication will not be clear, and thus it will not be effective. A reference is *ambiguous* when there is more than one possible noun referent for a pronoun.

Ambiguous reference:	I could not help overhearing Tim arguing with Justin. He seemed angry enough to throw a punch.
Explanation:	It is impossible to tell whether he refers to Tim or Justin.
Correction:	I could not help overhearing Tim arguing with Justin. Tim seemed angry enough to throw a punch.

2. Also, your communication will lose some of its effectiveness if your pronoun and noun referent are so far removed from each other that your reader must pause for a time to determine what the pronoun's referent is. This is an error called *remote reference*.

Remote reference:	By 5:00 I had started the stew. I left the room for a minute to get the newspaper, and then I quickly changed my clothes. When I returned to the kitchen, a strange hissing sound alerted me to the fact that it had boiled over.
Explanation:	It is too far removed from stew to provide a clear reference.
Correction:	When I returned to the kitchen, a strange hissing sound alerted me to the fact that the stew had boiled over.

3. Finally, be sure that each of your pronouns has a specifically stated noun referent or you will risk being unclear due to *implied reference*.

Implied reference:	Tom is so adventurous; it is a quality I greatly admire.
Explanation:	It has no noun referent. The adjective adventurous is used as a referent, but this is grammatically unacceptable. Actually the implied referent is spirit of adventure.
Correction:	Tom has such a spirit of adventure; it is a quality I greatly admire.
	or
	Tom is so adventurous; his spirit of adventure is a quality I greatly admire.

EXERCISE:
Ambiguous, Implied, and Remote Reference

Circle the pronouns below that are a problem because of ambiguous, implied, or remote reference. In the blanks, write the correction. The first one is done for you as an example.

1. My last history exam demonstrates just how unreasonable some tests can be. I am opposed to exams, for they don't always test students' knowledge. For example, although I studied, I'm sure I didn't score any higher than a D on (it.)

my history exam. _____

2. Janet walked into the room just as Ted and Marcus were finishing the decorations for her surprise party. He was so upset that his surprise was ruined that he stormed out the door.

_____

3. That nursery school teacher is quite attentive, and it makes her the best teacher in the school.

_____

4. Professor Harold and Professor DiBacco wrote two books, but they were never widely praised by the profession.

_____

5. My husband is such a failure in the kitchen that he couldn't even scramble eggs unless I wrote it out.

_____

6. To ensure the most attractive glassware display possible, wash and dry them carefully just before the sale begins.

_____

7. Mrs. Cohen first joined Mrs. Bosley as co-chairman of the charity ball when she was still the president of the YWCA.

_____

8. Dan is certainly musically inclined, but can he use it to make a living?

_____

9. When I arrived to pick up my car, I was horrified to see a dented fender and broken headlight. I soon learned that Maureen had been out for a ride without my permission. What else could I do but get in and drive it home?

_____

10. To create a perfect dinner party, you must plan the menu carefully, choosing foods that everyone will enjoy. Also, invite guests who get along well with each other. Select the correct wine and serve it at the right temperature. Then it will be a success.

_____

Dangling and Misplaced Modifiers

A *modifier,* as you recall, is a word or word group that describes. If you use a modifier but fail to provide a word for it to describe, you have written a *dangling modifier.* Often, dangling modifiers make for absurd sentences.

As you work for clarity in order to communicate effectively, you must be careful to avoid dangling modifiers because these will create confused and even silly sentences. Confused or silly sentences will distract your reader, causing your writing to lose its impact.

Dangling modifier: While scrambling the eggs, the toast burned.

Explanation: While scrambling the eggs is a modifier, yet it is impossible to find a word in the sentence for it to describe. As a result, the sense of the sentence is that the toast was scrambling the eggs.

There are two ways to correct a dangling modifier. First, you can add a word in the coordinate clause for the modifier to describe.

Correction: While scrambling the eggs, I burned the toast.

Explanation: While scrambling the eggs here has I as a logical word to refer to.

If you prefer, you may correct a dangling modifier by revising the modifier so that it includes the logical reference.

Correction: While I was scrambling the eggs, the toast burned.

Explanation: Here the modifier is reworked so it is clear just who was scrambling the eggs.

Note: You cannot correct a dangling modifier by reversing the order of the modifier and the coordinate clause.

Incorrect: The toast burned while scrambling the eggs.

When you use a modifier, be sure to place it as close as possible to the word it describes, or you will have a *misplaced modifier.* A misplaced modifier weakens your communication because it can cause a sentence to be confusing or silly.

Misplaced modifier: The man gave the box to his wife held together by string.

Explanation: Because of its placement, held together by string seems to describe wife.

To correct a misplaced modifier, move it as close as possible to the word it describes.

Correction: The man gave the box held together by string to his wife.

EXERCISE:
Dangling and Misplaced Modifiers

The following sentences are troublesome because they contain dangling and misplaced modifiers. Rewrite them to eliminate the problems and establish clarity. The first one is done for you as an example.

1. While riding on the bus, the neon signs flashed brightly.

While I was riding on the bus, the neon signs

flashed brightly.

2. Because of following the recipe exactly, the chicken came out tasty and tender.

_____

_____

3. At the garage sale, I sold a wagon to a man without wheels.

_____

_____

4. The youngster ran across the hot pavement that had no shoes on.

_____

_____

5. The instructions stated the paint should be kept away from heat clearly.

_____

_____

6. I hear that Gloria and Paul plan to be married by the grapevine.

_____

_____

7. Driving at 5:00 A.M., the sunrise was spectacular.

_____

_____

8. I was playing with my son when the doorbell rang on the floor.

_____

_____

9. Being a real science fiction buff, _Star Wars_ drew my immediate attention.

_____

_____

10. When sweet, my brother can eat an entire jar of pickles in one sitting.

_____

_____

Sentence Variety

Perhaps it is too obvious to say, but I'll say it anyway: No reader, unless forced, will follow a piece to its finish if the writing is boring. This is one reason writers search for interesting topics. However, it is not enough to have an interesting subject, for even the most fascinating topic will fail to hold a reader if it is expressed in a dull way. On the other hand, even a seemingly dull subject can fascinate a reader if the treatment is fresh and interesting. Consider the following passage:

Tina is eccentric, to say the least. She dyed her hair green once because green is her favorite color. Her boss told her she would lose her job if she didn't return her hair to a normal color. Tina felt her boss had no right to dictate her hair color. She quit her job. Her hair grew out to its natural color eventually. Tina found a job selling shoes. This job did not last very long, however. Tina felt the shoes were overpriced. She believed they were worth $5.00 less than they were marked. That is what she sold them for. Her manager fired her when he realized what she was doing. Tina has a new job now. She is a housekeeper and companion for an eighty-year-old man. The man is senile. He doesn't notice Tina's eccentricity. Tina is happy with her work.

Certainly Tina could be the subject of an interest-holding theme. But the passage above is likely to bore a reader because the sentence structure lacks variety. The passage is monotonous because every sentence begins with the subject. If you tend to write this way, your communication will not be very effective because it will be dull.

In your own writing, work for *sentence variety* by mixing the sentence structures you use. Doing that will give your style polish, sophistication, and interest. As a result, your written communication will be improved. To get a pleasing mix of sentence structures, do the following:

1. Use coordination in some sentences:

   Example: Tina may be eccentric, but she has a good heart.

2. Use introductory subordinate clauses in some sentences:

   Example: Although Tina is eccentric, she has a good heart.

3. Begin some sentences with modifying words:

   Example: Clearly Tina is eccentric, but she has a good heart.

4. Begin some sentences with modifying phrases:

   Example: As a shoe salesperson, Tina did not last long.

5. Begin some sentences with the subject:

   Example: Tina did not last long as a shoe salesperson.

6. Place transitions at the beginnings of some sentences:

   Example: However, Tina did not last long as a shoe salesperson.

7. Place transitions at the ends of some sentences:

   Example: Tina did not last long as a shoe salesperson, however.

8. Place transitions in the middle of some sentences:

   Example: Tina, however, did not last long as a shoe salesperson.

9. Place interrupters at the beginnings of some sentences:

   Example: By all standards, Tina must be considered an eccentric.

10. Place interrupters at the ends of some sentences:

    Example: Tina must be considered an eccentric by all standards.

11. Place interrupters in the middle of some sentences:

    Example: Tina, by all standards, must be considered an eccentric.

12. Strike a balance between long and short sentences:

    Example: Tina is clearly an eccentric. She has been known to wear her hair green as well as sell shoes for what she felt they were worth rather than what the price ticket said.

The paragraph about Tina lacks sentence variety because there are too many subject-first sentences. Too much of any particular sentence structure will cause sentence monotony, so remember to strive for a nice mix of structures. To ensure that your writing has enough sentence variety to prevent your reader from becoming bored by your style, check your writing when you revise and edit to be sure that you do not have too many sentences next to each other with the same structure. It is not difficult to reshape some of your sentences according to the twelve suggestions above in order to achieve variety. Remember, interesting ideas conveyed in a dull fashion will disturb a reader just as quickly as boring content.

EXERCISE:
Sentence Variety

1. Rewrite the paragraph about Tina to achieve sentence variety.

_____

_____

_____

_____

_____

_____

_____

_____

_____

_____

_____

_____

_____

_____

_____

2. Look through some of your earlier writings and select a paragraph that could benefit from some sentence variety. Then rewrite the paragraph according to the twelve suggestions for varying sentence structure.

_____

_____

_____

_____

_____

_____

_____

_____

_____

_____

_____

_____

_____

A Word about the Apostrophe

For some reason (I've never quite figured out why), the apostrophe (') is one of the most frequently misunderstood punctuation marks. Yet it is important to use this mark properly, because not doing so can cause confusion in your writing. So in the interest of improving written communication, let's look at the uses for the apostrophe.

1. Use an apostrophe in contractions to take the place of omitted letters. A _contraction_ is formed by making one word out of two. Below are some common contractions.

haven't (have not)	I'd (I had; I would)	it's (it has)
isn't (is not)	I've (I have)	who's (who is)
couldn't (could not)	it's (it is)	there's (there is)

Notice that you make a contraction by joining two words to form one and by leaving some letters out. The apostrophe signals the spot where the letters are omitted. As a writer, if you forget an apostrophe in a contraction, you may find that your reader stumbles a bit over the word. And any time your reader stumbles, your communication loses some of its effectiveness.

Note: The contraction form of <u>will not</u> is the irregular <u>won't</u>.

2. Use an apostrophe when letters or numbers have been left out of a longer form.

Example: The spirit of '76 will never be with us again.

Example: Joshua asked, "Who's goin' with us?"

Should composition be a required course? Why or why not?

What would you like to see changed in this course?

What would you like to see remain the same in this course?

Using your thoughts and feelings about the composition course and writing in general, write a well-developed, well-organized theme that communicates to your instructor your current attitude about writing and the composition course. This exercise in effective written communication is valuable for three reasons. First, it will give you the chance to sort and order your feelings and thoughts about something that is currently taking up a significant portion of your time, energy, and money. Second, it will provide your instructor with valuable feedback. Finally, with the feedback your instructor receives, he or she can come to understand you and your needs better and in that way provide you with the best instruction possible for the remainder of the term. Perhaps your instructor will be moved to write a response to some of your thoughts and feelings, which will improve the communication between the two of you even more.

As you work on this assignment, remember that for it to be of maximum value, you must communicate effectively and honestly. Be sure that you supply reasons for each thought and feeling you communicate. You must consider carefully and communicate honestly because I'm sure your instructor is more interested in honest communication than in a snow job. Below are some questions to answer before submitting your theme.

Questions to Answer before Submitting Your Theme

Before submitting your theme, be sure that you can answer yes to the following questions:

1. Is your diction precise and economical? Have you avoided clichés?
2. Have you checked for fragments and run-ons?
3. Have you checked your subject–verb agreement and your pronoun–referent agreement?
4. Have you avoided inappropriate tense shifts?
5. Have you avoided dangling and misplaced modifiers?
6. Have you checked your punctuation to be sure you have used commas, semicolons, colons, dashes, parentheses, and apostrophes correctly? Have you punctuated conversation correctly?
7. Have you shown the relationships among your ideas with coordination, subordination, and transitions?
8. Have you worked to achieve sentence variety?

9. Are your lead-in, thesis, topic sentences, and conclusion suitable?

10. Is your supporting detail adequate and relevant?

11. Did you use some new vocabulary words?

12. Did you proofread carefully, more than once?

WRITING ASSIGNMENT II

Malcolm X notes that he could communicate quite effectively when he was in the street. He even "commanded attention" when he spoke. Yet when he tried to write "simple English" to those who did not use street slang, he was not successful. This brings to our attention the fact that there are many varieties of a single language, not all of which are appropriate in all situations. Consider for a moment that you use one variety of language when communicating to your instructors and another when you are out with your friends. You probably use yet another variety of language when communicating with your parents and still another one when communicating with a young child.

To be effective communicators, we must be able to determine which variety of language to use according to the particular situation we happen to find ourselves in and the particular audience we are communicating with. Furthermore, we must be sufficiently fluent in enough varieties to be able to adapt our vocabulary, content, tone, and style to suit various situations and various audiences.

To appreciate that effective communication involves the ability to determine the variety of language to use as well as the ability to use it well, try this: Pretend you are a senior only one term away from graduation. You have decided that school is a bore, and the real education is to be had outside the classroom. Adding any other details that you care to, write a letter to your parents (who have always dreamed you would get your degree and have sacrificed much to pay your tuition) explaining that you are quitting school to travel across the country. Now write a letter to your closest friend (who goes to another school) and explain your plans. Finally, write a letter to your academic adviser (who has just written a recommendation for a scholarship to graduate school for you) and again explain your plans.

As you can tell, you will have to consider your audience when you write each letter and adjust what you do to suit that particular audience. In addition, your *purpose* for writing will be different for each reader, and this, too, will affect your writing. When you write to your parents, you will be trying to spare their feelings. You know they will be disappointed, but you love them and want to let them down as easily as possible. When you write to your adviser, you will be trying not to create a negative impression because you value that person's opinion of you. When you write to your best friend, your purpose is to make someone you care about understand your feelings.

After you have all written your letters, break into groups of four or five to discuss how audience and purpose affect vocabulary, sentence structure, approach, and content. One member of each group should keep a list of the group's conclusions so that each group's findings can be shared with the class as a whole. Below are three sample letters that illustrate this assignment, along with some questions for discussion.

Three Sample Letters

Dear Mom and Dad,

I know you expected to hear from me before now, but I've had a great deal on my mind, and I wanted to think things through before I wrote to you. I have spent the last weeks sorting things out, trying to figure out what I want in life. No, I don't have all the answers yet, but at least now I know the path I should follow to find those answers. I've made a decision, Mom and Dad. It's one you may have trouble understanding and one you may find disappointing. But let me assure you that I've thought this through carefully. There's no way to break this to you gently, so forgive my abruptness. My decision is to drop out of school for a time.

As you know, this last year has been difficult for me. Even though my grades are still pretty good, I haven't been working as I should. I've just been going through the motions. When I study, my heart's not in it. I have to force myself to go to class. When I get to class, I barely hear the lecture. I tried hard to figure out why I lost my enthusiasm, and at last I know—I'm really not interested in business administration anymore. At first I enjoyed my major, but lately I realize that I don't want to spend the rest of my life in a three-piece suit.

I know I'm only one quarter away from graduation, and I suppose there would be a certain logic to crossing the finish line, but how can I finish out with a major I don't even like? Believe me, I would stay and graduate if there was even a remote chance that I could find happiness in the business world, but I don't think that's possible.

Once I determined that business administration wasn't for me, I tried to find another course of study. I figured that I could switch majors and finish a year late. But, Mom and Dad, no matter how many times I read the catalog, I can't find a thing that excites me. I know I want to do something meaningful with my life; I just don't know what it would be right now.

I'm sure you can tell from this that I'm confused and in need of direction. I spoke to a counselor in the psych department, and she suggested that I didn't know what to do with my life because I haven't had enough experience with life. I thought about that carefully, and you know what? She was right. Almost all my life I've been in school. Everything I've learned has been secondhand. Knowledge has come to me filtered through books and teachers. I've learned so little through firsthand experience.

Well, I've got to change that. I've got to do some firsthand living. So I'm taking the money I've saved, and I'm going to travel the country. I'll work as I need to, but mostly I'll see things, people, and places—and I'll learn from it all.

At last I'm truly excited about something. Both my instincts and my mind tell me this is right. So please, Mom and Dad, be happy for me. You've raised me to do what I think is right, and this *is* what I think is right for me. Once I learn what to do with myself, who knows—I may come back to school and get my degree.

I can't close this until I tell you how much I appreciate all you've done for me and all you've sacrificed so I could go to school. Believe me, these past three and a half years have not been wasted. I *have* learned. It's just that now my education lies elsewhere.

I love you both. I will be home next week to see you before I head out on my journey.

> All my love,
> Hank

Dear Marco,

Well I hope you're sitting down, old buddy, because I'm about to drop a bombshell. I've decided to trade my book bag for a knapsack. Yep, you read it right—I'm quitting school to travel around for a while.

I know what you're thinking—that I'm the last person you'd expect to pull such a stunt—but believe me I haven't lost my senses. In fact, for the first time in a long while I'm thinking clearly. I'm tired of listening to boring lectures, taking notes, and attending classes that I don't really care about. And I've had it with exam anxiety. It took me a long time to figure it out, but now, one quarter from graduation, I realize that business administration is the ultimate pits.

You see, I've been conned, Man, and I'm mad as hell about it. The whole system has conspired to make me believe that money, power, and success are the means to happiness. The middle-class jive about ambition being the supreme motivation may be true, but I've lost mine, friend. I don't want money, power, or success. I just don't want to play in the button-down shirt league.

Unfortunately, I don't really know *what* I want to do. But I know I've got to find out. So I'm off to see the country. On the way I hope to learn about myself and others. I'm not sure *how* yet, but I know somehow I'll figure out what I want to do as a result. So wish me luck because I'm off to see the wizard—and if he can't give me a brain, a heart, and some courage, maybe I'll make my way back to Kansas.

By the way, Marco, I'd appreciate it if you'd give my folks a call and explain that this is not the end of the world. They respect you, and I think they may be in need of some reassurance.

> Your travelin' buddy,
> Hank

Dear Dr. DiBlasio:

Lately I have given serious thought to the direction my life should take. This soul-searching has not been easy, but I have reached a conclusion I would like you to be aware of.

I have decided that it is in my best interests to drop out of school for a time. I am aware that this is not a decision to make lightly, and believe me I thought hard before I settled on this path. I am convinced that I must get away from school for a time in order to reevaluate my goals. I'm sure you can understand this need to take stock.

I want you to know, Dr. DiBlasio, how much I appreciate your efforts in my behalf. I am sincerely sorry that I didn't reach my decision before you went to so much trouble. I will always remember the valuable advice you gave me. I have learned a great deal from you, and I thank you.

Sincerely,
Hank Shepherd

Questions for Discussion:
Three Sample Letters

1. How do you account for the difference in the length of the three letters?

_____

_____

_____

_____

2. In each letter, Hank presents his decision differently. Describe the three different approaches and explain why each is suited to its audience and Hank's purpose.

Letter to parents:

_____

_____

_____

_____

_____

_____

_____

Letter to Marco:

_____

_____

_____

_____

_____

_____

Letter to Dr. DiBlasio:

_____

_____

_____

_____

_____

_____

3. What differences do you note in the tone of each letter?

Letter to parents:

_____

_____

Letter to Marco:

_____

_____

Letter to Dr. DiBlasio:

_____

_____

_____

4. How does the word choice in the letter to Marco differ from the word choice in the other two letters? How do you explain this difference?

_____

_____

_____

_____

_____

WRITING ASSIGNMENT III

Has someone ever stopped you on the street and asked for directions? Sometimes we know how to get from point A to point B, but we have difficulty communicating the directions clearly. Or have you ever tried to explain to someone how to perform a task that you can do well, only to fumble around trying to communicate the procedure? Even when we try to explain how to do something we do all the time, we can have difficulty with the explanation. Most of us need to improve our skills at communicating simple directions. Here are two assignments of one or two paragraphs each to help in this area.

First, write directions for a classmate who is fairly new to your town and your campus. Explain how to get to where you live from your English class, so the two of you can study together. Be sure to include helpful landmarks. After writing the directions, follow them yourself to determine how clear and accurate they are.

Second, write instructions for an incoming freshman, explaining how to register for classes. Include any tips you have learned for streamlining the process. Save these instructions and follow them next time you register to determine how good they are. (As an alternative to the latter assignment, you may explain to someone who has never used a library how to locate and check out a book from your campus library.)

Although there are times when you will give directions in writing, more often you will do so orally. However, written practice such as these two assignments provide will improve your ability to communicate directions orally by exercising your powers of clarity and precision.

WRITING ASSIGNMENT IV

To improve your ability to communicate, you need experience writing for many different audiences. To get some of this experience, write a letter to the editor of your campus newspaper or the editor of your city newspaper.

In this letter you should express your view on an issue of interest to the readers of the paper. Check the letters page of the newspaper you are writing to in order to find out what guidelines the paper has established for such letters. After writing your letter, be sure to send it and watch for it in print. I'm sure you'll get a thrill from seeing your letter published. Also, I believe you'll be surprised to see how different your writing appears in print from the way it did on the page you wrote it.

A FINAL WORD

The relationship between writing and improving communication is an interesting one. The more we write and work to improve that writing, the more we find ourselves communicating effectively—both in writing and in speech. As our communication skills improve, many aspects of our lives become easier and better because we can get our ideas across to others with more ease and precision. This is important in our personal lives, when we communicate with those close to us; in our academic lives, when we communicate with instructors and students; and in our professional lives, when we communicate with our co-workers. Clearly, there is every reason for us to improve our writing skills, so when we communicate we can feel confident that we are doing so effectively.

Chapter 8
Understanding Others:
Writing about People

Because we live in a society, we interact with other people all the time. Sometimes these interactions are brief and businesslike, as when we pay a clerk for something we've bought. Sometimes these interactions last longer, but they are still rather formal, as when a teacher and students come together for one term in a classroom. And, of course, other times these interactions are long term and very personal, like those we have with our loved ones.

Any interaction, regardless of whether it's formal or personal, short term or long term, can have a significant impact on us. A clerk who gives us a hard time can ruin our mood for the rest of the day and maybe even cause us to be irritable with those we care about. A stranger who passes on the street and smiles warmly can brighten our mood for hours. And those we care about the most are often responsible for our greatest joys and our keenest disappointments.

At times, our relationships are troubled by friction and misunderstanding. Sometimes people just do not interact smoothly. They do not get along as well as they might because one does not understand the other's nature and personality well enough. How many times have you thrown up your hands in despair or disgust and announced, "I just don't understand that person"?

Well, sometimes we do not understand that person because we have not tried hard enough to understand aspects of his or her character, and we have not tried to determine what things can influence and explain behavior.

Certainly it is worth our while to work a bit harder to understand people in order to improve our relationships with them. This chapter is meant to help you use writing as a way to understand people better and thereby improve your relationships.

READING SELECTION:
"Birthday Party"

The first reading selection in this chapter is "Birthday Party" by Katharine Brush. Although short, the piece is interesting because of how effectively it reveals personality by telling a story. As you read, notice the details that describe personality. Also, decide what you think is responsible for the misunderstanding between the husband and wife.

Birthday Party
Katharine Brush

They were a couple in their late thirties, and they looked unmistakably married. They sat on the banquette opposite us in a little narrow restaurant, having dinner. The man had a round, self-satisfied face, with glasses on it; the woman was fadingly pretty, in a big hat. There was nothing conspicuous about them, nothing particularly noticeable, until the end of their meal, when it suddenly became obvious that this was an Occasion—in fact, the husband's birthday, and the wife had planned a little surprise for him.

It arrived, in the form of a small but glossy birthday cake, with one pink candle burning in the center. The headwaiter brought it in and placed it before the husband, and meanwhile the violin-and-piano orchestra played "Happy Birthday to You" and the wife beamed with shy pride over her little surprise, and such few people as there were in the restaurant tried to help out with a pattering of applause. It became clear at once that help was needed, because the husband was not pleased. Instead he was hotly embarrassed, and indignant at his wife for embarrassing him.

You looked at him and you saw this and you thought, "Oh, now, don't *be* like that!" But he was like that, and as soon as the little cake had been deposited on the table, and the orchestra had finished the birthday piece, and the general attention had shifted from the man and woman, I saw him say something to her under his breath—some punishing thing, quick and curt and unkind. I couldn't bear to look at the woman then, so I stared at my plate and waited for quite a long time. Not long enough, though. She was still crying when I finally glanced over there again. Crying quietly and heartbrokenly and hopelessly, all to herself, under the gay big brim of her best hat.

Vocabulary List:
"Birthday Party"

Record below any words from "Birthday Party" that you are unsure of. Next to each word, write a brief dictionary definition that fits the way the word was used in the selection. Finally, add one word and definition to your list in Appendix A, and continue your daily word study.

_____   _____

_____   _____

_____   _____

Questions for Discussion:
"Birthday Party"

1. "Birthday Party" is an example of writing that reveals character or personality by telling a story. What aspects of the husband's character are brought out?

_____

_____

2. What aspects of the wife's character are brought out?

_____

_____

3. We have all at some time been embarrassed by the good intentions of another. Why, then, do we not sympathize with the husband?

_____

_____

4. Write a paragraph describing what happens when the husband and wife drive home from the restaurant. Use some conversation.

_____

_____

_____

_____

_____

_____

_____

_____

_____

_____

_____

5. What do you think is responsible for the misunderstanding between the husband and wife?

_____

_____

_____

6. Why couldn't the speaker bear to look at the woman?

_____

_____

7. Record below three examples of descriptive language that you particularly like. What makes each description effective?

_____

_____

_____

_____

READING SELECTION:
"The Monster"

"The Monster," written by Deems Taylor, is an example of a *character sketch*, an essay that reveals the personality of someone. Notice as you read that Taylor uses topic sentences to present each aspect of character discussed. Then he explains each aspect, often using examples, in the body paragraphs.

The Monster
Deems Taylor

He was an undersized little man, with a head too big for his body—a sickly little man. His nerves were bad. He had skin trouble. It was agony for him to wear anything next to his skin coarser than silk. And he had delusions of grandeur.

He was a monster of conceit. Never for one minute did he look at the world or at people, except in relation to himself. He was not only the most important person in the world, to himself; in his own eyes he was the only person who existed. He believed himself to be one of the greatest dramatists in the world, one of the greatest thinkers, and one of the greatest composers. To hear him talk, he was Shakespeare, and Beethoven, and Plato, rolled into one. And you would have had no difficulty in hearing him talk. He was one of the most exhausting conversationalists that ever lived. An evening with him was an evening spent in listening to a monologue. Sometimes he was brilliant; sometimes he was maddeningly tiresome. But whether he was being brilliant or dull, he had one sole topic of conversation: himself. What *he* thought and what *he* did.

He had a mania for being in the right. The slightest hint of disagreement, from anyone, on the most trivial point, was enough to set him off on a harangue that might last for hours, in which he proved himself right in so many ways, and with such exhausting volubility, that in the end his hearer, stunned and deafened, would agree with him, for the sake of peace.

It never occurred to him that he and his doings were not of the most intense and fascinating interest to anyone with whom he came in contact. He had theories about almost any subject under the sun, including vegetarianism, the drama, politics, and music; and in support of these theories he wrote pamphlets, letters, books . . . thousands upon thousands of words, hundreds and hundreds of pages. He not only wrote these things, and published them—usually at somebody else's expense—but he would sit and read them aloud, for hours, to his friends and his family.

He wrote operas; and no sooner did he have the synopsis of a story, but he would invite—or rather summon—a crowd of his friends to his house and read it aloud to them. Not for criticism. For applause. When the complete poem was written, the friends had to come again, and hear *that* read aloud. Then he would publish the poem, sometimes years before the music that went with it was written. He played the piano like a composer, in the worst sense of what that implies, and he would sit down at the piano before parties that included some of the finest pianists of his time, and play for them, by the hour, his own music, needless to say. He had a composer's voice. And he would invite eminent vocalists to his house, and sing them his operas, taking all the parts.

He had the emotional stability of a six-year-old child. When he felt out of sorts, he would rave and stamp, or sink into suicidal gloom and talk darkly of going to the East to end his days as a Buddhist monk. Ten minutes later, when something pleased him, he would rush out of doors and run around the garden or jump up and down on the sofa, or stand on his head. He could be grief-stricken over the death of a pet dog, and he could be callous and heartless to a degree that would have made a Roman emperor shudder.

He was almost innocent of any sense of responsibility. Not only did he seem incapable of supporting himself, but it never occurred to him that he was under any obligation to do so. He was convinced that the world owed him a living. In support of this belief, he borrowed money from everybody who was good for a loan—men, women, friends, or strangers. He wrote begging letters by the score, sometimes groveling without shame, at others loftily offering his intended benefactor the privilege of contributing to his support, and being mortally offended if the recipient declined the honor. I have found no record of his ever paying or repaying money to anyone who did not have a legal claim upon it.

What money he could lay his hands on he spent like an Indian rajah. The mere prospect of a performance of one of his operas was enough to set him running up bills amounting to ten times the amount of his prospective royalties. On an income that would reduce a more scrupulous man to doing his own laundry, he would keep two servants. Without enough money in his pocket to pay his rent, he would have the walls and ceiling of his study lined with pink silk. No one will ever know—certainly he never knew—how much money he owed. We do know that his greatest benefactor gave him $6,000 to pay the most pressing of his debts in one city, and a year later had to give him $16,000 to enable him to live in another city without being thrown into jail for debt.

He was equally unscrupulous in other ways. An endless procession of women marches through his life. His first wife spent twenty years enduring and forgiving his infidelities. His second wife had been the wife of his most devoted friend and admirer, from whom he stole her. And even while he was trying to persuade her to leave her first husband he was writing to a friend to inquire whether he could suggest some wealthy woman—*any* wealthy woman—whom he could marry for her money.

He was completely selfish in his other personal relationships. His liking for his friends was measured solely by the completeness of their devotion to him, or by their usefulness to him, whether financial or artistic. The minute they failed him—even by so much as refusing a dinner invitation—or began to lessen in usefulness, he cast them off without a second thought. At the end of his life he had exactly one friend left whom he had known even in middle age.

He had a genius for making enemies. He would insult a man who disagreed with him about the weather. He would pull endless wires in order to meet some man who admired his work, and was able and anxious to be of use to him—and would proceed to make a mortal enemy of him with some idiotic and wholly uncalled-for exhibition of arrogance and bad manners. A character in one of his operas was a caricature of one of the most powerful music critics of his day. Not content with burlesquing him, he invited the critic to his house and read him the libretto aloud in front of his friends.

The name of this monster was Richard Wagner. Everything that I have said about him you can find on record—in newspapers, in police reports, in the testimony of people who knew him, in his own letters, between the lines of his autobiography. And the curious thing about this record is that it doesn't matter in the least.

Because this undersized, sickly, disagreeable, fascinating little man was right all the time. The joke was on us. He *was* one of the world's great dramatists; he *was* a great thinker; he *was* one of the most stupendous musical geniuses that, up to now, the world has ever seen. The world did owe him a living. People couldn't know those things at the time, I suppose; and yet to us, who know his music, it does seem as though they should have known. What if he did talk about himself all the time? If he had talked about himself for twenty-four hours every day for the span of his life he would not have uttered half the number of words that other men have spoken and written about him since his death.

When you consider what he wrote—thirteen operas and music dramas, eleven of them still holding the stage, eight of them unquestionably worth ranking among the world's great musico-dramatic masterpieces—when you listen to what he wrote, the debts and heartaches that people had to endure from him don't seem much of a price. Eduard Hanslick, the critic whom he caricatured in *Die Meistersinger* and who hated him ever after, now lives only because he was caricatured in *Die Meistersinger*. The women whose hearts he broke are long since dead; and the man who could never love anyone but himself has made them deathless atonement, I think, with *Tristan und Isolde*. Think of the luxury with which for a time, at least, fate rewarded Napoleon, the man who ruined France and looted Europe; and then perhaps you will agree that a few thousand dollars' worth of debts were not too heavy a price to pay for the *Ring* trilogy.

What if he was faithless to his friends and to his wives? He had one mistress to whom he was faithful to the day of his death: Music. Not for a single moment did he ever compromise with what he believed, with what he dreamed. There is not a line of his music that could have been conceived by a little mind. Even when he is dull, or downright bad, he is dull in the grand manner. There is a greatness about his worst mistakes. Listening to his music, one does not forgive him for what he may or may not have been. It is not a matter of forgiveness. It is a matter of being dumb with wonder that his poor brain and body didn't burst under the torment of the demon of creative energy that lived inside him, struggling, clawing, scratching to be released; tearing, shrieking at him to write the music that was in him. The miracle is that what he did in the little space of seventy years could have been done at all, even by a great genius. Is it any wonder that he had no time to be a man?

Vocabulary List:
"The Monster"

Record below any words from "The Monster" that you are unsure of. Next to each word, write a brief dictionary definition that fits the way the word was used in the selection. Finally, add one word and definition to your list in Appendix A, and continue your daily word study.

_____	_____
_____	_____
_____	_____

Questions for Discussion:
"The Monster"

1. The organization of this essay is unlike any other in this text. There is no introduction such as you are used to; instead Taylor lists some of his points about Wagner. What is the effect of this technique?

_____

_____

2. There is no stated thesis here. In fact, even the name of the monster is not given until paragraph 12. What is the effect of this delay?

_____

_____

3. There is no specifically stated thesis in this piece. If there were one, however, what might it be?

_____

_____

4. In the previous selection, a story was told to reveal character. In this selection, however, topic sentences usually provide statements that describe aspects of Wagner's character, and these statements are backed up with supporting detail that is often in the form of examples. List each aspect of Wagner's character that is pointed out this way.

_____   _____

_____   _____

_____   _____

_____   _____

_____   _____

_____   _____

5. This essay is divided into two parts. Where does part 1 end and where does part 2 begin?

_____

_____

6. Although this essay does not have a formal introduction, it does have a formal conclusion. What points does Taylor make in this conclusion?

_____

_____

_____

_____

7. The last sentence is a _rhetorical question_—a question that expects no answer because the answer is obvious. Is the rhetorical question an effective closing here? Why?

_____

_____

8. Do you agree with Taylor that Wagner's genius and what he contributed as the result of that genius excuse his "monstrous" behavior? Explain.

_____

_____

_____

9. Do you think Deems Taylor demonstrates an understanding of Wagner as a person? Explain.

_____

_____

_____

GETTING READY: ROLE PLAYING

Sometimes we don't understand someone as well as we might because we have not really tried to appreciate what it's like to be in that person's shoes. _Role playing_ is a technique that can show us what it's like to be in someone else's situation. So you can try your hand at role playing, let's begin with someone who is frequently misunderstood: the classroom teacher. To see if role playing will help you come to understand your composition instructor better, try this: Break into groups of four. Each group should pick one of the situations below and write a script for a five-minute dialogue between your composition instructor and a student. If you prefer, you may devise your own situation.

The student wants the instructor to raise his or her final grade so a scholarship isn't lost.

The student wants the instructor to accept a theme one week late.

The student wants the instructor to explain why the composition course is required.

The instructor is annoyed because the student rarely comes to class prepared.

The instructor is trying to convince the student to participate more in class.

The instructor is explaining why he or she must fail the student, although the student has tried very hard and has made some progress.

The instructor is explaining why the student's grammar and usage have earned him or her a D on a paper that is full of good ideas.

After the script is written, two group members should deliver the dialogue to the rest of the class. After each dialogue, your instructor may wish to indicate which points were accurate reflections of what he or she would say and which were not. If this is the case, you might ask your teacher to explain why he or she would react in these ways. Giving your instructor a chance to explain the reasoning behind certain actions will help you understand even more why a teacher behaves in certain ways.

Once all the dialogues are given, once all the teacher comments are made, and once all student questions are answered, you should write a paragraph that details any new understandings you have gained about your composition instructor.

GETTING READY: TRYING TO UNDERSTAND

If you're like the rest of us, at some time or another you have found yourself saying something like, "I don't see how anyone could do (like, believe, want) that." And then you probably shrugged your shoulders and dismissed the whole thing. But wouldn't it be better to try to understand rather than just let it go? I think so, because if we can come to understand, we can appreciate people more and be more sympathetic toward them. Of course it takes more effort to try to understand than it does to dismiss something, but it's worth that effort if understanding leads to better relationships.

Here's an opportunity to exert some of that effort and see if it pays off. Below is a list of sentences describing things some people may not understand about other people.

I don't understand how anyone can like football (or another sport).

I don't understand how anyone can be a Democrat (or a Republican).

I don't understand how anyone can be a teacher (or pick some other occupation).

I don't understand how anyone can like country music (or another type of music).

I don't understand how anyone can major in math (or another subject).

I don't understand how anyone can take drugs (or smoke).

I don't understand why anyone would (would not) join a sorority (or another group).

I don't understand why anyone would (would not) favor censorship.

I don't understand why anyone would (would not) favor abortion.

I don't understand why anyone would (would not) favor gun control.

I don't understand why anyone would (would not) favor capitol punishment.

I don't understand why anyone would (would not) favor mercy killing.

I don't understand how anyone can think money buys happiness.

Pick one of the sentences above that reflects the way you feel. Or form a similar sentence of your own. Then arrange to speak to someone you know who believes or acts or likes the opposite of what you do. For example, if you don't understand why anyone likes Ronald Reagan and your political science teacher likes Reagan, make arrangements to speak to your political science teacher.

When you speak to the person you have selected, your purpose will be to ask questions in an effort to come to understand why that person believes, acts, or likes whatever it is that is the issue. I suggest that you begin with the question, "Why do you believe (act, do) _____?" Thus, you would ask your political science teacher, "Why do you like Ronald Reagan?" The answer to this question should prompt another question. For example, if your teacher likes Reagan because of his economic policies, you could ask, "Which policies are these and why are they good?" Continue asking your questions until you feel you understand why the other person believes, acts, or likes whatever it is.

Once you feel you understand, write a paragraph explaining why the person you spoke to believes, acts, or likes whatever is under discussion. Then give the paragraph to that person and ask him or her to tell you whether what you wrote is accurate. If it is not, make the necessary changes. I have two hints for you. First, take notes during the interview. Second, keep in mind that you do not have to *agree* with something in order to *understand* it. Therefore, you do not have to come to like Reagan yourself—you only need to appreciate why your political science instructor likes him.

GRAMMAR AND USAGE

In this chapter you will learn about parallelism, and you will learn some additional comma rules. You will learn about parallelism so that you can continue to improve your writing style, and you will learn the comma rules to continue the practice of learning them a few at a time.

Parallelism

Just as a lack of sentence variety can annoy a reader, so, too, can awkward sentences. Very often awkwardness is a result of the writer's failure to achieve parallelism. *Parallelism* means that sentence elements serving the same function should be in the same grammatical form. As a writer you should strive for parallelism when you place items in a series, when you compare or contrast items, and when you use certain conjunctions.

Parallelism:
Items in a Series

Any time you place items in a series, you should be sure they are all in the same grammatical form because they serve the same function—they are part of the series.

Words not parallel:	Our new chemistry instructor is clever, witty, and has intelligence.
Words parallel:	Our new chemistry instructor is clever, witty, and intelligent.
Explanation:	In the first example, the first two elements in the series are adjectives (modifiers), but the third is a verb phrase. In the second example, the third element is changed to an adjective so that all items in the series have the same grammatical form.

Words not parallel:	My favorite winter sports are <u>skiing</u>, <u>skating</u>, and <u>to sled</u>.
Words parallel:	My favorite winter sports are <u>skiing</u>, <u>skating</u>, and <u>sledding</u>.
Explanation:	In the first example, the first two elements in the series are <u>ing</u> forms of verbs, but the third is the <u>to</u> form of a verb or the infinitive. In the second example, parallelism is achieved by changing the third element to an <u>ing</u> form so that all series elements have the same grammatical form.
Phrases not parallel:	Our constitution is founded on the principle of government <u>of the people</u>, <u>by the people</u>, and <u>that government is for the people</u>.
Phrases parallel:	Our constitution is founded on the principle of government <u>of the people</u>, <u>by the people</u>, and <u>for the people</u>.
Explanation:	In the first example, the first two elements in the series are prepositional phrases, but the third is a clause. In the second example, the third element is changed to a phrase so that all items in the series have the same grammatical form.
Clauses not parallel:	The instructor told us <u>to complete the exam in one hour</u>, <u>that we should use a pen</u>, and <u>that we should proofread carefully</u>.
Clauses parallel:	The instructor told us <u>that we should complete the exam in one hour</u>, <u>that we should use a pen</u>, and <u>that we should proofread carefully</u>.
Explanation:	In the first example, the first element in the series is a phrase, but the second and third elements are clauses. In the second example, the first element is changed to a clause so that all items in the series have the same grammatical form.

Parallelism:
Items Compared or Contrasted

1. When you compare or contrast two or more items in a sentence, they have the same function (comparison or contrast), and therefore they should be in the same grammatical form.

Contrast not parallel: I like <u>small group discussions</u> better than <u>attending big lectures</u>.

Contrast parallel: I like <u>small group discussions</u> better than <u>big lectures</u>.

Explanation: In the first example, a noun phrase is contrasted with a verb phrase. In the second example, parallelism is achieved by changing the verb phrase to a noun phrase.

Comparison not parallel: I enjoy <u>a day in the country</u> as much as <u>to spend a day at the beach</u>.

Comparison parallel: I enjoy <u>a day in the country</u> as much as <u>a day at the beach</u>.

Explanation: In the first example, a noun phrase is compared with a verb phrase. In the second example, parallelism is achieved by changing the verb phrase to a noun phrase.

2. Often when we compare things, we use correlative conjunctions. *Correlative conjunctions* are coordinate conjunctions that come in pairs:

> either . . . or
> neither . . . nor
> not only . . . but (also)
> both . . . and

It is important when you use correlative conjunctions that you place them as closely as possible to the items being compared, or you will not have parallel structure.

Not parallel: He not only does well in school, but also on the gridiron.

Parallel: He does well not only in school, but also on the gridiron.

Explanation: In the first example, <u>not only</u> is followed by a verb phrase, while <u>but also</u> is followed by a prepositional phrase. In the second example, parallelism is achieved by moving <u>not only</u> so that it is followed by a prepositional phrase.

EXERCISE:
Parallelism

Rewrite the following sentences to achieve parallelism.

1. To become a successful teacher you must have patience, understanding, and knowing the subject matter.

_____

_____

2. Either I will move out of the dorm and into an apartment or request a different roommate because I can't stand sharing a room with Margaret.

_____

_____

_____

3. I told Tim that if he wants to pass the exam, he should reread the text, make an outline, and to review the lecture notes.

_____

_____

4. Most of us like small classes better than going to large ones.

_____

_____

5. Ralph enjoys college for its social life and because of its athletic programs.

_____

_____

6. The president of the student body was required to preside at council meetings as well as supervising all committees.

_____

_____

7. The campaigning governor said he not only believed in the principle of states' rights but also in the right of the federal government to control certain state activities.

_____

_____

_____

8. To finance a trip to Daytona this spring, either you could get a part-time job, or you could borrow some money from your parents, or a bank loan could be taken out, or you could ask your rich uncle to give you the money.

_____

_____

_____

9. The poetry of neither T.S. Eliot nor the plays of Eugene O'Neill are covered in this course, but if you desire to read Eliot or O'Neill, their complete works are available in the library, at the bookstore, or I have copies I will lend.

_____

_____

_____

10. The faculty senate, a small but extremely powerful group, decides who will get promotions, the courses offered, and determines how many students can be in a class.

_____

_____

_____

A Word about Commas in a Series

1. After a discussion of parallelism, it makes sense to mention the most frequent use of the comma: Use commas to separate three or more items in a series or list.

   Example: By the time the final whistle sounded, our team had scored <u>two touchdowns</u>, <u>one field goal</u>, and <u>a safety</u> to win the game.

   Example: Our instructor explained that our themes would be graded on the basis of <u>organization</u>, <u>grammar</u>, <u>clarity</u>, and <u>originality</u>.

Explanation: In the above two sentences, there are series or lists composed of three or more items. Each item is separated by a comma.

Note: Do not place a comma before the first element of the series or after the last element of the series.

2. If each element in a series or list is joined by a cooordinate conjunction, no comma is used.

Example: <u>Neither</u> Janet <u>nor</u> Jack <u>nor</u> Martha will be able to come.

A Word about Commas for Clarity

There are times when commas must be used to ensure clarity. In these cases, the commas prevent confusion by signaling pauses that keep the reader from misreading.

Example: The speaker noted that in our efforts to explore space, programs for the poor have been neglected.

Explanation: The comma is necessary to keep the reader from reading <u>in our efforts to explore space programs</u>.

A Word about Commas for Emphasis or Contrast

Often a comma can be used to signal a pause that emphasizes what comes after the comma.

Example: Summer is passing quickly, far too quickly to suit me.

Other times, the pause that a comma signals serves to contrast what comes after the comma with what comes before it.

Example: There are some people who go to college to find a mate, not to learn.

Note: In both of the above example sentences, a dash could be used instead of the comma. Remember that a dash signals a long pause for emphasis or dramatic effect. Which mark you use depends on what kind of pause you want to signal to your reader.

EXERCISE:
The Comma

In the following sentences, place commas where they are needed. You will need to draw upon all the comma rules you have learned so far in this book. Be sure you can back up each comma you use with a rule.

1. This movie might be interesting but it also might be frightening.

2. Without so much as saying goodbye Joyce turned walked to the door and left.

3. Uncle Milt who happens to be seventy took up golf recently and does quite well considering his age.

4. Because Mom was unable to find a job she has decided to return to school but I fear that she will be uncomfortable around the younger students.

5. Jake and Marilyn had to cut their honeymoon short because Jake came down with measles and Marilyn got sun poisoning after four hours in the Florida sun.

6. The little boy who lives across the street is named Jonathan not John.

7. At the edge of the pier three adorable chubby boys sat holding fishing poles.

8. Ruth in my opinion is the most qualified candidate for the student government office because she has leadership experience intelligence and a real desire to serve.

9. Dr. Peters who is one of the most popular professors on campus believes in giving exams that allow students to show what they know not what they do not know.

10. While I am sure that geography is an important field of study I cannot become interested in the subject for the class meets at 8:00 much before I am totally awake.

WRITING ASSIGNMENT I

For this assignment, you have your choice of two topics, each based on one of the reading selections in this chapter. The first topic is based on "Birthday Party." If you choose this topic, you will write about an event that reveals something about the personality of someone you know. For example, perhaps you can show that a friend is considerate of others by telling the story of when that friend was kind to a newcomer to your group. Or maybe you can show how much Uncle Ned loves practical jokes by telling what happened last Halloween.

I urge you to write about an event that actually happened because if you make up a story you will not come to understand someone better as a result of your writing. When you write, try to make your story as vivid as "Birthday Party" by using precise description and by choosing detail carefully so that it reveals part of someone's character.

The second topic is based on "The Monster," which is a *character sketch*, an essay that describes the personality and nature of someone. For this assignment, write a character sketch of someone important in your life. (It might be a good idea to do some freewriting to bring to the surface your ideas about this person.) Your sketch can be organized in much the same way as "The Monster." That is, you can have the topic sentence of each body paragraph present one aspect of the person's character. The supporting detail for each body paragraph can be in the form of examples that illustrate the trait revealed in the topic sentence.

This writing will force you to look very closely at someone important in your life. And although you may already understand a great deal about this person, it is likely that you will come to understand him or her even more as a result of the careful consideration this assignment requires. Before handing in your work, be sure you can answer yes to the Questions to Answer before Submitting Your Theme, which appear below.

Questions to Answer before Submitting Your Theme

Before submitting your theme, be sure you can answer yes to the following questions.

1. Is your diction precise and economical? Have you avoided clichés?
2. Have you used commas, semicolons, colons, dashes, parentheses, and apostrophes correctly?
3. Have you punctuated correctly any conversation that you used?
4. Have you used capitals for titles of relatives used like names?
5. Have you checked for fragments and run-ons?
6. Have you checked for subject–verb agreement and pronoun–referent agreement?
7. Have you avoided dangling and misplaced modifiers?
8. Have you avoided inappropriate tense shifts?
9. Have you avoided dull prose by using sentence variety?
10. Have you achieved parallelism?
11. Have you shown the relationships among your ideas with coordination, subordination, and transitions?
12. Do you have an interesting introduction and suitable conclusion?
13. Is your thesis narrow?
14. Is your support adequate and relevant?
15. Did you use some new vocabulary words?
16. Did you proofread carefully and check spellings?

WRITING ASSIGNMENT II

One good way to increase your understanding of another person is to put yourself in that person's place. The role playing you did early in this chapter was meant to demonstrate this. This assignment is a variation of the role-playing theme. Select a person you do not like very much or do not understand very well and write a description of an unpleasant encounter you have had with that person. Then assume the identity of the other person and rewrite that account from his or her point of view.

For example, a woman who does not get along with her mother-in-law could discuss a recent visit she had with the mother-in-law when the two exchanged harsh words. The writer could discuss her own actions, words, and motivations. Then as the mother-in-law she would rewrite the description of the visit. Only this time she would attempt an honest explanation of the mother-in-law's point of view and motivations.

Sometimes this kind of effort to see the other person's side can lead to greater understanding of that person and improved relations with someone previously disliked or misunderstood. It's possible that you will be able to determine for sure what actually caused someone to act in a particular way, and that determination will lead to understanding. However, it is also possible that you will not be sure you have figured out what caused certain behavior. Even if this is the case, the fact that you have come up with a *possible* explanation can lead you to view someone more kindly and sympathetically— and this, too, can lead to a better relationship. If this writing does open your eyes to another person's point of view, record your insights at the end of your theme. Below is a sample theme that illustrates this assignment.

Sample Theme:
Role Playing

Below is a student paper that explains an event from two different points of view. The theme also records what understanding was achieved as a result of the writing.

My View

A few weeks ago I bummed a ride to school with my girlfriend Rita. It wasn't the first time I had to hitch a ride with her, for my car had been breaking down regularly all quarter. Anyway, that morning it was particularly cold out, and just the short walk from my apartment to her car was a killer. I remember that we were running late, so Rita agreed to drop me off since I had the earlier class. I was done that day at one o'clock, but Rita went until three. Before I got out of the car, we made plans to meet at her art class so

I could get the keys, because I was supposed to meet a guy at 1:30. With that settled, I hustled to my class, already five minutes late. It never occurred to me then that getting Rita's keys would cause as much trouble as it did.

I shot out of chemistry at 12:50 and headed for Bliss Hall, where Rita had art. I was moving pretty good because I didn't have any time to spare if I was to make my 1:30 meeting. The hike across campus was pretty uncomfortable because I was going against the bitter wind all the way, and in my morning rush I had forgotten my gloves. Still, I made it to Rita's class, got the keys, and was at the parking deck by 1:05, stinging hands and all.

At the deck, the problem became clear—I didn't know where Rita had parked. I figured she would park on the top level because that's were she *always* parked, but when I got there, there was no blue Nova in sight. I walked through the entire deck looking everywhere, my hands freezing from the subzero cold, my arms numb from my heavy load of books. I felt like an idiot with keys and no car. The frustration was enormous. Meanwhile, Rita was in art class painting some stupid picture.

When I realized I was going to have to walk all the way back across campus, I became furious. I wanted to kill someone, namely Rita. I just stood there for a moment with the blood pounding in my temples. No, there was no way around it, so I began the icy walk toward Bliss Hall.

By the time I got to Rita's class, I knew there was no way I could make my 1:30 meeting. This realization fueled my anger and frustration. An explosion was inevitable. I barged into the art room and cried, "Rita, come here!" I must say Rita looked a bit embarrassed as she headed into the hallway with me. Once in the hall I shouted, "Where's the stupid car? I just walked all over hell looking for it!" Rita just looked at me blankly, so I added, "Why didn't you park where you always do?" She then gave me the dumbest answer I ever heard: "Why didn't you ask me where I parked? It's not my fault." At that point I was so worked up I could barely speak. But I managed to ask her where her car was, and I turned and left without another word.

Once again, I raced across campus in the cold, without gloves. I found the car, but I missed the guy I was supposed to meet. Since that day Rita and I haven't spoken much. She's never apologized for the hassle she caused me, and frankly it's been okay with me if that's how she wants to be.

Rita's View

Hank called a while back and asked for another ride to school. He was doing that a lot because his car was screwed up, but I didn't really mind helping him out. He had to meet someone after school, so I said he could use my car since I'd be in class all afternoon anyway. I dropped him off on campus and arranged for us to meet at my art class so I could give him the keys. I suppose if I'd been thinking, I would have told him then that I stopped parking in the deck (it certainly would have eliminated a lot of trouble), but we were late that morning, and all I could think of was how rotten I felt because I missed my morning coffee.

Shortly before one I met Hank at my class and gave him the keys. I meant to tell him the car wasn't in the deck, but my mind was on my painting (which wasn't going very well), and I just plain forgot to say anything. By the time I remembered, it was too late to do anything about it. I felt bad, but what could I do?

I was working on my painting when Hank came back to the class. I couldn't believe it; he just stormed in and shouted, "Come here!" I wasn't sure what he would do, so I went out to the hall with him. I felt so embarrassed and self-conscious as I walked across the classroom. I hate being conspicuous, and I knew everyone's eyes were on me.

In the hall, Hank gave me all kinds of grief about the car not being in the deck. I knew he was probably that upset because he had to meet someone at 1:30, but I still couldn't believe the way he was treating me. Hank and I go way back, and I didn't think I deserved that. Anyway, I told him where the car was, and he left without apologizing. To this day, he hasn't apologized, and our relationship is pretty strained. I've thought of apologizing first, but I'm not the one who lost my temper and embarrassed a friend. I think Hank should make the first move.

What I Learned

As a result of writing down this incident from two points of view, I realize now that I came down pretty hard on Rita, mostly because I was so cold, frustrated, and concerned about that 1:30 appointment. This is one of those instances when things got blown out of proportion. I realize that when I spoke to Rita as I did in the hall, I made it impossible for her to apologize for not telling me where the car was because I really shocked her and put her on the defensive. I also recognize that I wanted to blame her because it was easier than blaming myself for my own stupidity in not asking where the car was. I will now call Rita and apologize for losing my temper. After all, she was doing me a favor in the first place by driving me to school and lending me her car.

WRITING ASSIGNMENT III

Sometimes when we interact with other people, their behavior puzzles, annoys, disturbs, depresses, angers, or frightens us. Most often we tend to ask ourselves, "Why did that person act that way?" Then we may search for answers in the person's actions, personality, and circumstances. Far less often do we ask, "What did *I* do to cause such a behavior?" Yet frequently our own actions may trigger unwelcome behavior in another.

For example, I recall one time writing in the margin of a student's paper that his vocabulary was far too sophisticated to suit his topic. As a result, his

A FINAL WORD

There is no doubt in my mind that writing can help us understand other people better and come to view them more sympathetically. The following letter, which appeared in Ann Landers' column, reveals how writing served this purpose for another person:

Dear Ann Landers:

I am a boy who is 12 years of age. I did something my parents didn't think was right and as punishment they made me stay home from a ball game I was dying to see. The tickets were bought and everything. They took my cousin instead of me.

I decided they were terrible to treat me so bad and I started to pack my suitcase to run away. I finished packing and I thought maybe I should write a goodbye letter. I wanted my folks to know why I was running away. I got to thinking about lots of things as I was writing and decided I ought to be very fair and apologize for a few things I had done that weren't right.

After I started to write I thought of lots of things that needed apologizing for. I then began to thank them for the nice things they had done for me and there seemed to be an awful lot of them.

By the time I finished writing the letter, I unpacked my suitcase and tore up what I wrote.

I hope all kids who think they want to run away from home will sit down and write a letter to their parents like I did and then they won't go.

A Rotten Kid

Chapter 9

Informing and Becoming Informed:
Writing and Research

Very often when we write, all the ideas we need are right there in our own minds. Sometimes it takes a bit of thinking and prewriting to bring these ideas to the surface, but they're nonetheless there in our heads waiting for us to use them. Other times when we write, we must look around before forming our ideas. Sometimes we spend time observing what goes on around us, and sometimes we talk to other people. So far, the writing you have been asked to do in this book has required you to draw on these kinds of ideas—the ones you already have, the ones you get by observing, and the ones you get by talking to other people.

Now, however, it is time to pause and discuss other sources of ideas for your writing: the facts and opinions to be found in books and articles in the library. This chapter will explain how you can locate what other people have to say about a subject, and it will describe how you can include some of that information in your own writing as supporting detail.

This kind of writing is exciting for both the writer and the reader. It is exciting for you as a writer because you will spend time discovering the ideas, facts, and opinions of knowledgeable people. You will have the opportunity to read what these people have written on a subject that interests you. Then you will be able to roll these ideas over in your mind and decide how you feel about them. Finally, you will make some thoughtful decisions about which of these ideas to include in your writing.

What all this means, then, is that you will become well informed about a subject that interests you. And you will gain this knowledge on your own.

You will find the information; *you* will read and consider it; *you* will decide what's important; *you* will select what to include in your paper. It is all very stimulating for a writer.

This kind of writing is exciting for your reader as well. First of all, your reader will become informed by reading your paper because he or she will be exposed to the ideas you included from the experts you read. But beyond that, your reader will also be exposed to your reactions to these ideas of others as well as your own ideas. Nowhere else can your reader get this combination but in *your* paper. That is why your reader will find this kind of writing both stimulating and informative.

For the most part, there are two kinds of writing that involve using material from other written sources. First, there is the research paper that takes an in-depth look at a subject. This kind of paper is made up mostly of material found in the library. Second, there is the paper that is made up mostly of the writer's ideas but that uses some library material as part of the supporting detail. It is this second kind of paper that you will be writing.

READING SELECTION:
"Should Instant Replay Cameras Aid in Officiating Football Games?"

The following paper was written by a college freshman. It is an example of a paper that contains mostly the writer's ideas, but it does use library material for some of the support. Notice as you read how the writer skillfully blends his own ideas with those he discovered through his reading.

```
         Should Instant Replay Cameras Aid

             in Officiating Football Games?


     It's the Super Bowl.  The New York Giants are

trailing by four points with three seconds left to

play.  Their only hope is the bomb.  The quarterback

lets the ball loose as time expires, and it is caught

in the end zone for a touchdown.  But wait, the ref-

eree is hesitant in making the call.  Was the receiver

out of bounds when he caught the ball?  The other of-

ficials gather around.  Meanwhile, the armchair quart-
```

erback, in front of his six-foot video screen, has
seen the play from fourteen different angles and knows
that he was definitely in bounds. The world has its
eyes on the referee. What will he call?

Fortunately, a situation like this hasn't occurred yet, but it may, and there are many people who
feel the referee on the field should have all the advantages of instant replay that the fans have at
home. I disagree. True, instant replay cameras would
be more reliable and less likely to make bad calls,
but the disadvantages of the system are far greater
than the advantages.

First, we would lose the human element of the
game. Everyone makes mistakes, and referees are no
exception. But imagine how dull a game would be if
the officiating were perfect. There would be no controversial calls that the fans could react to, no mistakes that the sportswriters could talk about in the
next day's column. And, as Joe Falls, columnist for
The Sporting News, states, ''We will be replacing people with machines, and that's never worked yet, in any
society, for any reason.''[1]

Another disadvantage of using the instant replay
system is the time delays that would be involved.
Many people think that it would take only a few seconds to look at a play and make a call, so it would
not be necessary to delay or stop the game. But when
Art McNally, supervisor of the National Football
League officials, placed two cameras in each end zone
of a Monday night game between Buffalo and Dallas for

experimental purposes, he reported that it took between twenty-seven seconds and two minutes to look for
a particular play, while the game continued on the
field. He continued to say, as quoted by Dave Brady
of the Washington Post:

> ''That gave us an idea of how long it would take
> with two cameras. [You can imagine what would
> happen] if we had to look at the pictures taken
> by three cameras, or maybe six, seven or eight.
> . . . The person in the monitoring booth would
> have to be a miracle man. You would have to stop
> the game and perhaps let the coaches ask to see a
> certain number of plays; let the officials see
> them; let the man in the booth judge the re-
> plays. You would have to stop the game because
> there might be a chance of changing the original
> official's decision.''[2]

Of course, there are those who argue that only
two or three plays will be affected in each game, but
any break in the continuity of the game would be unbearable, especially for the fans in the stadium.
Imagine sitting at a game, waiting for five minutes
while an unseen official views an unseen videotape of
a close play from ten different angles. Emotion is a
very important part of the game, and all that was
built up prior to that play will have been lost during
those five minutes.

But perhaps the greatest disadvantage of the instant replay system is the cost. Pete Rozelle, commissioner of the National Football League, cites a

1976 N.F.L. study and states it would cost the league
$46 million per year for a full system. Breaking that
down, it comes to approximately $150,000 for each
game.[3] Considering an average stadium seats 50,000
people, that would be about three dollars more per
ticket for you and me. After all, you don't think the
players are going to pay for it.

   Those who favor the instant replay system say the
cost could be cut down by using the cameras only in
crucial games, like the playoffs and Super Bowl. But
imagine a team winning a regular season game because
of a wrong call made by the official, when the cameras
weren't employed. Then imagine that team making the
playoffs by only a few percentage points, and had the
official made the correct call in that one game,
they'd be sitting at home watching on television instead of playing on the field. If that team goes on
to win the Super Bowl, you have an unjust winner,
which is what the use of replays is supposed to
avoid. So the cameras must be used in every game, no
matter what the seeming importance.

   Considering these drawbacks, I feel the instant
replay cameras have no business in the N.F.L. Maybe
in the future, with advanced technology, the system
would be feasible, but for now the referees on the
field are sufficient, and they're doing a fine job.
Dave Brady reports that during the 1975 season ''there
were 27,000 plays run off and . . . only six important
plays were called wrong.''[4] For every one play that was
called wrong, 4,000 plays were called right. That's a
record anyone can be proud of.

Notes

[1]Joe Falls, ''Instant Replay No Way to Settle Close Call,'' The Sporting News, 26 Jan. 1980, p. 7, col. 1.

[2]Dave Brady, ''NFL Tests Replays for Officials, Finds 'Obvious Drawbacks,' '' Washington Post, 9 March 1977, Sec. D., p. 7, col. 1.

[3]William N. Wallace, ''Rozelle Gives Promise of Improved Officiating,'' New York Times, 14 Jan. 1978, p. 13, col. 1.

[4]Brady, Sec. D., p. 7, col. 2.

Bibliography

Brady, Dave. ''NFL Tests Replays for Officials, Finds 'Obvious Drawbacks.' '' Washington Post, 9 March 1977, Sec. D., p. 7, cols. 1–2.

Falls, Joe. ''Instant Replay No Way to Settle Close Call.'' The Sporting News, 26 Jan. 1980, p. 7, col. 1.

Wallace, William N. ''Rozelle Gives Promise of Improved Officiating.'' New York Times, 14 Jan. 1978, p. 13, col. 1.

Note: For space considerations, the notes and bibliography appear here on the same page. However, in your paper, the notes and bibliography should each appear on separate pages.

Vocabulary List:
"Should Instant Replay Cameras Aid
in Officiating Football Games?"

Record below any words you are unsure of from the reading selection. Next to each word write a brief dictionary definition that fits the way the word was used in the selection. Then choose two words to add to your vocabulary list in Appendix A. Continue to study this list each day.

_____   _____

_____   _____

Questions for Discussion:
"Should Instant Replay Cameras Aid
in Officiating Football Games?"

1. Did you enjoy reading the selection? Explain why or why not. Consider content, style, and organization when you answer.

_____

_____

_____

_____

_____

2. Is it necessary to agree with the author's point of view to enjoy his writing? Explain.

_____

_____

3. What specific new information did you get as a result of reading this selection?

_____

_____

_____

_____

4. What kind of lead-in is used? How many paragraphs is the introduction?

_____

_____

5. What does the thesis indicate this paper will be about?

_____

6. What points are made to support the thesis? (**Hint:** Check the topic
sentences.)

_____

_____

_____

7. What is the function of the quotation in paragraph 3?

_____

8. What is the function of the summary of Art McNally's findings and
the quotation in paragraph 4?

_____

_____

9. What is the function of the summary of Pete Rozelle's statement in
paragraph 6?

_____

10. What is the function of the quote in the last paragraph?

_____

11. Cite two objections to the author's view that are raised in the paper.
How are these objections countered?

Objection: _____

Counter: _____

Objection: _____

Counter: _____

12. What kind of conclusion is used? Explain why it is or is not effective.

_____

_____

_____

GETTING READY: CHOOSING A TOPIC

The paper you will be working on is one that will show you how you can use writing to inform your reader and become informed yourself. Rather than have writing assignments at the end of this chapter, you will be working on your paper as you progress through this chapter. As your first step, you will settle on a broad subject that you would like to read, learn, and write about. To enjoy the writing and the research, it is important that you settle on a topic that you truly are interested in learning more about. Also, it is important that you choose a subject that you do not already know a great deal about. Otherwise, how will you become informed? Still, you should choose a subject that you have several ideas on, so you can put these in your paper.

Below is a list of some subject areas that may interest you.

The saccharine controversy	Shoplifting
Air, water, or noise pollution	Body language
Nuclear waste disposal	The electoral college
Adolescent suicide	Government support for private schools
The effects of television violence	
The social security system	Television advertising
The effects of divorce on children	Women's rights
Sexual harassment on the job	A mandatory retirement age
Teacher strikes	Barrier-free architecture
Drug abuse	Automobile safety
Violence in sports	School busing for racial balance

Pick one of the subjects listed above or pick some other one that interests you. Then go to your campus library and look up your topic in the _subject_ file of the card catalog. Find three books about your subject and write down the author's name, the title, and the number that appears in the upper left corner of the card. Use that number to locate each book in the stacks.

4. Look up your general topic in some general reference works, such as encyclopedias (see Appendix C for a list of general reference works). The entries in these books will give you ideas for narrowing.

5. Next, check to see what articles there are on your subject in journals, newspapers, and magazines. To do this, find the subject bibliographies and indexes relevant to your topic. (See Appendix D for a list of useful bibliographies and indexes.) These bibliographies and indexes will give you titles of articles on your subject.

6. Select three or four article titles that look interesting and go to the stacks to get the actual articles. These will be located away from the books, so ask a librarian to help you. Read all or parts of some of the articles to get ideas for narrowing your topic.

When you have completed these six steps, you will have an idea of how much your general topic takes in, and you will already have learned a few things about your general subject. On the basis of this knowledge, you will decide how you would like to narrow your topic.

As you do your preliminary reading, check to be sure of the following:

1. There is enough material listed in the card catalog, bibliographies, and indexes.

2. The book material has not already been checked out.

3. The articles are in periodicals (journals, magazines, and newspapers) your library has.

4. The material available to you is written so that you can understand it.

Step 3: Narrow Your Topic. After doing some preliminary reading, you will know enough about your subject and the material available to you to enable you to narrow your topic. As you decide how to narrow it, keep the following things in mind:

1. Make sure your topic is narrow enough to be handled in the required length. I usually expect the paper to run about 700 words, but your instructor will help you decide on a suitable length.

2. Remember that it is far more satisfying to treat a narrow subject in depth than a broad one on the surface.

3. Avoid a topic so recent that it will be hard to find material on it.

4. Avoid a topic of only local concern, for it may be hard to find enough material.

5. Make sure your topic is something that really requires research. For example, a paper about how the heart functions would not be

acceptable because a person would only need to look at one good book on the subject and that would cover all there is to say.

6. Narrow your topic in a way that allows *you* to have something to say. Remember, for this paper you will be supporting *your* views with the ideas of others.

EXERCISE:
Narrowing the Topic

For each topic below write *yes* if the topic is acceptable for a 700-word paper using research. Write *no* if the topic is unacceptable, and explain why it is not satisfactory.

1. The Cruelty of Hitler

_____

2. The Disadvantages of Being the Middle Child

_____

3. Saccharin Should Not Be Banned

_____

4. Pollution from the Steel Industry Is Killing the Mahoning River

_____

5. Television Shows Aimed at Children Should Be Free of Commercials

_____

6. The Life of Anwar Sadat

_____

7. How to Keep Your Plants Healthy

_____

8. Computers Are Ruining Our Lives

_____

9. Computers Help Students Learn

_____

10. Violence on Television Can Cause Violence in Real Life

_____

11. The Elderly Deserve Our Respect

_____

12. The Elderly Are Mistreated in This Country

_____

13. There Is Little Dignity for the Elderly in Many Homes for the Aged

_____

14. Japan after World War II

_____

15. How the Japanese Keep Their Factory Workers Happy

_____

16. The Symptoms of Heart Disease

_____

Progress Check: Narrowing the Topic

Now in the space below, write down the narrow topic you formed for yourself after your preliminary reading. Your instructor may wish to check this before you go on to your working bibliography.

_____

_____

Step 4: Compile Your Working Bibliography. A _working bibliography_ is a list of the sources you want to check for information. After narrowing your topic, it's time to put your working bibliography together. Each time you come across the title of a book or article that looks promising (that is, that looks as if it may contain useful information), make a bibliography card. Each title should appear on a separate index card.

Appendix E shows you how to write these cards. There you will see that bibliography cards for books have the author's name, the book title, place and date of publication, and publisher. In addition, if such information applies, the editor's or translator's name, the edition used if not the first, the series number, and the volume number are given. For periodicals the bibliography cards cite author, title of article, title of periodical, volume number, date, and pages.

Notice that bibliography cards contain specific information in a specific order and form. Be sure to write your cards in the way shown in the appendix with all the necessary information. This is not a way to make more work for you. Instead, it is a way to ensure that you have all the information you will need later when you write your final bibliography. In addition, be sure to include the Library of Congress number or the Dewey decimal number (whichever your library uses). One of these will be needed so you can get the book or article at note-taking time.

To compile your working bibliography, do the following:

1. Return to the subject file of the card catalog and check book titles.
2. Return to the bibliographies and indexes and check article titles.
3. Return to the general reference works and check any titles listed there.

When you are putting your working bibliography together, you are looking only at titles, titles of books in the subject file of the card catalog and titles of periodicals in the bibliographies and indexes. This means that you will make a decision about the usefulness of a source on the basis of the title. Use your judgment here. If in doubt, add the source to your bibliography just to be safe; you can always discard it later if it doesn't work out.

Progress Check: The Working Bibliography

In the spaces below, write complete, correct bibliography citations for four sources you will check for information. Your instructor may wish to check your work before you go on to the preliminary outline.

1. _____

_____

2. _____

_____

3. _____

_____

4. _____

_____

Step 5: Write Your Preliminary Outline. Now that you have your topic narrowed and a list of sources to check, it's time to pause and think about what you would like to cover in your paper. The preliminary outline will help you do this. A *preliminary outline* need be nothing more than a brief list of the aspects of your topic that you believe you will cover. You form your preliminary outline on the basis of what you know about your topic after narrowing your subject, doing your preliminary reading, and putting together your working bibliography. For example, if your topic is The Advantages of the 55 mph. Speed Limit, your preliminary outline might look like this:

Fuel economy

Safety

Less wear and tear on cars

Yes, your preliminary outline can be just that simple. Yet it is a very important part of your work because it makes your note taking more manageable. You see, if you do not have a preliminary outline, you may be tempted to take notes on everything. This could happen because you would fear leaving out something you might need in your paper. However, with a preliminary outline, you have an idea of what will be in your paper, so you need only take notes on what you find that relates to the items in your preliminary outline. That makes your note taking much easier.

Do keep one thing in mind, however. You are not married to this outline. If you decide later to change it, go right ahead. That's why it's called *preliminary*.

Progress Check: The Preliminary Outline

In the spaces below, write out your preliminary outline. Your instructor may wish to check your progress before you move on to taking notes.

_____

_____

_____

_____

_____

Step 6: Take Notes.   Now it is time to take a close look at the sources in your working bibliography. Take your first bibliography card and, using the Library of Congress number or the Dewey decimal number you wrote in the corner, find the source in your library. Examine the source and decide if there is material in it useful to your paper. If there is, begin taking notes on index cards. To make it as easy as possible to blend your borrowed material into your paper, you should follow these two suggestions:

1. Label each note card with the source of information and the page number the borrowing comes from, so you will be able to footnote easily when the time comes.
2. Put only one piece (or two related pieces) of information on each card so that you can easily arrange your cards later in the order in which the information will appear in your paper.

There are two ways you can take notes. You can put the information in your own words (paraphrase), or you can copy the exact words that are in the source (direct quotation). Since you will want to use both of these methods, we will discuss both kinds of note taking.

Paraphrasing

Most of the time you should paraphrase information when you write it on your note cards. When you *paraphrase,* you write the information in your own words, being very careful not to change the original meaning. A simple rearrangement of the word order is *not* a paraphrase because you have not put the information in your own words.

A good way to paraphrase is to read several sentences (a paragraph at the most) several times until you are sure you understand the meaning. Then look away from the material and rewrite it on your card in your own words. Finally, check your card against the source to be sure you have kept the original meaning but not the original wording and style.

Another good way to paraphrase is to read several sentences (never more than a paragraph) several times. Then imagine yourself explaining to a friend the meaning of what you just read. Finally, write your paraphrase on your note card the way you imagined yourself saying it.

Note: Do not use quotation marks around a paraphrase.

Quoting

Most of your note cards should be in paraphrase form so your paper has your own personal style and flavor. However, if you cannot paraphrase something for some reason, or if an author has stated something so nicely that you want to keep the original wording, you can write down a direct quotation on a note card. When you write down a *direct quotation,* you have a card with the exact wording that appears in the source.

When using a direct quotation, you should remember a few things.

1. The spelling, capitalization, and punctuation of your quotation must be just as it is in the original.
2. Sometimes when you quote you wish to omit a portion of the material. To do this, use *ellipses*—a series of three spaced dots—in place of the omitted words.

    Original: All mothers, especially those with preschool children, should consider the issue carefully before returning to work.

    Quotation with ellipses: One authority believes, "All mothers . . . should consider the issue carefully before returning to work."

Note: Notice that the ellipses stand for the omitted commas as well as the omitted words.

When an ellipses comes at the end of a sentence, add a fourth dot for the period (unless, of course, a question mark is called for).

Original:	All mothers should consider the issue carefully before returning to work, especially those with preschool children.
Quotation with ellipses:	One authority believes, "All mothers should consider the issue carefully before returning to work. . . ."

It is customary not to use ellipses when words are omitted from the beginning of a quotation.

Original:	All mothers, especially those with preschool children, should consider the issue carefully before returning to work.
Incorrect:	One authority believes that ". . . mothers, especially those with preschool children, should consider the issue carefully before returning to work."
Correct:	One authority believes that "mothers, especially those with preschool children, should consider the issue carefully before returning to work."

3. Sometimes when you quote it is necessary to add your own word or phrase to clarify or to work the quotation smoothly into your sentence. In such a case, use brackets to note the addition.

Original:	The working mother often finds herself at the mercy of whatever facilities exist in her area.
Quotation with brackets:	According to one source, "The working mother often finds herself at the mercy of whatever [child-care] facilities exist in her area."

4. When you wish to quote material that contains some italicized words, underline on your card whatever appears in italics in the original.

Original:	Working mothers *must* experience satisfaction on the job, or their frustrations will affect their relationships with their children.
Quotation with underlining:	Fredrickson notes, "Working mothers <u>must</u> experience satisfaction on the job, or their frustrations will affect their relationships with their children."

5. If you wish to quote material that is already quoted in the source or contains some direct quotation, use single quotation marks to indicate what was quoted in the original.

Original:	Most researchers share Dobb's view that "children who watch television constantly have short attention spans."
Quotation with single quotation marks:	Rice states, "Most researchers share Dobb's view that 'children who watch television constantly have short attention spans.' "

Note: The period comes inside both the single and double quotation marks.

EXERCISE:
Paraphrasing and Quoting

This exercise is meant to give you some practice with paraphrasing and quoting.

1. Paraphrase below Robin Roberts' reasons for suggesting a softball be used in Little League (see p. 127, paragraph 8).

_____

_____

_____

_____

_____

2. Paraphrase below what Roger Williams believes should happen to athletic scholarships (see p. 132, paragraph 2).

_____

_____

3. Paraphrase below what Roger Williams believes should happen to football coaching staffs (see p. 132, paragraph 4).

_____

_____

_____

4. Paraphrase Roger Williams' response to the argument that "many young men get a college education who otherwise would have no chance for one" (see p. 133, paragraph 1).

_____

_____

_____

5. Quote directly the last sentence of Roger Williams' essay (see p. 133).

_____

_____

_____

6. Quote directly the last sentence of paragraph 3 on page 133 (the one that begins with "Vanderbilt University").

_____

_____

_____

7. Quote directly the following sentence: Nancy Reagan looked _quite_ elegant at the wedding of Prince Charles and Lady Diana last week.

_____

_____

8. Quote the same sentence that you did for No. 7, but this time leave out the last two words.

_____

_____

9. Quote the following sentence, leaving out in this country: There is substantial evidence to support the claim that the Vietnam veteran in this country has not been treated fairly.

_____

_____

10. Quote the following sentence, adding your own definition of stillborn: When natural childbirth techniques are used, fewer babies are stillborn.

_____

_____

Progress Check: Note Taking

Copy in the space below one paraphrase and one quotation from your note cards. Make a copy of the pages from the sources you used for these notes so your instructor can check your work before you go further.

Paraphrase: _____

_____

_____

_____

_____

Quotation: _____

_____

_____

_____

_____

Step 7: Write Your Final Outline.   A paper that uses research for some of its support must be planned as carefully as any other theme. In chapter 4 you learned about outlining (see p. 86). Once you have finished your note taking, it is time to outline your paper. When you are satisfied with your outline (and you may draw up and throw away several outlines before you work out one that pleases you), arrange your note cards in the order they will be used in your paper. This will make writing the first draft easier. It is quite possible that you will not use all your note cards in your final outline and paper.

Progress Check: The Final Outline

Fill in the blanks below after completing your final outline. Your instructor may want to check your work before you write your first draft.

1. My thesis will be something like this: _____

_____.

2. My first topic sentence will be something like this:

_____

_____.

3. I will use the following support to develop my first topic sentence:

_____

_____

_____

_____

4. My second topic sentence will be something like this:

_____

_____

5. I will use the following support to develop my second topic sentence:

_____

_____

_____

_____

6. My third topic sentence will be something like this:

_____

_____

7. I will use the following support to develop my third topic sentence:

_____

_____

_____

_____

8. My fourth topic sentence will be something like this:

_____

_____

9. I will use the following support to develop my fourth topic sentence:

_____

_____

_____

Step 8: Write Your First Draft.   With your final outline complete, you are now ready to begin your first draft. As you write, there are a few things about research writing you should know.

1. When you paraphrase or quote, it is customary to introduce the borrowing with a short phrase so the reader can tell immediately that the material is from another source. Below is a list of some phrases you can use.

   As *Time* reports,

   According to J. B. Rhine,

   One author notes,

   A prominent sociologist tells us,

   Rollo May acknowledges that

   Margaret Mead points out that

   The NEA suggests,

   One critic states that

   The National Rifle Association contends,

   A respected psychiatrist believes,

   A recent article in the *Journal of Applied Psychology* reveals,

   Notice that all the verbs in the above list are in the present tense. When referring to the printed word, people generally use the present tense, even when paraphrasing or quoting words written at some point in the past. It is conventional to view written words as "living now," even if their author has long been dead.

2. If a quotation begins with a capital letter, follow the introduction with a comma. However, if the quotation does not begin with a capital letter, follow the introduction with the word *that* and do not use a comma.

   Example: One member of the National Rifle Association believes, "Gun control legislation is unconstitutional."

   Example: A former high school teacher explains that "violence in the classroom makes learning impossible."

   Explanation: In the first example, <u>Gun</u> was capitalized in the source, so a comma comes after the introduction. In the second example, <u>violence</u> was not capitalized in the source, so the word <u>that</u> is added to the introduction and no comma is used.

3. A quotation that is less than five typed lines is worked into your paper like anything else. However, a quotation that is five or more typed lines gets some special handling. You should set off such a quote by skipping a line before and after the quote (triple space if you are typing). Indent the quote on the left (ten spaces if you are typing).

Also, do not use quotation marks for these long quotes, unless there are quotation marks in the source. If quotation marks appear in the source, place double quotation marks around the long quote. Usually the introduction for a long quote is followed by a colon. (For an example of how to handle the long quote, see p. 256 of the reading selection.)

4. Whenever one writer borrows information from another writer, it is absolutely necessary that the borrowing be acknowledged in a note. You will therefore need to provide a note for the paraphrases and quotations that appear in your paper. After all, fair is fair, so you will want to make it clear when you use another person's words and ideas. Your notes will do this. Be sure to check Appendix F and Appendix G to learn how to handle these notes.

5. The last page of your paper should be a bibliography page, which lists all the sources cited in your paper. If you were careful to write your bibliography cards in the correct form, you will have all the information you need to write the bibliography page easily and in the proper manner. However, do check Appendix E and Appendix G when you write this important part of your paper.

Step 9: Revise and Edit.   With your first draft complete, you are ready to review your work and make any necessary changes. When you revise and edit, I suggest that you do the following:

1. Go away from the first draft for at least a day before beginning any changes so you can be more objective and think more clearly.
2. Look at the Questions to Answer before Submitting Your Theme Using Research Material on p. 282.
3. Review the proofreading and editing checklist in Appendix B.
4. Review What to Notice about a Theme Using Research Material on p. 277.
5. Review the Six Sins of Research Writing on p. 282.

Step 10: Write Your Final Draft.   Once your revising and editing work is done, you can put your final draft together. At this stage you will no doubt be feeling a real sense of pride and accomplishment—and well you should. To give this special paper a special touch, I suggest that you type it. When typed, a paper using research looks attractive and seems to reflect all the work you put into it and all the pride you feel as a result of writing it. If you type, remember the following guidelines:

1. Leave about a 1-inch margin on each side and at the top and bottom.
2. Double-space the text, notes, and bibliography.

3. You may make minor corrections neatly in ink, but a page with many corrections should be retyped.

4. Number your pages in the upper right-hand corner.

WHAT TO NOTICE ABOUT A THEME USING RESEARCH MATERIAL

The paper using research that you read early in this chapter is repeated below. This time comments are added to call your attention to examples of what was explained in this chapter.

Should Instant Replay Cameras Aid
in Officiating Football Games?

It's the Super Bowl. The New York Giants are trailing by four points with three seconds left to play. Their only hope is the bomb. The quarterback lets the ball loose as time expires, and it is caught in the end zone for a touchdown. But wait, the referee is hesitant in making the call. Was the receiver out of bounds when he caught the ball? The other officials gather around. Meanwhile, the armchair quarterback, in front of his six-foot video screen, has seen the play from fourteen different angles and knows that he was definitely in bounds. The world has its eyes on the referee. What will he call?

        Fortunately, a situation like this hasn't occurred yet, but it may, and there are many people who feel the referee on the field should have all the advantages of instant replay that the fans have at home. I disagree. True, instant replay cameras would be more reliable and less likely to make bad calls,

but the disadvantages of the system are far greater
than the advantages.

First, we would lose the human element of the
game. Everyone makes mistakes, and referees are no
exception. But imagine how dull a game would be if
the officiating were perfect. There would be no controversial calls that the fans could react to, no mistakes that the sportswriters could talk about in the
next day's column. And, as Joe Falls, columnist for
The Sporting News, states, [borrowing introduced in
present tense with comma after the introduction] ''We
[first word of quote capitalized] will be replacing
people with machines, and that's never worked yet, in
any society, for any reason.''[1] [note number elevated
at end of borrowing, period inside quotes]

Another disadvantage of using the instant replay
system is the time delays that would be involved.
Many people think that it would take only a few seconds to look at a play and make a call, so it would
not be necessary to delay or stop the game. But when
Art McNally, supervisor of the National Football
League officials, placed two cameras in each end zone
of a Monday night game between Buffalo and Dallas for
experimental purposes, he reported [introduction for
borrowing; notice the need for past tense here] that
it took between twenty-seven seconds and two minutes
to look for a particular play, while the game continued on the field. He continued to say, as quoted
by Dave Brady of the Washington Post: [colon introducing long quote; triple space before and after the
quote and indent 10 spaces]

''That [double quotes because quotation marks appeared in source] gave us an idea of how long it would take with two cameras. [You can imagine what would happen] [brackets for words added to quote] if we had to look at the pictures taken by three cameras, or maybe six, seven or eight. . . . [ellipses for omission; fourth dot for period] The person in the monitoring booth would have to be a miracle man. You would have to stop the game and perhaps let the coaches ask to see a certain number of plays; let the officials see them; let the man in the booth judge the replays. You would have to stop the game because there might be a chance of changing the original official's decision.''[2] [double quotes because quotation marks appeared in the original source]

Of course, there are those who argue that only two or three plays will be affected in each game, but any break in the continuity of the game would be unbearable, especially for the fans in the stadium. Imagine sitting at a game, waiting for five minutes while an unseen official views an unseen videotape of a close play from ten different angles. Emotion is a very important part of the game, and all that was built up prior to that play will have been lost during those five minutes.

But perhaps the greatest disadvantage of the instant replay system is the cost. Pete Rozelle, commissioner of the National Football League, cites a 1976 N.F.L. study and states [introduction in present tense] it would cost the league $46 million per year

for a full system. Breaking that down, it comes to
approximately $150,000 for each game.[3] Considering an
average stadium seats 50,000 people, that would be
about three dollars more per ticket for you and me.
After all, you don't think the <u>players</u> are going to
pay for it.

Those who favor the instant replay system say the
cost could be cut down by using the cameras only in
crucial games, like the playoffs and Super Bowl. But
imagine a team winning a regular season game because
of a wrong call made by an official, when the cameras
weren't employed. Then imagine that team making the
playoffs by only a few percentage points, and had the
official made the correct call in that one game,
they'd be sitting at home watching on television instead of playing on the field. If that team goes on
to win the Super Bowl, you have an unjust winner,
which is what the use of replays is supposed to
avoid. So the cameras must be used in every game, no
matter what the seeming importance.

Considering these drawbacks, I feel the instant
replay cameras have no business in the N.F.L. Maybe
in the future, with advanced technology, the system
would be feasible, but for now the referees on the
field are sufficient, and they're doing a fine job.
Dave Brady reports that during the 1975 season ''there
[no capital letter for first word of quote and <u>that</u>
used because <u>there</u> was not capitalized in the source]
were 27,000 plays run off and . . . [ellipses for
omission] only six important plays were called
wrong.''[4] For every one play that was called wrong,

there were 4,000 plays called right. That's a record
anyone can be proud of.

Notes

[notes are double—spaced and in form shown in
Appendix F]

[1]Joe Falls, ''Instant Replay No Way to Settle
Close Call,'' The Sporting News, 26 Jan. 1980, p. 7,
col. 1.

[2]Dave Brady, ''NFL Tests Replays for Officials,
Finds 'Obvious Drawbacks,' '' Washington Post, 9 March
1977, Sec. D., p. 7, col. 1.

[3]William N. Wallace, ''Rozelle Gives Promise of
Improved Officiating,'' New York Times, 14 Jan. 1978,
p. 13, col. 1.

[4]Brady, Sec. D., p. 7, col. 2.

Bibliography

[Bibliography is double—spaced, alphabetized, and
in form shown in Appendix E]

Brady, Dave. ''NFL Tests Replays for Officials, Finds
  'Obvious Drawbacks,' '' Washington Post, 9 March
  1977, Sec. D., p. 7, cols. 1—2.

Falls, Joe. ''Instant Replay No Way to Settle Close
  Call.'' The Sporting News, 26 Jan. 1980, p. 7,
  col. 1.

Wallace, William N. ''Rozelle Gives Promise of Im—
  proved Officiating.'' New York Times, 14 Jan. 1978,
  p. 13, col. 1.

Note: For space considerations, the notes and bibliography appear here
on the same page. However, in your paper the notes and bibliography should
appear on separate pages.

Chapter 10
Getting and Keeping a Job:
Writing at Work

Like most college students, you are probably seeking a degree for many reasons. No doubt one of those reasons is that you expect the degree to help you land an appealing job. But to get that job you're after, your degree alone may not be enough. Let's be realistic—you will have to compete with many other people out there who also have college educations. Although your degree can put you in the running for the job you want, you will need other skills to *keep* you in the competition. One of the skills you will no doubt need is the ability to write well. Your writing skills will serve you not only as you apply for a job, but very often as you work at that job as well.

In addition, there are various kinds of business writing you may become involved in off the job. Writing business letters, for example, is something we all must do at times. Also, when we join an organization, we often find ourselves handling reports, minutes for meetings, and the like. And so it is that many kinds of business writing become a part of our lives both at work and away from the job. This chapter will introduce you to some of this kind of writing.

GETTING READY: HOW MUCH WRITING WILL YOU HAVE TO DO?

I admit that some jobs require a person to do more writing than others, but I stand firm in the belief that every job that requires a college degree holds the possibility of involving a person in some writing. When I mention this to my students, there are always some disbelievers: A future professional artist cannot imagine writing until I suggest that an artist may wish to write to the curator of a museum about a one-person show; a budding CPA cannot see writing anything beyond numbers until I mention interoffice communications and letters to clients; a nursing student predicts little on-the-job writing beyond chart entries until I offer the possibility that she or he may wish to submit an article to a professional journal. And so it goes. No student has yet suggested a job that does not hold the possibility of some writing.

But just how much writing will you do in your chosen profession? To get an idea, interview one or two people who currently hold the kind of position you are working toward. Ask these people the following questions:

1. What kind of writing do you do on a daily basis?
2. Who reads what you write?
3. Does the quality of this writing influence the opinion people have of your competence? How?
4. What kind of writing do you do on a weekly basis?
5. Who reads this writing?
6. Does the quality of this writing influence the opinion people have of your competence? How?
7. What kind of writing do you do on a monthly basis?
8. Who reads this writing?
9. Does the quality of this writing influence the opinion people have of your competence? How?
10. What kind of writing do you do on an irregular basis?
11. Who reads this writing?
12. Does the quality of this writing influence the opinion people have of your competence? How?
13. How many writing courses do you think a person who seeks a position such as yours should have?
14. How well can a person with weak writing skills function in a position such as yours?

Even if you think you are already aware of the amount and kind of writing your future job will demand, conduct the interview. You may still learn a few things about what will be expected of you. After the interview, write a paragraph or two that explains the amount and kind of writing your future job will require. Also explain how that writing will affect the view your co-workers will form of you and your ability.

The following selection by Nona Aguilar explains how the right kind of business letter can lead to just the right job. Notice as you read the role strategy plays in composing the tailored letter of application.

How to Write a Letter That Will Get You a Job
Nona Aguilar

Whether you're just getting back into the job market after years out of it or you're looking for a better job to advance your career, you can double your chances of success by using a "tailored" letter.

What's a tailored letter? It's simply a brief letter highlighting background elements which most relate to the needs of a prospective employer. In other words, you "tailor" your experience to meet the needs of the person or company you want to work for. By following our simple guidelines, you can write a persuasive, concise letter that gets results.

Here's an example of the power of a tailored letter: My friend's mother, Mrs. Kinley, had been widowed for almost three years. She was 54 years old, her children were grown and she hadn't worked during the 29 years of her marriage. Now, with time on her hands, she wanted a job, but employment agencies discouraged her because, she was told, she didn't have skills or work experience.

Since she knew that I had always managed to rustle up a job no matter what or where, she talked to me about her problem. She realized that she didn't really want a full-time job; she had looked for one because it was the only type of work available through the agencies. And her only work experience

was the hospital and Red Cross volunteer work she'd done throughout her marriage. We used that experience in composing her tailored letter, which she sent to 30 doctors (found in the "Physicians" section of the Yellow Pages).

What Were the Results?

Within three days of mailing the letter, Mrs. Kinley had received four telephone calls. One wanted someone to work full time for five doctors in practice together; she declined that interview request but went on the other three.

While trying to decide which of two opportunities she might take—one of the positions wasn't offered to her after the interview—the mail brought a written reply asking her to call for an interview. On a hunch, she decided to make the call. That last interview turned out to be THE job: four days a week, from 9 to 1:30.

A postscript to the story: She received two more calls after she started working. She also got a few P.B.-O.s (Polite Brush-Offs) in the mail plus a "not right now but maybe in six months" letter. *That* is what I mean about the power of a tailored letter!

Measurable Accomplishments

Take a look at the letter Mrs. Kinley wrote. She used the Four Elements that form the basic structure of a good tailored letter: (1) an opening grabber, (2) an appeal to the self-interest of the reader, (3) a number of examples of her experience and (4) a good closing. The Four Elements are detailed . . . here, but as you can see, *specific accomplishments* are at the letter's heart. If your accomplishments are measurable in any way, you will look that much more impressive.

Here's what I mean by measurable. I landed a job teaching English in a language school in Italy. I was not a professional teacher; I had never taught in a school—obviously I had never been certified! However, one summer while I was still in high school, I started a little brush-up school in our family dining room to help three of my kid brothers and sisters. Four neighborhood kids joined my "class" and, through tutoring, I literally boosted English grades by about 13%.

The opening line of my tailored letter to the directress of the language school—the "grabber"—read: "I raised students' grades in English an average of 13% during a summer-school program which I began in my neighborhood." The letter made an impression, sailing past almost 100 weighty epistles and résumés sent by teaching professionals listing schools, courses, degrees, and experience in abundance. When I came in for my interview, the directress was already anxious to meet me. My letter had shown an awareness of her major problem: finding teachers who could actually teach—and could then prove it.

March 1, 197–

Marvin Willis, M.D.
488 Madison Avenue
New York, NY 10022

Dear Dr. Willis:

In the past several years, I have worked over 6,000 hours in hospitals handling bookkeeping and billing.

I am writing to you because your office may be in need of a woman with my background and experience to work on a part-time basis. If so, you may be interested in some of the things I have done.

For example, I was responsible for handling Wednesday receipts for a volunteer-operated hospital gift shop.

I sorted 500 pieces of patient mail per week.

I handled all bookkeeping for the gift shop, insuring payment of suppliers and disbursement of profits to the hospital by the 30th of each month.

If such experience would be valuable to your office to help with bookkeeping or billing, I would be happy to talk to you in more detail. My telephone number is EL 6-0000.

Sincerely yours,

Mrs. Kinley's letter

The Four Elements

1. An Opening Grabber. Mrs. Kinley's letter begins with a short sentence listing a memorable figure: 6,000 hours of work experience in a hospital. This grabs the reader's interest.

2. Self-Interest Appeal. She appeals to his self-interest right away in her second sentence by letting the doctor know that those 6,000 hours are part of valuable experience which might be useful to him.

3. Examples. Mrs. Kinley gives three specific examples of accomplishments to further appeal to the self-interest of a would-be employer.

4. The Closing. Mrs. Kinley does not plead for an interview. She doesn't even ask for one. Rather, she lets the recipient know she's a worthwhile professional person and that "if such experience would be valuable to your office . . ." she'd be happy to discuss it in an interview.

Specific Accomplishments

So I can't stress it enough: *The heart of a successful tailored letter is specific accomplishments.* When your accomplishments are measurable, you look even more impressive—but don't equate *paid* with *measurable*. Mrs. Kinley does not apologize for her lack of paid business experience. That isn't even mentioned, nor is the fact that her work had been on a volunteer basis. Instead she casts all her experience in terms of *accomplishment*. Each separate accomplishment that relates to working in a medical environment is placed in its own brief, one-sentence paragraph. Indeed, the whole letter is brief, only eight sentences in all, so busy recipients—in this case doctors—are more inclined to read the letter straight through to the end.

It's important that your letter be short and crisp. Work and rework the letter so that your grabber is brief and punchy. Appeal right away to the self-interest of the recipient. In the Examples section of your letter, cover each accomplishment in one short sentence in its own paragraph. The succession of short, accomplishment-laden paragraphs makes a greater impact on the reader than long, cumbersome prose. Make your closing sharp and clean. And *don't beg* for an interview.

Finding Job Prospects

Of course, you have to find prospects for your letter!

It was easy with Mrs. Kinley: We just opened the phone book and picked physicians whose offices were convenient to her home.

If you already have a job but want a better one, you're probably aware of where and for whom you want to work. All you have to do is send letters to the companies on your "list."

If you use the help-wanted ads in the paper, send a tailored letter *instead* of a ré-sumé, even if a résumé is asked for. All résumés tend to look alike, so your letter will stand out, considerably increasing your chances of getting an interview—*the* crucial first step toward getting a new job.

If you're interested in a particular business or industry, check with your librarian to see if a directory exists for it. There you'll find listings complete with spellings, business titles, and addresses. You can also pick up ial handbook in your library will show you nesses. Ask for the name and correct spelling of the owner or president—if it's a small company—or the district manager, if it's a large company and you're calling the regional office in your city. If a secretary insists on knowing why you're calling before she gives the information, simply say that you're writing the man or woman a letter and need the information.

How many letters will you have to send out? That's hard to say.

When you send letters to companies that aren't specifically advertising or looking for someone, you can expect to send a lot. I did that some years ago; I sent over 60 letters to advertising agencies. Some of the letters drew interviews; only one interview finally resulted in a job. But I only needed *one* job, and I got the job I wanted!

As a general rule, your letter is a good one when requests for an interview run about 8% to 10%. If Mrs. Kinley had received just two or three interview requests, she would have been doing fine. If she had received only one reply, or none, we'd have reworked the letter. As it turned out, she got six interview requests out of 30 letters—that's an exceptionally high 20%.

If you send a tailored letter when you know a company is hiring—for instance, in reply to a help-wanted ad—you will increase your chances of being called for an interview at least 30% to 50%, sometimes more. Once I was the only person called for an interview for an advertised editorial job, even though I had never worked on either a newspaper or a magazine in my life—there's the power of a tailored letter!

Look Professional!

Once you've composed your short, punchy, accomplishment-laden letter and decided who's going to get it, make sure you're careful about three things:

First, *type*—don't handwrite—the letter, following standard business form; a secretarial handbook in your library will show you examples. Or follow the form Mrs. Kinley used.

Second, use plain white or ivory-colored stationery. Very pale, almost neutral, colors are okay too, but nothing flashy or brightly colored. I've found that it is helpful to write on monarch-sized stationery, which is smaller than the standard 8½″ × 11″ paper; the letter looks much more personal and invites a reading.

Finally, do *not* do anything gimmicky or "cute." I remember the laughter that erupted in an office when a job-seeking executive sent a letter with a small, sugar-filled bag carefully stapled to the top of the page. His opening line was: "I'd like to sweeten your day just a little." He came across looking foolish . . . and the boss didn't sweeten his day by calling him for an interview.

These are the basics that add up to a professional business letter. I've worked in a lot of offices and seen some pretty silly letters tumble out of the mailbag. Don't let yours be one of them; especially not if you're a woman of specific accomplishments who's ready for a job!

Vocabulary List:
"How to Write a Letter That Will Get You a Job"

In the spaces below, record any words you are unsure of in "How to Write a Letter That Will Get You a Job." Next to each word write a brief dictionary definition that corresponds to the way the word was used in the selection. Add two words to your vocabulary list in Appendix A and continue to study your words each day.

_____   _____

_____   _____

_____   _____

Questions for Discussion:
"How to Write a Letter That Will Get You a Job"

1. What is a tailored letter?

_____

_____

2. What are the four elements of a tailored letter?

_____   _____

_____   _____

3. What is the most important part of a good tailored letter?

_____

4. After composing a tailored letter, what three things should you be careful of?

_____

_____

_____

WRITING ASSIGNMENT I

Write a tailored application letter in an effort to get a part-time job while you are in school. Before you do this, decide what kind of job you would like and make a list of employers to send the letter to. Then make a list of your accomplishments—the ones that would appeal to the self-interests of the employers on your list. If you already have a job and don't care to change, or if you do not have a job and are not interested in one, write the letter for a job you might like to have in the future.

THE ROLE OF GRAMMAR AND USAGE IN BUSINESS WRITING

As you already know, grammar and usage rules are important. They are the conventions—the writing etiquette—that writers are expected to follow (see p. 70). A writer who doesn't follow these rules will create an unfavorable impression in the mind of the reader.

When writing business communications, whether on the job or not, you must continue to be careful of your grammar and usage for several reasons. First, business writing calls for you to make a special effort to communicate clearly. Often you are writing to seek specific action or information, so you want to do all you can to ensure that you get what you're after. Using the appropriate grammar and usage can help you achieve the clarity that can get results. Also, imagine for a moment writing a letter applying for a job. What do you think your chances would be if you made several errors in spelling, punctuation, and subject–verb agreement?

Second, there is the fact that the reader of your business writing will form an impression of you based in part on the quality of your writing. How do you think your boss will react if you send her or him a memo with apostrophes left out of noun possessive forms? That person will surely lose at least a bit of confidence in your ability. Also, a business communication can be filed away as a permanent record, so whatever impression you create is likely to be around for a while. Off the job, the impression you create can be equally important. Let's say you write a letter to a manufacturer seeking a refund. I suspect a letter correctly done is more likely to get you the refund than one that is full of errors—just because of the impression created in the mind of the reader.

Third, on the job "time is money." This means that if your business writing does not follow the grammar and usage conventions, someone may have to spend time correcting your mistakes. This will cost your employer money and make you a less valuable employee.

Finally, when you understand and can apply the grammar and usage rules, you have a sense of confidence in your ability. This confidence can come through to the reader, which generally makes him or her more likely to pay attention to what you have to say. So in your business writing, be sure to give some special attention to the grammar and usage rules you have already learned. In addition, you will learn the differences among some frequently confused words in this chapter, so that you can avoid the pitfalls these words present.

Frequently Confused Words

In our language there are groups of words that writers sometimes confuse. Often this confusion occurs because the words sound alike or look similar. Study the list of these words below. And be sure that you understand how to use each word in the list. If you were to confuse these words in your business writing, you would risk weakening the impact of your communication, and you would risk creating an unfavorable impression of yourself.

Accept	to receive or approve of
Except	excluding; but
	I cannot <u>accept</u> your offer of help because I must do this alone.
	Everyone felt a picnic was a good idea <u>except</u> Len, who preferred to go swimming.

Advice   a noun meaning a suggestion or help

Advise   a verb meaning to give suggestions or help

Anita's <u>advice</u> helped me decide which job to take.

As your best friend, I <u>advise</u> you to stay in school.

Affect   a verb meaning to influence

Effect   a noun meaning result; a verb meaning to bring about

All the tension in my life is <u>affecting</u> my health.

The <u>effects</u> of agent orange are only now becoming known.

To <u>effect</u> a change in curriculum, a faculty vote is necessary.

All ready   fully prepared

Already   previously

The scout troup is <u>all ready</u> to leave on the hike.

By the time you left, I had <u>already</u> cleaned the garage.

All right   the correct spelling

Alright   an unacceptable form

It's <u>all right</u> with me if you take the car.

Among   refers to more than two items

Between   refers to two items

The difference in price <u>among</u> these four sets of golf clubs is hard to understand.

You must choose <u>between</u> going to the movie and going to the concert.

Could have   the correct form

Could of   unaceptable form

Do not use <u>of</u> for <u>have</u>.

should have   N<u>OT</u>   should of
might have   NOT   might of
would have   NOT   would of
can't have   NOT   can't of

Different from	the usual form
Different than	generally used to avoid awkwardness
	This $50 camera is not much <u>different from</u> the $75 one.
	Eating in a restaurant calls for a <u>different</u> set of manners <u>than</u> eating at home does.
Fewer	refers to things that can be measured or counted
Less	refers to degree or amount
	<u>Fewer</u> people came to the garage sale today because of the rain.
	The <u>less</u> said the better.
Hear	to notice with the ear
Here	in a particular spot
	I can <u>hear</u> the rain against the window.
	<u>Here</u> is where I'd like you to put the couch.
Hole	an opening
Whole	entire or complete
	This <u>hole</u> in the wall must be plastered.
	I read the <u>whole</u> book, but I still don't see why you liked it.
Its	possessive
It's	it is; it has
	The floor has lost <u>its</u> shine, and is in need of some wax.
	<u>It's</u> about time you arrived since <u>it's</u> been hours since you said you would be here.
Knew	past tense of know
New	not old
	Johnny <u>knew</u> how much I wanted to come.
	The <u>new</u> bar on the corner is doing quite well.
Passed	past tense of pass
Past	before the present; by
	When Eric <u>passed</u> the ketchup, he put his elbow in the jello.

I went <u>past</u> your house yesterday, but no one seemed to be home.

Forget the <u>past</u>; today is all that matters.

Peace	calm; opposite of war
Piece	a portion

<u>Peace</u> in the Middle East will not be achieved easily.

The child cried when she got the smallest <u>piece</u> of cake.

Principal	chief or most important; a school official
Principle	a rule or belief

The <u>principal</u> cause of the fight was Jeffrey's irritability.

The <u>principal</u> of John Adams High retired after twenty years.

Karla refused to back down because there was a <u>principle</u> involved.

Quiet	without noise
Quit	to stop
Quite	completely; rather

It's so <u>quiet</u> in these woods.

<u>Quit</u> that nonsense now.

The young couple was <u>quite</u> happy with their new home.

Reason is because	an unacceptable form
Reason is that	the correct form

The <u>reason</u> Juan didn't come <u>is that</u> he is studying for finals.

Than	used for comparisons
Then	indicates a certain time

I did much better in French <u>than</u> I did in biology.

We finished the yard work, and <u>then</u> we took a break.

There	indicates a certain place; a frequent sentence opener
Their	possessive form of <u>they</u>
They're	they are

Bring the boxes into the kitchen and place them <u>there</u> in the corner.

There are three stores opening in the new mall this week.

The children looked so cute in their new party clothes.

The Youngs are unable to be here because they're in Washington on business.

Threw	past tense of throw
Through	in one end and out the other; finished

The shortstop threw the ball to complete the double play.

The ride through the car wash delighted three-year-old Gregory.

After her last dreadful experience, Ingrid announced, "I'm through with blind dates forever!"

To	a preposition meaning toward; part of a verb form as in to swim
Too	also; more than enough
Two	the number

Going to Grandmother's for Thanksgiving is a real treat.

Dad left after breakfast to catch his plane.

Doris felt she should have been invited too.

The beach was deserted because it was too cold to swim.

I want only two eggs for breakfast this morning.

Your	possessive form of you
You're	you are

Your gloves were left in the classroom, so I picked them up for you.

You're not at all clear in this paragraph; please try it again.

Wear	to have on
Where	asks about or indicates a location
Were	the past tense of are
We're	we are

Wear your heavy sweater today because it's quite cold.

Where did you see that movie?

We were planning to go, but then the storm hit.

We're late as it is, so we should leave right away.

Weather	what it's like outside
Whether	if

If the <u>weather</u> holds, let's leave at noon for the state fair.

<u>Whether</u> we can come depends on how Erika is feeling.

Whose	possessive form of who
Who's	who is

I've been wondering <u>whose</u> coat this is.

<u>Who's</u> going to the meeting with you?

EXERCISE:
Frequently Confused Words

In the sentences below, circle the correct words.

1. Choosing (between–among) college and a job after high school is a decision that can (affect–effect) a person for the rest of his or her life.

2. My (advice–advise) to you is to take route 76 because (there–their–they're) are (fewer–less) cars on it.

3. I should (of–have) listened to you in the first place, and this (whole–hole) mess wouldn't (of–have) happened.

4. When David (passed–past) his school (principle–principal), he looked away rather (than–then) wave.

5. The three judges (knew–new) (whose–who's) essay had won the prize, but they had to keep it a secret (between–among) themselves.

6. (Its–It's) (all right–alright) with me if you go now as long as (your–you're) back in time for supper.

7. Noreen was unwilling (to–too) (accept–except) such an expensive gift, so she returned it (to–too) Pat and explained that she just couldn't (where–wear) it.

8. (Whether–Weather) we go will depend on how soon the (whether–weather) clears.

9. The people (here–hear) are different (than–from) the people in the South (where–were–wear–we're) everyone is so polite and pleasant.

10. The reason (its–it's) so difficult to carry that (piece–peace) of lumber is (that–because) (its–it's) such an odd shape.

11. The police were (quit–quiet–quite) sure they had (there–their–they're) man because he was found (there–their–they're) at the scene of the crime.

12. The (effects–affects) of (your–you're) surgery will last (no–know) longer (than–then) (two–to–too) weeks.

THE LETTER OF APPLICATION

The tailored letter you read about is a variation of the traditional letter of application and can serve very well, particularly when you are applying to employers who have not announced specific openings. When, however, you wish to apply for a specific job that you know is available at a specific company, you may wish to write a more traditional letter of application. Such a letter typically includes the following information:

1. How you heard about the opening
2. Why you are interested in the position
3. The qualifications and past experience that qualify you for the job
4. Any other information you have been asked to supply
5. When you can go in for an interview
6. Your address, phone number, and the times you can be reached by phone

When you write your application letter (or any other business letter, for that matter), keep in mind that the person you are addressing is busy. Therefore, keep your letter brief and to the point. Also, be aware that your application letter will influence a potential employer's first impression of you. And because you will want that first impression to be a positive one, be sure that your letter is neatly typed, clear, and businesslike. Keep the tone of your letter professional and do not include any unnecessary detail. Also, you will want to put your application letter in a standard business letter form. This will help impress your reader with your professionalism. Below is a sample application letter in business letter form for you to study.

A Sample Application Letter

Notice in the following application letter that all six items of information listed above are included. Also notice that the information is presented briefly and directly. Letters of application should always be brief and to the point so as not to annoy busy personnel directors by wasting their time.

8209 Southington Court
West End, Ohio 49982
October 30, 1981

[**Triple space**]

Personnel Manager
Wessex Corporation
802 Deerfield Place
West End, Ohio 49982

Dear Personnel Manager:
    I noticed your ad for a newsletter editor in the October 29 Dispatch-Chronicle. Because writing and publication work have long been interests of mine, I wish to apply for this position.
    I believe both my education and work experience qualify me for the job. In 1979 I earned my B.A. degree with a major in English and a minor in journalism. While in school, I was the sports editor on the campus newspaper and the senior editor for the campus literary magazine. Since graduation, I have written and edited the monthly bulletin of the Main Street Methodist Church.
    Your ad noted that applicants must be able to start immediately and be willing to relocate. I am in a position to do both of these.
    I am currently available for an interview any weekday after 3:00 p.m. You can reach me at my home phone, 555-7390, any day after 3:00 p.m.
    I look forward to hearing from you, and I thank you for your attention.

Sincerely,

Douglass Van Cleef

Douglass Van Cleef

Note: For a discussion of the form a business letter should take, see p. 303.

RÉSUMÉS

A résumé is a sheet or two that outlines information about yourself and your background. Often employers request that résumés accompany letters of application because they provide at a glance much of the information they need when considering applicants' qualifications. If a potential employer requests your résumé, neatly type the following information:

1. Name.
2. Address.
3. Telephone number.
4. Educational background with dates, degrees, and fields of study. Provide most recent schooling first and work back to high school; indicate your grade point average in college (GPA) if it is a good one—above a 2.7.
5. Work history with dates. Put most recent job first and include your positions and duties performed.
6. Relevant special experiences if not covered in No. 4 or No. 5.
7. Names and addresses of three references. These should not be relatives, but other people who can speak to your work ability and character—perhaps former employers and teachers.

In a résumé, do not include your age, sex, marital status, race, or religion. Such information is now irrelevant due to equal opportunity legislation. Also, do not include salary expectations, as this is better dealt with during an interview. Finally, do not mention your hobbies because this information is not relevant.

A Sample Résumé

On the following page is a sample résumé for you to examine. Notice that the information is attractively arranged in a way that allows the reader to get a sense of the applicant's qualifications easily.

Résumé for Douglass Van Cleef

Name   Douglass Van Cleef

Address 8209 Southington Court
        West End, Ohio 49982

Phone   (216) 555-7390

Educational   Oxblood University 1975-79, B.A.
  Background   degree; English
                                  major, journalism
                                  minor; GPA 3.6
              Alma Mater High School 1971-75

Work History Main Street Methodist Church: 1979-
                present; editor, monthly church
                bulletin
              My duties include soliciting,
              writing, and editing items for the
              bulletin as well as typing,
              proofing, and distributing the
              bulletin. Also, I regularly review
              other church bulletins to get ideas
              for improving our publication.
              Wilson's Market: 1973-1975, stock boy
                My duties included bagging
                groceries, stocking shelves, and
                receiving incoming goods.

Special   Sports Editor, Oxblood Newsworthy,
  Experiences   1977-79
                My duties included making
                assignments to the sports reporters,
                reviewing and editing their writing,
                and reporting on the football
                games. Also, I determined which
                sports articles to include in the
                weekly campus newspaper.
              Senior Editor, Oxblood Creative
                Chronicle, 1977-79
                My duties included supervising a
                staff of twelve in the compiling,
                editing, and publishing of this
                quarterly literary campus magazine.
                I also decided which contributions
                to accept, checked galley proofs,

-2-

and coordinated the efforts of my
staff, the publisher, and the
contributors. In addition, I
contributed three short stories and
a poem.

Special
Skills

In addition to the writing, editing,
and proofing skills I learned as
sports editor, senior editor, and
church bulletin editor, I gained an
ability to supervise and coordinate
the efforts of people in my charge.
I believe this organizational
ability is one of my best assets.

References

Dr. Janet Kasinsky, faculty adviser to
the Oxblood Newsworthy
Journalism Department
Oxblood University
Orange Grove, Ohio 48798

Dr. Jerome Patterson, faculty adviser
to the Oxblood Creative Chronicle
English Department
Oxblood University
Orange Grove, Ohio 48798

Pastor Theodore Maloney
Main Street Methodist Church
9620 Fourth Street
West End, Ohio 49983

Note: Never list a person as a reference until you have permission to do so. Also, rather than list references on your résumé, you may state, "References will be furnished upon request." However, this can slow the processing of your application somewhat because before the references can be secured, a personnel director must ask you to furnish the names of your references so they can be contacted.

WRITING ASSIGNMENT II

This assignment will give you some experience with application letters and résumés. Select a position that appeals to you from the Sunday help-wanted ads in your local newspaper. Type a traditional letter of application for that position and include a résumé. Be sure to see the following page for the form a business letter should take.

A Business Letter and Envelope

[Heading: your address and date]
1814 North Lyon Street
Delmar, Virginia 77371
December 10, 1981

Mr. George Roberts
General Manager
Roberts Department Store
802 Wyand Avenue
Delmar, Virginia 77374

[Inside address: name, title, and address of person receiving letter]

[Double space here]
Dear Mr. Roberts: **[Salutation, followed by colon]**

[Double space here]
    The Delmar Civic Club is currently planning its programs for 1982. We would very much like to have you speak to us about shoplifting, its cost to the consumer, and methods of prevention. We understand you have given this lecture in the past and that it has been most informative.   **[Body]**

    Typically, our speakers lecture for thirty minutes and answer questions for fifteen minutes. However, if you desire, this format can be altered. At this time, we can offer you a choice of dates. We have openings January 30, March 18, April 13, and June 16. All our meetings are held at 384 Dearborn Street and begin at 8:00 p.m.

    Because we do not have a large budget, we can pay you only $25.00. However, we can also offer you refreshments and entertainment following your lecture.

[Double space here]

Sincerely,   **[Closing]**

Patricia Donnelly
Patricia Donnelly
Program Director

[Signature, typed and written]

Patricia Donnelly
1814 North Lyon Street
Delmar, Va. 77371

Mr. George Roberts
General Manager
Roberts Department Store
802 Wyand Avenue
Delmar, Va. 77374

BUSINESS LETTERS

There will probably be a number of times when you will need to write a business letter. On the job, depending upon the nature of your work, you may frequently need to compose such letters. However, off the job as well, you will probably write business letters. For example, letters of application are business letters. So, too, are letters seeking information about products, letters complaining about incorrect bills, bad service, or faulty products, letters ordering products, letters thanking business and professional people for special attention, and letters requesting information from a business or agency.

Whether you are writing a business letter on or off the job, you will want to write it in such a way that it gets the results you are after as promptly as possible. Furthermore, you will want to create an impression of yourself as a responsible, reasonable person. Therefore, you will want to follow all the conventions of business-letter writing. These conventions fall under two headings: content and format.

The content of your business letters should always be courteous, clear, accurate, economical, and complete. The person who reads your letter is likely to be a busy individual who has no time to waste on rude, wordy, vague, or inaccurate letters that lack the necessary information for follow-through. Such letters will only annoy a business or professional person and make him or her less willing to take the action you desire. Also, be sure to type your business letters. Typing will give them a neat, professional appearance.

There are several forms for business letters, and they are all standard and conventional. Because a standard form is expected, you will want to follow one of them to create a favorable impression of yourself. On page 302 is a sample business letter illustrating one of these forms as well as proper content.

About the Heading

1. Give your full address.
2. Provide the date.
3. Use commas between the city and state and between the day of the month and the year.
4. Do not use abbreviations.
5. Type the heading in the upper right-hand corner.
6. If your stationery has a letterhead with address, type the date centered below this information.

About the Inside Address

1. Give the name and title (if known) and the address of the person or firm to whom the letter is addressed.
2. Use a comma between the city and state.
3. Do not use abbreviations.
4. Type the inside address at the left-hand margin, three spaces below the heading.

About the Salutation

1. Type the salutation at the left margin, two spaces below the inside address.
2. Follow the salutation with a colon.
3. Capitalize "Dear."
4. If you do not know the name or sex of the person you are writing to, use "Dear Sir or Ms." or use the person's title, as in "Dear Manager."

About the Body

1. Type the body two spaces below the salutation.
2. Single-space the body and double-space between paragraphs.
3. Indent the first word of each paragraph.
4. Keep your content courteous, businesslike, clear, accurate, and as brief as possible.

About the Closing

1. Capitalize the first word.
2. Place a comma at the end.
3. Position the closing under the heading; double-space after the body before typing the closing.
4. Standard closings are:

Sincerely yours,	Yours truly,
Sincerely,	Yours very truly,
Yours sincerely,	Cordially,

About the Signature

1. Type your name four spaces under the closing.
2. Sign your name above the typed signature.
3. You may type your title or position under your typed name.

About the Envelope

1. Single-space the address and return address in block form.
2. Place a comma between the city and state.
3. Use the two-letter state abbreviations to take advantage of the new mail-sorting equipment.
4. Fold 8½ × 11 paper horizontally in thirds to fit in a long business envelope.

WRITING ASSIGNMENT III

Below are six suggestions for various kinds of business letters. Choose three of them and type three separate letters with envelopes.

1. Type a letter to the admissions officer of a college you might like to transfer to. Request an application, a catalog, and information about financial aid. Inform the college of the date you would like to enter and the subject you plan to major in. (You can get the address from your library.)

2. Type a letter to the Government Printing Office in Washington, D.C., requesting information about toy safety for a school report. Explain the kind of information you want and why you want it. (Your library will have the address.)

3. Type a letter to Acme Business Machines, 179 Gaylord Street, Whitehouse, Minnesota 32190. Explain that the calculator the company mailed you is not working properly. Explain the nature of the problem and the kind of adjustment you desire, and include any other information you think is necessary (the order number, for example).

4. As personnel director for O'Hare Industries, 8890 Jackson Avenue, Milford, Arizona 09934, type a letter to Nathan Burkey offering him a position as foreman of the afternoon shift. Include any information you think is necessary (salary, benefits, duties, for example).

5. Type a letter to the manager of a local store informing her or him of a pleasant experience you had with one of the store's employees. Describe what happened and explain that you would like your letter to be placed in the employee's personnel file. (**Hint:** You could describe special help or particularly courteous treatment that you were given.)

6. Type a letter to a local store explaining that you have received an incorrect bill. Include all the information that would be needed in order to resolve the problem.

COMMITTEE REPORTS

On your job you may be called upon from time to time to write reports. One kind of report you may be asked to handle is the committee report. The purpose of the committee report is to inform people of the findings of a committee. It typically includes:

A statement of the problem or area the committee investigated

A statement of the procedures the committee followed

A statement of the findings of the committee

A statement of the committee's recommendations

Away from the job, you may also find yourself writing committee reports. Many organizations that we belong to form committees to look into various things and report back in writing.

Read the accompanying sample committee report. Notice that it is economical and that it includes no unnecessary detail.

Report of the English Department
Curriculum Committee, January 1981
The English Department curriculum committee, having been asked to determine the need for a freshman-level remedial reading course, arranged for the testing of incoming freshmen during the 1979-80 academic year. The Nelson-Denny Reading Test was administered to 874 freshmen. In addition, questionnaires were sent to all faculty members requesting their opinions of the reading abilities of their students.

The results of the testing indicate that many of our new students have inadequate reading skills. Forty-two percent of the tested students read below the tenth-

```
grade level.  We had a 75 percent response rate to our
questionnaire.  Of the respondents, 55 percent said that
their students have some difficulty reading and
comprehending their textbooks.
     As a result of these preliminary findings, this
committee recommends that the university establish an
elective remedial reading course and requests
authorization to determine the nature of such a course.
```

FORMAL REPORTS

Report writing can be required in many different situations for many different reasons. For example, in business there are progress reports, annual reports, survey reports, cost estimates, new project proposals, policy recommendations, and so on. In science there are grant proposals, reports of findings, and reports similar to those that occur in business (cost estimates, progress reports, and so on). In school, too, reports are a fact of life. If you haven't yet, you probably will in the future be asked to write something like a biology or psychology report. It is worthwhile, then, to take a look at the report as one kind of writing project you may be asked to handle.

Because reports can be written on so many different subjects for so many different reasons, I'm sure you can understand that there is a great deal of variety to formal reports. The format, the kind of information included, and the amount of detail required will all vary according to the purpose, subject, and audience of the report. Thus, a report a stockbroker writes to a company's board of directors explaining the need to change the firm's stock holdings will be very different from the report a charge nurse writes for the chief of nurses explaining the causes of low employee morale in the intensive care unit. Yet despite the fact that one report can vary greatly from another, there are some useful generalizations that can be made.

First, there are basically two kinds of reports: the informational report and the analytical report. The *informational report* presents all the relevant facts about a subject in order to inform the reader. The *analytical report* also presents the relevant facts about a subject, but it goes a step further to analyze and evaluate those facts and perhaps make some suggestions.

Regardless of whether you are writing an informational report or an analytical report, there are five steps you should follow.

1. Define precisely the subject you are investigating.
2. Decide where you will get your information (the library, interviews, questionnaires, company files, and so on).

3. Gather your information.

4. If your report is analytical, decide on your evaluation of the information you found.

5. Write your report (using all the writing principles you have learned).

EXERCISE:
Informational and Analytical Reports

Below are sentences from different reports. Read each sentence and on the basis of its content decide whether the report it came from is informational or analytical. Write an *I* in the blank for informational and an *A* for analytical.

1. _____ The fastest way to increase sales of the HX40 power mower is to run a two-week rebate campaign tied to the May anniversary sale.

2. _____ In 1981–82, the number of reported instances of classroom violence in the Keegan County schools was up 30 percent over the 1980–81 academic year.

3. _____ The 30 percent increase in the number of reported instances of classroom violence in the Keegan County schools in 1981–82 can be attributed to the Board of Education's insistence that all violent episodes be reported within 24 hours.

4. _____ To reduce the violent episodes in Keegan County school classrooms, a private security force should be retained to patrol all high school buildings during school hours.

5. _____ The least expensive way to create 100 additional parking spaces within a quarter mile of campus is to tear down West Hall and turn the land into a parking lot.

A Sample Formal Report

Report on the Advisability of
Changing Insurance Companies

Submitted by Joshua Portage,
Benefits Officer

On June 16, 1981, Beverly Osgood, finance officer, asked me to determine whether Orion United Industries was purchasing the most economical insurance coverage for our employees. My investigation has shown that we are paying more than we have to for our group insurance plan and that there are less expensive plans available that provide the same or better coverage.

Between June 17, 1981, and July 3, 1981, I spoke to representatives of fifteen major insurance companies either in my office or on the phone. Of this number, three companies (Manufacturers' Mutual, Inc., Group Health Care Corp., and Eastern Insurance Co.) claimed they could provide coverage identical to what our employees currently have at an annual savings of $12,000–$19,000. One company, Bell Insurance Company, claims to be able to provide the same program we currently have and add dental coverage without exceeding the premiums we now pay.

On the basis of these findings, I recommend that we solicit bids from as many insurance companies as possible. Once we select the most economical plan for the necessary coverage, we should not renew our present contract with Insurance Industries International.

Below are some things about the sample formal report that you should notice.

1. The report is analytical. That is, the findings are evaluated and a suggestion is made.
2. The report is written in a clear, economical way using precise diction.
3. The report has an introduction that supplies background information and defines the area investigated.
4. The introduction includes a thesis sentence.
5. The report explains how the information was gathered.
6. The report explains what information was discovered.
7. The evaluation or suggestion based on the information discovered appears in the conclusion.

Although it is true that every report cannot be handled in the same way as the sample report, some principles are shown there that always hold true. Any report, whether informational or analytical, should:

1. Be well organized
2. Be complete
3. Be clear
4. Be economical
5. State the area studied
6. State how the information was gathered
7. State what information was found

WRITING ASSIGNMENT IV

Below are six report topics. The first three topics are for the kinds of informational reports you write in school. To write one of these, you will have to go to the library to get a book on the subject you are dealing with. (Your report should give the author, title, and publication data of the source you are using.) The second three topics are for analytical reports. To gather information for one of these, you will have to talk to people on your campus, check articles in the school newspaper, and observe situations on your own.

I suggest that you pick one topic for an informational report and one for an analytical report. Be sure you check the steps for report writing on p. 307 and the list of what to notice about the sample formal report on p. 309.

Topics for Informational Reports
1. **Psychology.** Explain the purpose of defense mechanisms. Also describe three of these mechanisms and how they work.
2. **Biology.** Describe the function of white blood cells and explain how they perform this function.
3. **History.** Explain what "manifest destiny" means and describe the role it played in American history.

Topics for Analytical Reports
1. Evaluate whether your school's parking facilities are adequate and make a recommendation.
2. Evaluate whether the student advisement at your school is adequate and make a recommendation.
3. Determine how safe your campus is at night and make a recommendation.

A FINAL WORD

As you can tell, not all business writing is done on the job. Letters to the editor of a newspaper or magazine, letters to senators and representatives, letters of complaint or praise to businesses, letters seeking information, committee reports—all these can be a part of our nonworking lives. However, on the job your business writing skills may well affect how well you perform. Your letters, memos, and reports will all be a measure of just how sharp you are. Furthermore, the job hunt itself may succeed or fail, at least partly on the basis of your application letters and résumés. So once again it is clear that writing is important far beyond your classroom walls.

Appendix **A**
Vocabulary List

_____

_____

_____

_____

Throughout this book you are asked to look up the words you do not know
the meanings of from the various reading selections. Some of these words
are to be recorded in the spaces below for daily study. Each word is to be
written in the left-hand column, and the dictionary definition that fits the
way the word is used in the selection is to be written in the right-hand column.
In addition, you may use this appendix to record other words that you come
across in your reading and studying.

Vocabulary Word	**Definition**
1. _____	_____
2. _____	_____
3. _____	_____
4. _____	_____
5. _____	_____
6. _____	_____
7. _____	_____
8. _____	_____

9. _____   _____

10. _____   _____

11. _____   _____

12. _____   _____

13. _____   _____

14. _____   _____

15. _____   _____

16. _____   _____

17. _____   _____

18. _____   _____

19. _____   _____

20. _____   _____

21. _____   _____

22. _____   _____

23. _____   _____

24. _____   _____

25. _____   _____

26. _____   _____

27. _____   _____

28. _____   _____

29. _____   _____

30. _____   _____

31. _____   _____

32. _____   _____

33. _____   _____

34. _____   _____

35. _____   _____

36. _____   _____

37. _____   _____

38. _____   _____

39. _____   _____

40. _____   _____

41. _____   _____

42. _____   _____

43. _____   _____

44. _____   _____

45. _____   _____

46. _____   _____

47. _____   _____

48. _____   _____

49. _____   _____

50. _____   _____

51. _____   _____

52. _____   _____

53. _____   _____

54. _____   _____

55. _____   _____

56. _____   _____

57. _____   _____

58. _____   _____

59. _____   _____

60. _____   _____

Appendix **B**
Proofreading, Revising, and Editing Checklist

After writing a first draft, the wise writer examines his or her work carefully to make improvements in organization, content, and style. This is the revising and editing process, the point at which the first draft is worked and reworked from rough form through intermediate drafts to finished copy (see p. 91). The wise writer will leave the first draft for several hours—or even a day or more—to regain objectivity. After the revising and editing are complete and the writer is satisfied with the organization, content, and style, it is time to check carefully for mistakes in grammar and usage. This is the proofreading stage (see pp. 91–92). Once again, the wise writer will leave the work for a time to clear the head and regain objectivity before beginning to proof.

To help you with your revising, editing, and proofreading, a checklist is provided here for you to consult each time you write. The page numbers refer you to the first page of discussions in this text in case you wish to check anything.

REVISING: ORGANIZATION

1. Does your introduction have a lead-in and thesis (pp. 60 and 56)?
2. Is your thesis narrow (p. 58)?

3. Is your lead-in appropriate (p. 60)

4. Do you have at least two body paragraphs (p. 63)?

5. Does each body paragraph have a topic sentence (p. 63)?

6. Do you have a concluding paragraph that brings your theme to a satisfying close (p. 66)?

Hint: Try outlining your theme after you have written it to be sure each detail has a logical placement. If something doesn't "fit" in the outline, rework it, place it somewhere else, or eliminate it.

REVISING: CONTENT

1. Do all your topic sentences relate clearly to your thesis (pp. 56 and 63)?

2. Do all the details in each body paragraph relate clearly to their topic sentence (pp. 38 and 64)?

3. Do you have enough body paragraphs to develop your thesis adequately (p. 63)?

4. Do you have enough detail to develop each of your topic sentences adequately (p. 64)?

Hint: Have someone else read your theme to check for relevant, adequate detail.

EDITING: STYLE

1. Is your diction economical (p. 24)?

2. Is your diction precise (p. 26)?

3. Is your diction free of clichés (p. 27)?

4. Have you achieved sentence variety (p. 214)?

5. Have you used transitions to show relationships between ideas (p. 146)?

6. Have you used coordination to show relationships between ideas (p. 174)?

7. Have you used subordination to show relationships between ideas (p. 176)?

8. Have you considered your audience (p. 199)?

Hint: Read your theme aloud to get a better sense of its flow and rhythm.

PROOFREADING: GRAMMAR AND USAGE

1. Is your writing free of fragments (p. 74)?
2. Is your writing free of run-ons (p. 93)?
3. Do your subjects and verbs agree (p. 103)?
4. Do your pronouns and referents agree in person (p. 208)?
5. Do your pronouns and referents agree in number (p. 206)?
6. Have you avoided ambiguous, implied, and remote pronoun referents (p. 210)?
7. Have you achieved parallelism (p. 239)?
8. Have you avoided inappropriate tense shifts (p. 110)?
9. Have you avoided misplaced and dangling modifiers (p. 212)?
10. Have you punctuated conversation correctly (p. 71)?
11. Have you used captial letters for titles of relatives used like names (p. 73)?
12. Have you used commas between coordinate clauses joined by coordinate conjunctions (pp. 96 and 101)?
13. Have you used commas after introductory subordinate clauses (pp. 99 and 101)?
14. Have you used commas before subordinate clauses showing separation from coordinate clauses (pp. 99 and 101)?
15. Have you used commas to set off interrupters (p. 151)?
16. Have you used commas after long introductory phrases (p. 181)?
17. Have you used commas for items in a series (p. 243)?
18. Have you used commas to set off nonessential relative clauses (p. 180)?
19. Have you used commas between coordinate modifiers (p. 29)?
20. Have you used semicolons correctly (pp. 95 and 102)?
21. Have you used colons correctly (p. 182)?
22. Have you used dashes correctly (p. 183)?
23. Have you used parentheses correctly (p. 183)?
24. Have you used apostrophes correctly (p. 217)?
25. Have you used the frequently confused words correctly (p. 291)?
26. Have you checked spellings?

Hint: For tips on how to proofread, see p. 91.

Appendix C

A Selected List
of General Reference Works

Note: In addition to the works cited below, there are general knowledge and specific subject encyclopedias that provide useful information as well as bibliographic entries. It is a good idea to check these for additions to your working bibliography.

Bibliographic Index: A Cumulative Bibliography of Bibliographies

Biography Index: A Quarterly Index to Biographical Material on Books and Magazines

Book Review Digest

British Humanities Index

Congressional Information Service

Cumulative Book Index

Cumulative Magazine Index

Current Biography

Dictionary of American Biography

Dictionary of American History

Dictionary of National Biography

Essay and General Literature Index

Guide to Reference Books

Humanities Index

International Encyclopedia of the Social Sciences

International Index

McGraw-Hill Encyclopedia of Science and Technology

Monthly Catalog of U.S. Government Publications

Moody's Industrial Manual

New York Times Index

Poole's Index to Periodical Literature

Public Affairs Information Service Index

Reader's Guide to Periodical Literature

Social Sciences Citation Index

Social Sciences and Humanities Index

Social Sciences Index

Subject Guide to Books in Print

Times of London Index

Vertical File Index: A Subject and Title Index to Selected Pamphlet Material

Wall Street Journal Index

Who's Who

Who's Who in America

Who's Who in Finance and Industry

Who's Who of American Women

A Selected List
of Bibliographies and Indexes

APPLIED SCIENCE AND TECHNOLOGY

Applied Science and Technology Index

Bibliography of the Philosophy of Technology

Industrial Arts Index

Nursing Literature Index

Technical Book Review Index

ART

Annotated Bibliography of Fine Art: Painting, Sculpture, Architecture, Arts of Decoration and Illustration

Art Books: A Basic Bibliography on the Fine Arts

The Art Index

Art-Kunst: International Bibliography of Art Books

A Bibliography of Aesthetics and of the Philosophy of the Fine Arts from 1900 to 1932

A Biographical Index of American Artists

The Index of Twentieth Century Artists

Index to Art Periodicals

Index to Reproductions of American Paintings

Index to Reproductions of European Paintings

BIOLOGICAL SCIENCES

Bibliography and Index of North American Carboniferous Brachiopods

Biological and Agricultural Index

Botanical Bibliographies: A Guide to Bibliographic Materials Applicable to Botany

Botany Subject Index

Contributions to a Biosystematic Literature Index

Index to American Botanical Literature

BUSINESS

A Bibliography of Methods of Social and Business Research

Business Periodicals Index

Literature of Executive Management: Selected Books and Reference Sources for the International Businessman

Sources of Business Information

CHEMISTRY

A Guide to the Literature of Chemistry

How to Find Out in Chemistry

Literature Resources for Chemical Process Industries

ECONOMICS

Cumulative Bibliography of Economic Books: 1954–1962

Cumulative Bibliography of Economic Books: 1963–1967

Developmental Change: An Annotated Bibliography

Economics: Bibliographic Guide to Reference Books and Informational Resources

Index to Economic Journals

International Bibliography of Economics

National Development 1776–1966: A Selective and Annotated Guide to the Most Important Articles in English

Select Bibliography of Modern Economic Theory 1870–1929

Special Bibliography in Monetary Economics and Finance

EDUCATION

Bibliographies and Summaries in Education to July 1935

Current Index to Journals in Education

Early Childhood Education: An ERIC Bibliography

Education Index

Educational Documents Index

Educational Finance: An ERIC Bibliography

Educational Media Index

The Literature of Education: A Critical Bibliography, 1945–1970

Philosophy of Education: A Select Bibliography

ELECTRONICS

Annotated Bibliography of Electronic Data Processing

Bibliography of the History of Electronics

Electronics: A Bibliographical Guide

International Computer Bibliography

KWIC Index: A Bibliography of Computer Management

ENGINEERING

Engineering Index Annual

ENGLISH LANGUAGE AND LITERATURE: GENERAL

Annual Bibliography of English Language and Literature

Bibliographical Dictionary of Modern Literature

Bibliography of Comparative Literature

Book Review Index

A Concise Bibliography for Students in English

Comtemporary Authors

Film Index

MLA International Bibliography of Books and Articles on the Modern Languages and Literature

National Library Service Cumulative Book Review Index, 1905–1974

New York Times Book Review Index

Selective Bibliography for the Study of English and American Literature

ENGLISH LANGUAGE AND LITERATURE: AMERICAN LITERATURE

American Bibliography

Articles on American Literature, 1900–1950

Articles on American Literature, 1950–1967

Bibliographical Guide to the Study of Literature of the U.S.

Bibliography of American Literature

Bibliography of Bibliographies in American Literature

Index to American Author Bibliographies

ENGLISH LANGUAGE AND LITERATURE: BLACK LITERATURE

A Bibliography of the Negro in Africa and America

Black African Literature in English since 1952: Works and Criticism

Black Image on the American Stage: A Bibliography of Plays and Musicals, 1770–1970

Index to Periodical Articles by and about Negroes

No Crystal Stair: A Bibliography of Black Literature

ENGLISH LANGUAGE AND LITERATURE: BRITISH LITERATURE

Bibliographical Resources for the Study of Nineteenth Century English Fiction

Bibliography of British Literary Bibliographies

British Authors before 1800

British Literary Resources: A Bibliographical Guide

Cambridge Bibliography of English Literature

A Descriptive Catalogue of the Bibliographies of Twentieth Century British Writers

English Theatrical Literature 1559–1900: A Bibliography Incorporating Lowe's Bibliographical Account

A Register of Bibliographies of the English Language and Literature

ENGLISH LANGUAGE AND LITERATURE: DRAMA

A Bibliographical Guide to Research and Dramatic Art

Bibliography of American Theatre

Bulletin of Bibliography and Dramatic Index

Cumulated Dramatic Index

Dramatic Bibliography

Dramatic Criticism Index

Modern Drama: A Checklist of Critical Literature on Twentieth Century Plays

Play Index

Theatre and Allied Arts: A Guide to Books Dealing with the History, Criticism, and Technic of the Drama and Theatre, and Related Arts and Crafts

ENGLISH LANGUAGE AND LITERATURE: LANGUAGE

American English: A Bibliography

Annual Bibliography of English Language and Literature

A Concise Bibliography for Students of English

English Stylistics: A Bibliography

ENGLISH LANGUAGE AND LITERATURE: MYTH AND FOLKLORE

A Bibliography of North American Folklore and Folksong

Index to Fairy Tales, Myths and Legends

Index to Fairy Tales, 1949–1974; Including Folklore Legends, and Myths in Collections

Motif Index of Folk Literature: A Classification of Narrative Elements in Folktales, Ballads, Myths, Fables, Mediaeval Romances . . .

Religion Mythologies, Folklores: An Annotated Bibliography

ENGLISH LANGUAGE AND LITERATURE: NOVEL

American Fiction: A Contribution towards a Bibliography

American Fiction 1900–1950: A Guide to Information Sources

The American Novel 1789–1959: A Checklist of Twentieth-Century Criticism

The Contemporary English Novel: An Annotated Bibliography of Secondary Sources

The Contemporary Novel: A Checklist of Critical Literature on the British and American Novel since 1945

The Continental Novel: A Checklist of Criticism in English, 1900–1966

English Novel Explication: Criticism to 1972

The English Novel, 1578–1956: A Checklist of Twentieth-Century Criticisms

ENGLISH LANGUAGE AND LITERATURE: POETRY

English Poetry: Select Bibliographical Guides

Granger's Index to Poetry

Poetry Explication: A Checklist of Interpretations since 1925 of British and American Poems Past and Present

Poetry Index

Subject Index to Poetry

Subject Index to Poetry for Children and Young People

ENGLISH LANGUAGE AND LITERATURE: SHORT STORY

Short Fiction Criticism: A Checklist for Interpretations since 1925 of Stories and Novelettes (American, British, Continental) 1800–1958

Short Story Index

Twentieth-Century Short Story Explication: Interpretations, 1900–1966

GEOGRAPHY

International Bibliography of Geography

Introduction to Library Research in Geography

GEOLOGY

Bibliography and Index of Geology Exclusive of North America

Geologic Reference Sources: A Subject and Regional Bibliography to Publications and Maps in the Geological Sciences

Geology, Bibliography and Index

Index of State Geological Survey Publications Issued in Series

HEALTH AND PHYSICAL EDUCATION

Annotated Bibliography on Perceptual-Motor Development

A Bibliography of Dancing

Bibliography of Swimming

Directory of Selected References and Resources for Health Instruction

Guide to Books on Recreation

Health and Development: An Annotated Indexed Bibliography

Index to Folk Dances and Singing Games

HISTORY

Bibliographer's Manual of American History

Bibliographies in American History: Guide to Materials for Research

Bibliography of Modern History

Bibliotheca Americana: A Dictionary of Books Relating to America from Its Discovery to the Present Time

Historical Bibliographies: A Systematic and Annotated Guide

International Bibliography of Historical Sciences

HOME ECONOMICS

Basic Books and Periodicals in Home Economics

Bibliographic Gastronomique

Bibliography of American Cookery Books, 1742–1860

Bibliotheca Gastronomica: A Catalogue of Books and Documents on Gastronomy

Gastronomic Bibliography

Guide to the Literature of Home and Family Life

Recipe Index—1970: The Eater's Guide to Periodical Literature

Regional American Cookery, 1884–1934: A List of Works on the Subject

MATHEMATICS

Cumulative Index: The Mathematics Teachers, 1908–1965

Current Information Sources in Mathematics: An Annotated Guide to Books and Periodicals, 1960–71

Guide to the Literature of Mathematics and Physics

How to Find Out in Mathematics

An Index of Mathematical Tables

Index to Translations Selected by the AMS

International Catalogue of Scientific Literature 1901–1914

Mathematical Reviews Cumulative Indices

MUSIC

American Music: An Information Guide

"The Bibliography of Music." *Musical Quarterly,* 5 (1919), 231–54.

General Bibliography for Music Research

General Index to Modern Musical Literature in the English Language Including Periodicals for the Years 1915–1926

Music and Edgar Allan Poe: A Bibliographical Study

Music Article Guide

The Music Index

Music Reference and Research Materials

Musicalia: Sources of Information in Music

Popular Music: An Annotated Index of American Popular Songs

Seventy-Five Years of New Music: An Information Guide

PHILOSOPHY

Bibliography of Philosophy

Bibliography of Philosophy, 1933–36

Bibliography of Philosophy, Psychology, and Cognate Subjects

Guide to Philosophical Bibliography and Research

PHYSICS

Guide to the Literature of Mathematics and Physics

How to Find Out about Physics

An International Bibliography on Atomic Energy

Physics Literature

Solid State Physics Literature Guides

POLITICAL SCIENCE

Advanced Bibliography of Contents: Political Science and Government

The Information Sources of Political Science

International Bibliography of Political Science

The Literature of Political Science: A Guide for Students, Librarians, and Teachers

Methodology and Research in Political Science: An Annotated Bibliography

Political Science: A Bibliographical Guide to the Literature

Political Science: Bibliographies

PSYCHOLOGY

Annotated Bibliography on Creativity and Giftedness

Bibliography of Bibliographies on Psychology, 1900–1927

Cumulated Subject Index to Psychological Abstracts, 1927–1960

Guide to Library Research in Psychology

Handbook of Psychological Literature

The Harvard List of Books in Psychology

The Index of Psychoanalytic Writings

Mental Health Book Review Index

Psychological Abstracts

Psychological Index, 1894–1935

RELIGION

Annotated Bibliography in Religion and Psychology

A Bibliographical Guide to the History of Christianity

A Bibliography of Bibliographies in Religion

The Catholic Periodical and Literature Index

The Ecumenical Movement in Bibliographical Outline

Index to Religious Periodical Literature

International Bibliography of the History of Religion

A Theological Book List

SOCIAL SCIENCES: GENERAL

Bibliography for Teachers of Social Studies

Book Review Index to Social Science Periodicals

Checklist of Books and Pamphlets in the Social Sciences

International Encyclopedia of the Social Sciences

Jewish Social Studies Cumulative Index

Literature and Bibliography of the Social Sciences: A Guide to Search and Retrieval

Literature of the Social Sciences

London Bibliography of the Social Sciences

Methodology of Social Science Research: A Bibliography

Monthly Catalog of United States Government Publications

Monthly Checklist of State Publications

Research Materials in the Social Sciences

Social Science Citation Index

Social Sciences and Humanities Index

Social Sciences Index

Sources of Information in the Social Sciences

SOCIOLOGY

International Bibliography

Social Sciences Index

Sociological Abstracts

SPEECH AND DRAMA

Bibliography of Costume

Bibliography of English Printed Tragedy

Bibliography of Medieval Drama

Bibliography of Speech and Allied Areas

Bibliography of Speech Education

Bibliography of the American Theatre

A Bibliography of the English Printed Drama to the Restoration

A Bibliography of the Restoration Drama

Britain's Theatrical Periodicals

Chicorel Theater Index to Plays in Anthologies, Periodicals, Discs, and Tapes

Cumulated Dramatic Index, 1909–1949: A Cumulation of the F. W. Faxon Company's Index

Drama Bibliography

Index of Plays, 1800–1926

Index to Full-Length Plays

An Index to One-Act Plays, 1900–1924

Index to Plays in Collections

Index to Plays in Periodicals

Music and Drama

The New York Times Theater Reviews, 1920–1970

Ottemiller's Index to Plays in Collections

Radio and Television: A Selected Bibliography

Rhetoric and Public Address: A Bibliography: 1947–1961

WOMEN'S STUDIES

Bibliography on Women: With Special Emphasis on Their Roles in Science and Society

Guide to Sources of Data on Women and Women Workers for the United States and for Regions, States, and Local Areas

Index to Women of the World from Ancient to Modern Times: Biographies and Portraits

Womankind Media: Current Resources about Women

Women: A Bibliography

Women: A Serial Bibliography

Women's Rights Movement in the U.S., 1948–1970: A Bibliography and Sourcebook

Appendix **E**
How to Make Bibliography Cards

Taken together, your bibliography cards form your working bibliography— the list of sources you will check for information to take notes on. Chapter 9 explains how to find these sources and what information to put on the bibliography cards. Appendixes C and D list works to check for periodical material to include in your working bibliography. In addition, you should check the subject file of the card catalog in your library for book material to add to your working bibliography. This appendix describes the form your bibliography cards should take.

It is wise to be sure that your cards follow the proper format for two reasons. First, it makes putting together the final bibliography for your paper much easier because you will need only to copy from your cards. Second, it ensures that you have all the information you need for the final bibliography, so you do not find yourself frantically searching the library at the last minute for missing information that you must have.

For a book your bibliography card will include the author, title, place of publication, publisher, and date of publication. For a journal your card will include the author, title of the article, title of the journal, volume number, date, and page numbers. In addition, a bibliography card will include the name of the editor or translator, edition if not the first, and series number, if any of these are applicable.

Your bibliography card should also have the Library of Congress or Dewey decimal number in the upper right-hand corner so you can find the work easily in the library without backtracking. Also, you may if you wish write a note to yourself about the content of the work. Below is a sample card for a book and one for a periodical.

HV
5035
.C 36

Carroll, Charles R. *Alcohol: Use, Nonuse, and Abuse*. Dubuque: William C. Brown, 1970.

Check for info. on teen abuse

Book

HQ
769
.M 913

Davidson, Margaret. "When You Both Work." *Parents' Magazine*, April 1977, pp. 66-68.

Periodical

The form your bibliography cards take will depend upon the information relevant to the source. Below are sample forms for various instances. Model your cards after the appropriate form, being sure to copy indentation and punctuation precisely.

SAMPLE BIBLIOGRAPHY FORMS FOR BOOKS

Author, One

Birren, Faber. Color Psychology and Color Therapy.
New York: University Books, 1965.

Authors, Two

Berke, Joseph, and Calvin C. Hernton. The Cannabis
Experience. London: Bristol Typesetting, 1974.

Authors, Three

Richardson, Charles E., Fred V. Hein, and Dana L. Farnsworth. Living: Health, Behavior, and Environment. 6th ed. Glenview, Ill.: Scott, Foresman, 1975.

Authors, More Than Three

Shafer, Raymond P. et al. Marijuana: A Signal of Misunderstanding. New York: New American Library, 1972.

Edition

Langacker, Ronald W. Language and Its Structure: Some Fundamental Linguistic Concepts. 2nd ed. New York: Harcourt, Brace, Jovanovich, 1973.

Editor

Stubbs, Marcia, and Sylvan Barnet, eds. The Little, Brown Reader. 2nd ed. Boston: Little, Brown, 1980.

Encyclopedia

"Abraham Lincoln." The World Book Encyclopedia. 1973 ed.

Reprint

Morton, Frederic. A Nervous Splendor: Vienna 1888/ 1889. 1979; rpt. Boston: Little, Brown, 1980.

A Work in a Series

Bree, Germaine, ed. Camus: A Collection of Critical Essays. Twentieth Century Views. Englewood Cliffs, N.J.: Prentice-Hall, 1962.

Translator

Cervantes, Miguel. Don Quixote. Trans. Peter Matteux. New York: Random House, 1946.

Volumes, A Work of More Than One Volume

> Gottesman, Ronald et al., eds. The Norton Anthology
> of American Literature. 2 vols. New York: W.
> W. Norton, 1979.

Volumes, One of Several Volumes

> Watson, George, ed. The New Cambridge Bibliography
> of English Literature. Vol. II. Cambridge,
> England: Cambridge University Press, 1971.

Note: When the volumes are all published in the same year, the volume number comes after the publication date.

SAMPLE BIBLIOGRAPHY FORMS FOR PERIODICALS

Author, Anonymous

> "Is the CIA Hobbled?" Newsweek, 5 March 1979, pp.
> 41–44.

Author, One

> Marks, John. "Sex, Drugs, and the CIA." Saturday
> Review, 3 Feb. 1979, pp. 12–16.

Authors, Two

> Sweet, Charles A., Jr., and Harold R. Blythe, Jr.
> " 'Try It; You'll Like It': A Primer for Edu-
> cational Television in the Classroom." College
> English, 39 (Jan. 1978), 608–616.

Journal with Continuous Pagination

> Cramer, Phebe. "Defense Mechanisms in Adolescence."
> Developmental Psychology, 15 (1979), 476–77.

Journal with Separate Pagination

> Donovan, Edwin J., and John F. Sullivan. "Police
> Response to Family Disputes." FBI Law Enforce-
> ment Bulletin, 43 (Sept. 1974), 3–6.

Magazine, Monthly

> Mayer, Jean. "Food Fortification: How Much Is
>   Enough?" Family Health, Feb. 1979, pp. 48–49.

Magazine, Weekly

> Greenfield, Meg. "A Test of Imagination." Newsweek,
>   23 March 1980, p. 88.

Newspaper

> "Philadelphia Electric Says Unit Closed Down on Its
>   Nuclear Plant." The Wall Street Journal,
>   6 March 1980, p. 1.

How to Write Footnotes and End Notes

Every paraphrase and quotation in your paper should be acknowledged in a note so the reader knows the exact location of every borrowing in case she or he wishes to investigate any material further. To signal that a note is supplied, place a raised note number after the paraphrase or quotation. These numbers run consecutively throughout your paper; do not begin over again with number 1 on each page. Notes can be footnotes at the bottoms of pages, or they can be end notes at the end of the paper. Ask your instructor which method you should use.

As with bibliography citations, note citations have a standard form. For the most part, bibliography and note forms have much in common. However, there are significant differences in content, punctuation, and indentation. A note for a book is different from a bibliography citation because the note has a raised note number, the author's first name appears first, a comma follows the author's name, the publication information appears in parentheses, the specific pages used are cited, and the first line is indented. A periodical note differs from a bibliography citation because the note has a raised note number, the author's first name appears first, a comma follows the author's name, a comma appears after the title of the article, the specific pages used are cited, and the first line is indented.

When writing a note, you should model your form after the appropriate form below.

SAMPLE NOTE FORMS: BOOKS

Author, One

 [1] Faber Birren, <u>Color Psychology and Color Therapy</u>
(New York: University Books, 1965), p. 31.

Authors, Two

 [2] Joseph Berke and Calvin C. Hernton, <u>The Cannabis</u>
<u>Experience</u> (London: Bristol Typesetting,
1974), p. 122.

Authors, Three

 [3] Charles E. Richardson, Fred V. Hein, and Dana L.
Farnsworth, <u>Living: Health, Behavior, and En-</u>
<u>vironment,</u> 6th ed. (Glenview, Ill.: Scott,
Foresman, 1975), pp. 35–36.

Authors, More Than Three

 [4] Raymond P. Shafer et al., <u>Marijuana: A Signal of</u>
<u>Misunderstanding</u> (New York: New American Li-
brary, 1972), p. 97.

Edition

 [5] Ronald W. Langacker, <u>Language and Its Structure:</u>
<u>Some Fundamental Linguistic Concepts,</u> 2nd ed.
(New York: Harcourt, Brace, Jovanovich, 1973),
pp. 9–10.

Editor

 [6] Marcia Stubbs and Sylvan Barnet, eds., <u>The Little,</u>
<u>Brown Reader</u> (Boston: Little, Brown, 1980), p.
80.

Encyclopedia

 [7] William G. Sinnigen, ''Lombard,'' <u>The World Book</u>
<u>Encyclopedia,</u> 1973 ed.

Reprint

⁸ Frederic Morton, <u>A Nervous Splendor: Vienna 1888/ 1889</u> (1979; rpt. Boston: Little, Brown, 1980), p. 13.

A Work in a Series

⁹ Germaine Bree, ed., <u>Camus: A Collection of Critical Essays,</u> Twentieth Century Views (Englewood Cliffs, N.J.: Prentice-Hall, 1962), pp. 8-9.

Translator

¹⁰ Miguel Cervantes, <u>Don Quixote,</u> trans. Peter Matteux (New York: Random House, 1946), pp. 148-151.

Volumes, One of Several Volumes

¹¹ George Watson, ed., <u>The New Cambridge Bibliography of English Literature,</u> II (Cambridge, England: Cambridge University Press, 1971), pp. 133-34.

Note: When the volumes are all published in the same year, the volume number comes after the publication date.

SAMPLE NOTE FORMS: PERIODICALS

Author, Anonymous

¹² "Is the CIA Hobbled?" <u>Newsweek,</u> 5 March 1979, p. 42.

Author, One

¹³ John Marks, "Sex, Drugs, and the CIA," <u>Saturday Review,</u> 3 Feb. 1979, pp. 15-16.

Authors, Two

[14] Charles A. Sweet and Harold R. Blythe, Jr., " 'Try It; You'll Like It': A Primer for Educational Television in the Classroom," <u>College English,</u> 39 (Jan. 1978), 610–11.

Journal with Continuous Pagination

[15] Phebe Cramer, "Defense Mechanisms in Adolescence," <u>Developmental Psychology,</u> 15 (1979), 476.

Journal with Separate Pagination

[16] Edwin J. Donovan and John F. Sullivan, "Police Response to Family Disputes," <u>FBI Law Enforcement Bulletin,</u> 43 (Sept. 1974), 5–6.

Magazine, Monthly

[17] Jean Mayer, "Food Fortification: How Much Is Enough?" <u>Family Health,</u> Feb. 1979, p. 48.

Magazine, Weekly

[18] Meg Greenfield, "A Test of Imagination," <u>Newsweek,</u> 23 March 1980, p. 88.

Newspaper

[19] "Philadelphia Electric Says Unit Closed Down on Its Nuclear Plant," <u>The Wall Street Journal,</u> 6 March 1980, p. 1.

Sample End Notes
and Bibliography Pages

Below are sample end notes and bibliography pages for you to study. At the end of each, there is a list of points to notice about the way these pages are set up.

END NOTES

1 James Fixx, <u>The Complete Book of Running</u> (New York: Random House, 1977), p. 23.

2 Fixx, p. 15.

3 William Glasser, M.D., <u>Positive Addiction</u> (New York: Harper & Row, 1976), p. 104.

4 George Sheehan, M.D., <u>Dr. Sheehan on Running</u> (New York: Bantam Books, 1978), p. 189.

5 Glasser, p. 104.

6 Glasser, pp. 104–105.

7 Glasser, p. 2.

8 Glasser, p. 123.

[9] A. H. Ismail and L. E. Trachtman, "Jogging the Imagination," Psychology Today, March 1978, p. 79.

[10] Ismail and Trachtman, pp. 81–82.

[11] Glasser, p. 49.

[12] Hal Higdon, "Can Running Cure Mental Illness?" Runner's World, Jan. 1978, p. 39.

[13] Hal Higdon, "Can Running Cure Mental Illness?" p. 39.

[14] Fixx, p. 16.

[15] Hal Higdon, "Can Running Cure Mental Illness?" p. 36.

[16] Hal Higdon, "Can Running Put Mental Patients on Their Feet?" Runner's World, Feb. 1978, p. 36.

[17] Hal Higdon, "Can Running Put Mental Patients on Their Feet?" p. 38.

[18] Hal Higdon, "Can Running Put Mental Patients on Their Feet?" p. 39.

[19] Hal Higdon, "Can Running Put Mental Patients on Their Feet?" p. 40.

[20] Hal Higdon, "Can Running Put Mental Patients on Their Feet?" p. 38.

[21] Hal Higdon, "Can Running Cure Mental Illness?" p. 39.

[22] David A. Mathison, "Running the Blues Away," Runner's World, Dec. 1978, p. 8.

[23] "Psychiatrists Tell Depressed Patients to Hit the Road," Executive Fitness Newsletter, 1 July 1978, p. 3.

[24] "Psychiatrists Tell Depressed Patients to Hit the Road," p. 3.

25 John H. Greist et al., "Running Out of Depression," The Physician and Sports Medicine, 6
(Dec. 1978), 55.

26 Roy Hattersley, "Jogging Along," New Statesman,
31 (March 1978), 431.

27 Fixx, p. 15.

28 George Sheehan, M.D., Running and Being: The Total Experience (New York: Simon and Schuster,
1978), p. 56.

29 Fixx, pp. 15–16.

30 Fixx, p. 14.

31 Sheehan, Dr. Sheehan on Running, p. 205.

What to Notice about the End Notes

The pages are headed End Notes because the notes are compiled separately at the end of the text of the paper rather than at the bottom of pages.

1. The first line of each note is indented five spaces, and subsequent lines are at the left margin.

2. The note number is typed slightly above the line—roll the carriage one notch toward you.

3. The lines of each note are double-spaced and there is a double-space between each note.

4. The notes are numbered consecutively throughout the paper and on the note page(s).

5. After a first complete note citation has been given for a source, the next citations for that source may be in a short form consisting of the author's last name and the page number. See note 2 for an example of this.

6. If more than one source by the same author is used, the short form must also contain the title. See note 17 for an example of this.

7. When a note cites more than one page (except for a journal), pp. precedes the numbers. See note 6 for an example of this.

8. When a question mark or exclamation point appears at the end of an article title, that mark takes the place of the comma that ordinarily appears. See note 12 for an example of this.

BIBLIOGRAPHY

Fixx, James. The Complete Book of Running. New York:
    Random House, 1977.

Glasser, William, M.D. Positive Addiction. New York:
    Harper & Row, 1976.

Greist, John H. et al. "Running Out of Depression."
    The Physician and Sports Medicine, 6 (Dec. 1978),
    49–56.

Hattersley, Roy. "Jogging Along." New Statesman, 31
    (March 1978), 431.

Higdon, Hal. "Can Running Cure Mental Illness?" Run-
    ner's World, Jan. 1978, pp. 36–43.

Higdon, Hal. "Can Running Put Mental Patients on Their
    Feet?" Runner's World, Feb. 1978, pp. 36–43.

Ismail, A. H., and L. E. Trachtman. "Jogging the Imag-
    ination." Psychology Today, March 1978, pp. 79–
    82.

Mathison, David A. "Running the Blues Away." Runner's
    World, Dec. 1978, p. 8.

"Psychiatrists Tell Depressed Patients to Hit the
    Road." Executive Fitness Newsletter, 1 July 1978,
    p. 3.

Sheehan, George, M.D. Dr. Sheehan on Running. New
    York: Bantam Books, 1978.

Sheehan, George, M.D. Running and Being: The Total Ex-
    perience. New York: Simon and Schuster, 1978.

What to Notice about the Bibliography Page

1. The bibliography appears in alphabetical order according to the last name of the author.

2. If no author is given for a source, the source is alphabetized by the first important word in the title. See the ninth citation for an example of this.

3. The first line of each citation is at the left margin, and subsequent lines are indented five spaces.

4. Each line of the citations is double-spaced and there is a double-space between citations.

5. Raised numbers are not used.

6. Citations for articles in periodicals note all the pages the article spans.

7. Citations for books contain no page references.

Appendix **H**
Additional Exercises

SENTENCE FRAGMENTS

A. Some of the word groups below are sentences because they express complete thoughts. However, some of the word groups are sentence fragments because they do not express complete thoughts. In the space provided, write an *S* if the word group is a sentence. If the word group is a fragment, rewrite it to make it a sentence.

Example: Since Marcus was always so kind.

Correction: Since Marcus was always so kind, everyone thought highly of him.

1. After finishing her last exam. _____

_____

2. His favorite fishing spot, which is not very far from here. _____

_____

3. When I walked into the kitchen, I instantly smelled the leaking gas. _____

_____

4. Before a student can register. _____

_____

5. The worst thing about being in a hospital. _____

_____

6. Who would have thought Dr. Belson could make geology so interesting? _____

_____

7. The nurse explaining the proper diet for someone with diabetes. _____

_____

8. Only if my grades are high enough this term. _____

_____

9. In the middle of the yard behind the oak tree. _____

_____

10. Whenever you can make it. _____

_____

11. My youngest brother being the best tennis player on his high school team. _____

_____

12. Before leaving please turn off the lights. _____

_____

13. After the last customer had left the drugstore. _____

_____

14. By the time I get to class in the morning. _____

_____

15. Juan, who is the only one who has a van. _____

_____

16. Perhaps it would be better if you took someone with you to carry the boxes. ____

_____

17. While Kevin was giving his German shepherd a bath. _____

_____

18. My sister who married her childhood sweetheart. _____

_____

19. The pressure of taking final exams. _____

_____

20. The happy toddler playing in the sandbox and making sand pies. _____

_____

B. The paragraph below contains some sentence fragments. Rewrite it in the space provided to eliminate the fragments.

When Carl walked into his first college class that September morning. He felt alone and afraid. Quickly he surveyed the room, but he saw not one familiar face. The only empty chair in the front, so he took it. Because the professor had not arrived yet. There was a sound of quiet chatter among the students. Carl being too shy and nervous to strike up a conversation. He just sat, wondering if he had made a mistake enrolling in school. Then a studious-looking guy next to Carl leaned over and asked, "Is this History 101?" Instantly Carl felt relieved. At least someone else seemed as unsure as he did. "Yes," Carl replied, "it is." Just then Dr. Stout entered the room. He moved his eyes across the rows of students. And smiled broadly. Then Carl knew he had made the right decision.

_____

_____

_____

_____

_____

_____

_____

_____

_____

_____

_____

RUN-ON SENTENCES

A. Some of the word groups below are correct sentences. However, some of them are run-on sentences because they contain at least two complete thoughts (coordinate clauses) that are not correctly joined. In the space provided, write a *C* if the word group is a correct sentence and *RO* if the word group is a run-on.

1. _____ Breakfast is served at 7:00 A.M. in my dorm, I can never manage to be up that early.

2. _____ Phil was never one to enjoy dancing; his wife loves it but never gets to go because Phil won't take her.

3. _____ I could never afford to pay my own tuition that's why I'm so grateful for this scholarship.

4. _____ Michael has two tickets to the Raiders' game on Sunday, however, he can't go, so he's giving them to me.

5. _____ Whenever you decide if you want to go, let Maureen know.

6. _____ Joyce is completely out of money, therefore, she has to quit school and work for a while.

7. _____ First we must decide whether we really need a new car, then we can worry about how to pay for it.

8. _____ Cal and Nick are leaving tomorrow for the Smoky Mountains that's just the kind of vacation spot I'd enjoy.

9. _____ Although the winters here have been fairly mild, Mom and Dad still want to move to a warm climate.

10. _____ When Paul said he was quitting his job, I was amazed because he always said that he loved his work.

B. Each of the word groups below is a run-on sentence. Correct each one according to the directions given. The first one is done for you as an example.

1. Paulette left work at 5:00 because she didn't get home until 8:00, everyone was worried.

Use a comma and coordinate conjunction: ___Paulette left work at 5:00, but because she___

___didn't get home until 8:00, everyone was worried._____

2. I don't understand why you suddenly changed your mind yesterday you seemed so anxious to go.

Use a semicolon: _____

_____

3. The young bride's first meal was a disaster she was so anxious to do well that she got nervous and burned everything.

Use a period and capital: _____

_____

_____

4. The rain held off until late afternoon we were able to complete seven innings of the game.

Use an introductory subordinate clause: _____

_____

5. Beth decided to go on for her master's degree she felt it would help her get a higher paying job.

Use a comma and a coordinate conjunction: _____

_____

_____

6. Now is not the best time to invest in the stock market the economy is just too unpredictable.

Use a semicolon: _____

_____

7. If I were you, I would wait a year before buying a house interest rates just may come down.

Use a period and a capital: _____

_____

_____

8. Andy just cannot be depended on it would be a mistake to put him in charge of organizing the fund raiser.

Use an introductory subordinate clause: _____

_____

_____

9. I think Julie is the best person for the job Greg agrees with me.

Use a comma and coordinate conjunction: _____

_____

10. Jeffrey believes he can get a part-time job without much trouble I have my doubts about that.

Use an introductory subordinate clause: _____

_____

_____

C. Rewrite the following paragraph to eliminate the run-on sentences.

I never understood why anyone would want a big wedding, it always seems to cause so many problems. In the first place someone's feelings always get hurt.

No matter how big the guest list is, some people are left out they end up feeling slighted and angry. Then there's the hassle of all the preparations. The caterer, the band, the flowers, the hall, the invitations, the clothes, the countless details— by the time these are all arranged, the bride, the groom, and their families are nervous wrecks. And you can be sure that at the last minute at least six things will go wrong, causing complete hysteria. Of course, the bride's family gets to pay for the privilege of experiencing all this aggravation. The cost is thousands of dollars. This is money that often must be borrowed the family of the bride spends years paying off the debt. And it's all for just a one-day event. If you ask me, all couples should elope, it's cheaper, easier on the nerves, and just as legal.

_____

_____

_____

_____

_____

_____

_____

_____

_____

_____

_____

_____

_____

SUBJECT—VERB AGREEMENT

A. In the following sentences, circle the correct verb.

1. Both your sister and my brother (believe/believes) that our relationship will not last.

2. The object of these exercises (are/is) to give you extra practice.

3. It's very clear that each of us (want/wants) something different from life.

4. Either the man next door or the teenagers down the street (is/are) watching the house while we're on vacation.

5. All the kittens in the litter (are/is) black with touches of white.

6. The membership committee (maintain/maintains) that we should have twelve new members by September.

7. Lying by the side of the road (was/were) a set of old tires.

8. There (is/are) a group of antinuclear demonstrators picketing outside the state office building.

9. The tablecloths that I made (is/are) selling well at the church flea market.

10. Neither my parents nor my sister (understand/understands) why I want to join the Peace Corps.

11. My collection of antique chairs (is/are) now worth several thousand dollars.

12. One of the members of our team (is/are) sure to be voted the most valuable player.

13. Six gallons of milk (were/was) drunk by our family in just one week.

14. There (is/are) three of us beginning work this week.

15. Thirty minutes (is/are) plenty of time to complete this exam.

16. The boys who (sing/sings) in the church choir are all sopranos.

17. Either Ted or his sister (delivers/deliver) our newspaper each evening.

18. Apple pie and coffee (is/are) a favorite American snack.

19. At the edge of the crowd (was/were) the scout troup waiting to see if help would be needed.

20. All of us (need/needs) a chance to get away at least once a year.

B. Below is a list of phrases. Write an *S* in the blank if the phrase takes a singular verb. Write a *P* in the blank if the phrase takes a plural verb.

1. _____ The crowd of shoppers

2. _____ Either Jim or his parents

3. _____ The sled and the toy cars

4. _____ Six of us

5. _____ Everyone who

6. _____ A pie and two cakes

7. _____ One of them

8. _____ Neither my children nor my husband

9. _____ Each of us

10. _____ The pile of dirty socks

TENSE SHIFT

A. In the following paragraphs, circle the verb forms that are incorrect because they represent inappropriate shifts in tense.

The moment we pulled out of the driveway, I knew the simple trip to the grocery store wouldn't be so simple. For no apparent reason five-year-old Nathan punched his three-year-old brother Bobby, which caused Bobby to let out that glass-shattering scream of his. "Stop it right now," I hollered to Nathan over Bobby's yells. "Mommy, make him stop looking at me," is Nathan's response. I took a deep breath.

Less than a block from the house, Bobby takes off his seat belt and starts to climb into the front seat. (Since I read once that children ride safer in the back seat, I never allow Nathan and Bobby to sit in the front.) I pulled down a side street, stopped the car, and returned Bobby to his place. But each time I buckled him in, he unbuckles the belt. Finally I had no choice—I slapped his hand. There's another glass-shattering scream.

As I started up the car again, I turned on the radio to drown out the boys' bickering. It doesn't work, so I resort to bribery. "If you two can keep quiet all the way to the store," I said, "I'll buy you each a pack of gum." Ah, it was quiet at last.

But it doesn't last. Once we were inside the store, the nagging began. "Buy me a toy, Mommy." "Buy some Kool Aid, Mommy." "I wanna get some candy, Mommy." That was all I could stand, so I took both little monsters by the hand and dragged them to the car. Of course, they are crying all the way—but then so was I. We drove home, all of us upset. But once we were in the house, everything got back to normal. Nathan ran to me and said, "Mommy, make him stop looking at me."

B. In the following sentences, there are some inappropriate tense shifts. Cross out the incorrect verb forms and write the correct verb forms above the incorrect ones.

1. Maureen stormed into the room, slammed the door, and angrily takes her seat.

2. When Willis finished his second piece of chocolate cake, he said, "If there is any more, I'd like a third helping." Mrs. French gets up to cut him yet another piece.

3. By the time I completed the exam, everyone had already left, except one other student who is sitting in the back sound asleep.

4. I went home to visit during Christmas vacation, but I discovered that everything there seems strange and unfamiliar.

5. When I come to the end of a book, I always feel that I had learned something and was a better person for it.

6. Before Lucille leaves, the gang planned a surprise going-away party at her favorite restaurant.

7. At the beginning of each class, Professor Simon always tells a joke. That's one of the things that made him such a popular teacher.

8. After he opened the beautifully wrapped gift, Steve asks, "How did you know I wanted a ski sweater?"

9. At first I thought college was impossible. Next I realize that it was rather enjoyable. Now I believe it is a totally satisfying experience.

10. The telephone rang, but by the time I ran in from the yard, it stops.

TRANSITIONS

A. In the following paragraphs, circle each transition and write above it the relationship it signals. The first one is done for you as an example.

Admitting a point

(Although) we had been warned about them, my husband and I were not prepared for the panhandlers in New York City. During the early days of our honeymoon, we managed to brush off these freeloaders, but the last afternoon of our stay, we succumbed. We were sitting in a steak house—one of those places that operates like a cafeteria. All around us were what we presumed to be native New Yorkers. I was just beginning to cut my steak when I noticed an elderly woman in shabby clothes. She approached a couple across from us; they shook their heads—a definite no. Next, the woman slowly made her way to the couple one table over from us. Just like the other couple, they shook their heads—another definite no. Now my husband saw her too. We both realized it was only a matter of time before the woman reached our table.

We tried to focus on our food; however, neither one of us felt much like eating. As a result we decided to leave. Certainly that would solve our problem—we would leave before the beggar reached us. We stood and Brian left a dollar to the right of his plate for the waitress who filled our coffee cups. Then we headed for the door. But we hadn't moved quickly enough.

The old lady met us as we walked between the tables. "A few pennies please, kind sir," she pleaded to Brian. Brian and I exchanged painful glances. We didn't want to be taken for suckers in this sophisticated town, so we both shook our heads no and kept walking.

Once outside, Brian and I felt dreadful. Inside we had felt awkward, but now we felt hardhearted. It was for this reason that we turned at the same time and walked back into the restaurant. We found the old woman, quickly gave her a dollar, and left once again.

Had we been suckers? Maybe, but we undoubtedly felt relieved.

B. Rewrite each pair of sentences below to include a transition that demonstrates the relationship given at the left. If you wish, you may combine sentences. Try mixing the placement of your transitions so that some appear at the beginning, some at the end, and some in the middle of your sentences. The first one is done for you as an example.

1. Contrast: Timing is very important to a comedian. Good material is more important.

Timing is very important to a comedian. Good material is more important, however.

2. Addition: Our rose garden is doing very well. Our vegetable garden is doing even better.

_____

_____

3. Comparison: Paul has always been bothered by heights. Crowds have always made him nervous.

_____

_____

4. Time: The homecoming game was over by 4:00. Everybody met at Kilcawley Center for cider and donuts.

_____

_____

5. Cause and effect: Katie researched her paper carefully. Professor Walton found it well detailed and interesting.

_____

_____

6. Purpose: To stay on the team, Ralph must raise his grades by November. He is studying four hours every night.

_____

_____

7. Emphasis: _Inherit the Wind_ is the best play I've seen at the Community Playhouse. It's the best play I've seen anywhere.

_____

_____

8. Illustration: Tuition costs are rising faster than students expected. At our school they are up 40 percent from five years ago.

_____

_____

9. Summary or classification: In our city there is more armed robbery, assault, rape, and murder than ever before. Crime seems to be running out of control.

_____

_____

10. Admitting a point: The life of a teacher is not an easy one. The job is gratifying in many ways.

_____

_____

11. Contrast: This is the furniture I would like to have in my apartment. It is far too expensive for me.

_____

_____

12. Addition: My job as a waitress does not pay very well. The hours are inconvenient.

_____

_____

13. Cause and effect: Jan worked a double shift at the hospital today. He looks exhausted.

_____

_____

14. Illustration: A campus job has many advantages. Work hours can easily be scheduled around class time.

_____

_____

15. Admitting a point: Living at home has its disadvantages. You can't beat the rent.

_____

_____

COORDINATION

A. Connect the following pairs of coordinate clauses with the coordinator at the left. Remember to use a comma before the coordinate conjunction.

1. And: The trip to Nashville through Kentucky is a beautiful one. It can be made in only nine hours.

_____

_____

2. But: I was able to get almost all my books used this quarter. My zoology book is newly published, so I had to pay the full price.

_____

_____

_____

3. Or: The restaurant at the Holiday Inn serves good food. You may enjoy eating at the new place that opened downtown.

_____

_____

_____

4. Nor: I never liked roller coasters very much. I do not care for ferris wheels.

_____

_____

5. For: You will have to tell Dwight he can't ride with us. There is no room left in my car.

_____

_____

6. So: Good writing skills are necessary throughout college. I suggest you take a composition course in your freshman year.

_____

_____

7. Yet: Of course flying is the fastest way to travel. I still dread the flight because I fear a crash.

_____

_____

8. Semicolon: Lying on this beach is so relaxing. I wish I could spend the rest of the week here.

_____

_____

B. Write sentences using each of the eight coordinators. Subjects are suggested for you, but you may choose your own if you like. Remember to use a comma before a coordinate conjunction that connects coordinate clauses.

1. Summer _____

_____

2. Your best friend _____

_____

3. Traffic _____

_____

4. Adolescence _____

_____

5. Television _____

_____

6. Eating out _____

_____

7. Getting up in the morning _____

_____

8. Receiving a present _____

_____

SUBORDINATION

A. Below are pairs of coordinate clauses. Make each pair one sentence by using subordination. The subordinate conjunction you should use is written at the left. Remember to use commas after an introductory subordinate clause and before a final subordinate clause that shows separation from the rest of the sentence. The first one is done for you as an example.

1. When: The eleven o'clock news came on. Joey switched off the set and went to bed.

When the eleven o'clock news came on, Joey _____

switched off the set and went to bed. _____

2. Although: Kate's grade point average dropped last term. She managed to keep her scholarship.

_____

_____

3. Since: The price of movies these days is outrageous. Fewer people are seeing them.

_____

_____

4. Because: Jackie has been so irritable lately. Most of her friends are growing annoyed with her.

_____

_____

5. While: I understand the point you are making. I still find it hard to agree with you.

_____

_____

6. As if: She didn't have a care in the world. Jane hummed as she walked down the street.

_____

_____

7. Until: The police levy cannot pass. Voters have a change of heart.

_____

_____

8. Where: Unemployment is high. Morale will be low.

_____

_____

9. As long as: The public withholds support. Our schools will be second-rate.

_____

_____

10. Unless: You change your mind and decide to come. I will be forced to go alone.

_____

_____

B. For each of the topics below, write two sentences. One sentence should have a subordinate clause at the beginning (place a comma after the clause). One sentence should have a subordinate clause at the end (place a comma before the clause if it shows some separation from the rest of the sentence).

1. Pizza: a. _____

_____

b. _____

_____

2. Soap operas: a. _____

_____

b. _____

_____

3. Dancing: a. _____

_____

b. _____

_____

4. Baseball: a. _____

_____

b. _____

_____

5. Grades: a. _____

_____

b. _____

_____

6. Snow: a. _____

_____

b. _____

_____

7. A new car: a. _____

_____

b. _____

_____

8. Cleaning: a. _____

_____

b. _____

_____

9. Homework: a. _____

_____

b. _____

_____

10. Grammar: a. _____

_____

b. _____

_____

PRONOUNS AND REFERENTS

A. In the following sentences, circle the correct pronoun.

1. When a person feels depressed, (he or she, they) should seek out the company of others.

2. Anybody who wishes to join us should be at the church parking lot with (their, his or her) skiing equipment at 6:00 A.M.

3. Both doctors felt that (her or his, their) long years of study were worthwhile.

4. Each of the mothers brought (their, her) children to the park in the morning.

5. Some of the football players felt that (their, his) losing season was due to poor coaching.

6. Either Don or Carlo can bring (his, their) boat so we can water-ski.

7. If everybody does (his or her, their) share, we can clean up this mess in an hour.

8. Anyone who works while attending school must budget (her or his, their) time carefully.

9. People who like to brag about (his or her, their) accomplishments really bother me.

10. If someone arrives before I get back, tell (them, her or him) I'll be home by noon.

B. Each of the following groups of sentences has a problem with remote reference, implied reference, or ambiguous reference. Write an *R* if the problem is remote reference; write an *I* if the problem is implied reference; write an *A* if the problem is ambiguous reference. Then rewrite just the sentences you have to in order to eliminate the problem. The first one is done for you as an example.

1. I put the baby in her crib for a nap and decided to rest for a while myself. As I walked to the bedroom, the phone rang. It was my sister, who needed a recipe I promised her. After I gave her the recipe, she asked me to talk for a bit. I hated to say no and ended up on the phone for an hour. Finally we hung up and just as I closed my eyes, she woke up ready to eat.

R. Finally we hung up and just as I closed my

eyes, the baby woke up ready to eat.

2. The kindergarten teacher was shocked to see Denise and Karen fighting. She was pulling her hair and screaming quite loudly.

_____

_____

3. Matt and Joey are two of the most thoughtful children I know; it is the main reason I enjoy being around them so much.

_____

_____

4. When Mother entered the room, she was surprised to see David and Mickey cleaning. He has never before cleaned up without being told to.

_____

_____

5. Denise had left the children for only five minutes, but when she returned she couldn't believe the mess they had made with their toys in the mud. They were absolutely filthy.

_____

_____

6. Little Bobby walked into the kitchen, put his popsicle on the counter, and headed for the den. He switched on the television and was delighted to find his favorite cartoon show on. After the cartoons were over, he headed back to the kitchen and was dismayed to discover it had melted into a pool of orange.

_____

_____

7. Greg is a beautifully sensitive child. If encouraged, it should help him grow into a warm, compassionate adult.

_____

_____

8. Heidi brought her doll and her doll carriage. It was one of the cutest toys I had seen for a girl that age.

_____

_____

9. Little Jeffrey is such a lovable child. It is why everyone enjoys him so much.

_____

_____

10. When I opened the refrigerator door, two fresh eggs and a bottle of ketchup fell out and broke all over the floor and wall. I was furious because I had just cleaned it the day before.

_____

_____

DANGLING AND MISPLACED MODIFIERS

A. Write sentences beginning with each of the modifiers shown. To avoid a dangling or misplaced modifier, write the words the modifier describes immediately after the modifier. The first one is done for you as an example.

1. While washing the car: *While washing the car I wore my* *bathing suit and got a bad burn.*

2. Driving down the country road _____

_____

3. Before eating supper _____

_____

4. Unaware that Gary hated practical jokes _____

_____

5. Being the understanding instructor that he is _____

_____

6. Confused by Lee's anger _____

_____

7. When teaching a child to swim _____

_____

8. Singing as she worked _____

_____

9. Fearful that the baby would wake up _____

_____

10. After studying for five hours _____

_____

B. Some of the following sentences are correct, and some contain dangling or misplaced modifiers. If a sentence is correct, write *C* in the space provided. If a sentence contains a dangling or misplaced modifier, rewrite the sentence to eliminate the problem.

1. While eating breakfast, my sociology book was open so I could study. _____

_____

2. After washing windows all day, my back was aching.

_____

3. The young mother stood at the hospital's nursery window and admired her infant daughter with her head pressed against the glass. _____

_____

4. Rumbling down the country road, the ancient pickup truck sputtered and backfired.

_____

5. The child sobbed as she picked up the pieces of the broken doll I was watching in the park.

_____

_____

6. After counting the change carefully, the piggy bank was placed on the shelf by the boy.

_____

_____

7. Before beginning such a long vacation, my car must have a tune-up and oil change.

_____

_____

8. Walking home at night, my nervous whistle was the only sound I could hear. _____

_____

9. If they are grape, my children can eat a dozen popsicles at one time. _____

_____

10. Although Fred was fired for being late too often, I'm sure he has learned his lesson and will do well in our firm.

_____

_____

PARALLELISM

A. In the space provided, write *P* if the sentence has parallel structure and *NP* if the sentence has nonparallel structure.

1. _____ Philip was having trouble deciding whether he should stay in school, get a job, or move in with his folks.

2. _____ The senior class decided having a class picnic would be more fun than to have a prom.

3. _____ When the nurse entered the examining room, she told Mrs. Summers that she would have to lose five pounds, get more exercise, and that she should avoid salt.

4. _____ Mom always did like small family gatherings better than having large reunions.

5. _____ I've always admired Jennifer because she is both intelligent and popular.

6. _____ Becoming a professional dancer requires dedication, years of practice, and you must be willing to sacrifice.

7. _____ Tom explained that he would either join the navy after graduation, or he would go to a trade school to study electronics.

8. _____ We checked in the field, behind the garage, and looked behind the shed, but we couldn't find Snoopy.

9. _____ A vacation at home can be not only inexpensive but also relaxing.

10. _____ You must either buy a car that uses less gasoline, or you must join a car pool if you are to save any money.

B. The following sentences lack parallel structure. Rewrite them so that the parallelism problems are eliminated.

1. The caterer explained that roast chicken would be less expensive than serving roast beef at the reception.

_____

_____

2. Poor Gwen was having a terrible day; she lost her doll, broke her wagon, and she fell and bruised her forehead.

_____

_____

3. I have found as I've gotten older that I must exercise regularly, eat less, and that I must get more sleep.

_____

_____

4. Buddy was amazed that Pat would neither help fix the car nor would he lend him a wrench.

_____

_____

5. When he learned that tickets for the big play-off game were still available, Tad decided he would either borrow the money from his roommate, or he would dip into his savings to get the money to buy the tickets.

_____

_____

_____

6. I never could understand why some people find baseball more exciting than watching a football game.

_____

_____

7. Walking is by far the most pleasant form of exercise for me because it is relaxing, it doesn't cost anything, and because it doesn't require a partner.

_____

_____

8. Although learning to operate a computer isn't difficult, you must concentrate as well as be able to learn from your mistakes.

_____

_____

9. After looking under his bed, behind the television, and checking to see if it was in the basement, Jimmy found his baseball glove on the shelf, where it was supposed to be.

_____

_____

_____

10. Smoking is not only harmful to the person who smokes, but also to the people around the smoker.

_____

_____

Acknowledgments

Nona Aguilar, "How to Write a Letter That Will Get You a Job." Reprinted from the March 8, 1977, issue of *Family Circle Magazine.* Copyright © 1977 The Family Circle, Inc. All rights reserved.

Sherwood Anderson, "Discovery of a Father." Reprinted by permission of Harold Ober Associates, Incorporated. Copyright © 1939 by the Reader's Digest Association. Renewed 1966 by Eleanor Copenhaver Anderson.

Gwendolyn Brooks, "Life for My Child Is Simple, and Is Good." From *The World of Gwendolyn Brooks* by Gwendolyn Brooks. Copyright © 1949 by Gwendolyn Brooks Blakely. Reprinted by permission of Harper & Row, Publishers, Inc.

Katharine Brush, "Birthday Party." Reprinted from *The New Yorker,* March 16, 1946. Copyright © by Thomas S. Brush. Used with permission of Thomas S. Brush.

Victor B. Cline, "How TV Violence Damages Your Children." Copyright © 1975 by LHJ Publishing Inc. Reprinted with permission of Ladies Home Journal.

Ann Landers, Excerpts from columns. Reprinted by permission of Ann Landers and Field Newspaper Syndicate.

Malcolm X from *The Autobiography of Malcolm X,* by Malcolm X, with the assistance of Alex Haley. Copyright © 1964 by Alex Haley and Malcolm X. Copyright © 1965 by Alex Haley and Betty Shabazz. Reprinted by permission of Random House, Inc.

"Rah! Rah! Sell! Sell!" *Time,* May 4, 1981. Reprinted by permission from *Time,* The Weekly Newsmagazine. Copyright © 1981 Time, Inc.

Paul Roberts, "How to Say Nothing in Five Hundred Words," pages 404–421. From *Understanding English* by Paul Roberts. Copyright © 1958 by Paul Roberts. Reprinted by permission of Harper & Row, Publishers, Inc.

Robin Roberts, "Strike Out Little League," *Newsweek,* July 21, 1975. Copyright © 1975 by Newsweek, Inc. All rights reserved. Reprinted by permission.

Deems Taylor, "The Monster." Reprinted by permission of the author's estate and its agent, Curtis Brown Associates, Ltd. Copyright © 1937 by Deems Taylor. Copyright © renewed 1965 by Deems Taylor.

John Updike, "Central Park." Copyright © 1956 by John Updike. Reprinted from *Assorted Prose,* by John Updike, by permission of Alfred A. Knopf, Inc. First appeared in *The New Yorker.*

Roger M. Williams, "Away with Big-Time Athletics," *Saturday Review World,* March 6, 1976. Reprinted by permission of the publisher.

Index

Accept, except, 291

Advice, advise, 292

Affect, effect, 292

Agreement (*see* Pronoun-referent agreement; Subject-verb agreement)

Aguilar, Nona, "How to Write a Letter That Will Get You a Job," 286–289

All ready, already, 292

All right, alright, 292

Ambiguous pronoun reference, 210–211, 361–362

Among, between, 292

Analytical reports, 307–310

Anderson, Sherwood, "Discovery of a Father," 48–51

Apostrophe, 217–219

Application letter, 297–299

Audience, 199–204

Autobiography of Malcolm X, The, 193–195

"Away with Big-Time Athletics," 130–133

Between, among, 292

Bibliographies:

in final draft, 276

and indexes, selected list of, 319–331

Bibliographies *(Cont.):*

in research paper, 262–267

sample pages, 344–345

Bibliography cards, making, 332–336

"Birthday Party," 229

Body paragraphs, 55, 63–68

Brooks, Gwendolyn, "Life for My Child Is Simple, and Is Good," 81

Brush, Katharine, "Birthday Party," 229

Business letters, 302–305

Business writing:

application letters, 297–299

business letters, 302–305

committee reports, 306–307

formal reports, 307–310

grammar in, role of, 290–291

résumés, 299–301

Capitalizing, 73

"Central Park," 14–15

Character sketch, 231, 245

Clauses (*see* Coordinate clauses; Relative clauses; Subordinate clauses)

Clichés, 28–29

Cline, Victor B., "How TV Violence Damages Your Children," 185–189

Closing sentences, 35, 40–41

Colon, 182, 184

Commas:
  for clarity, 244
  for contrast, 244
  with coordinate clauses, 96,
    101
  with coordinate modifiers,
    29–31
  for emphasis, 244
  with interrupters, 151–153
  with introductory phrases,
    181–182
  with introductory subordinate
    clauses, 99, 101
  with items in a series,
    243–244
  with relative clauses, 180,
    181
  with terminal subordinate
    clauses, 99, 101
  with transitions, 146–151

Committee reports, 306–307

Conclusions, 55, 66–68
  (*See also* Closing sentences)

Conjunctions (*see* Coordinate
  conjunctions; Correlative
  conjunctions; Subordinate
  conjunctions)

Connotation, 205

Contractions, 217

Conversation, punctuating,
  71–73

Coordinate clauses, 96–97, 101,
  174–176, 356–358

Coordinate conjunctions,
  96–97, 174–175

Coordinate modifiers, 29–31

Coordination (*see* Coordinate
  clauses)

Correlative conjunctions, 241

Countering objections, 135,
  138–139
  (*See also* Persuasion)

Dangling modifiers, 212–214,
  362–364

Dash, 182, 183, 244

Denotation, 205

Description:
  image, 17, 26
  plan for detail selection,
    19–22
  revising, 19–20
  (*See also* Detail; Diction;
    Modifiers;
    Personification)

Detail:
  adequate, 38, 40, 64
  plan for selection, 19–22
  relevant, 38–39, 56, 64

Diction:
  clichés, 28–29
  connotation, 205
  definition of, 24
  denotation, 205
  economical, 24–26
  precise, 16, 26–27
  (*See also* Vocabulary)

Different from, different than, 293

Discovering ideas (*see*
  Prewriting)

"Discovery of a Father," 48–51

Economical diction, 24–26

Editing (*see* Revising and
  editing)

Effect, affect, 292

Emotion, 21–22

End notes and footnotes, 276,
  337–344

Essay examinations:
  key words in questions, 166
  organization, 167
  outlining answers, 167
  practicing, 171
  proofreading, 167

Essay examinations *(Cont.):*
 tips for handling, 164—167
Except, accept, 291

"Fear of Death," 111—112
Fewer, less, 293
Final draft of research paper,
 276
Final outline of research paper,
 273—274
First draft, 90, 275—276
Footnotes and end notes, 276,
 337—344
Formal reports, 307—310
Fragments, 74—78, 346—348
Freewriting, 6—7, 53—55, 83
 (See also Prewriting)
Frequently confused words,
 291—296

"Give Me the Home Life,"
 153—154
Grammar:
 reasons for, 70—71
 role in business writing,
  290—291

Haley, Alex, *The Autobiography of
 Malcolm X,* 193—195
Have, of, 292
Hear, here, 293
Hole, whole, 293
"How to Say Nothing in Five
 Hundred Words,"
 123—124
"How to Write a Letter That
 Will Get You a Job,"
 286—289
"How TV Violence Damages
 Your Children," 185—189

Ideas about writing, 4—5
 (See also Tips, for writers;
  Writing strategies)
Image, 17, 26
Implied pronoun reference,
 210—211, 361—362
In-class themes, 171—174
Indefinite pronouns, 106—107,
 207—208, 218
Indexes and bibliographies,
 selected list of, 319—331
Informational reports,
 307—310
Interrupters, 151—153
Introductions, 55—63
 lead-in, 56, 60—63
 thesis, 56—60
Introductory phrases, 181—182
Introductory subordinate
 clauses, 99, 101
Its, It's, 293

Journal writing, 12, 198—199
 (See also Prewriting)

Knew, new, 293

Landers, Ann, column, 115, 252
Lead-in *(see* Introductions)
Less, fewer, 293
Letters, three sample, 222—224
 (See also Business writing)
"Life for My Child Is Simple,
 and Is Good," 81
Listing in prewriting, 10—11

Malcolm X, *The Autobiography of
 Malcolm X,* 193—195
Mental image, 17, 26

Misplaced modifiers, 212−214, 362−364
Modifiers:
  commas between coordinate, 29−31
  coordinate, 29−31
  dangling, 212−214, 362−364
  definition of, 16
  misplaced, 212−214, 362−364
  stringing, 16−17
"Monster, The," 232−234
Mood, 21−22
"My Awakening," 42−43
"My Bedroom," 32−33

New, knew, 293
Notetaking for research paper, 268−273

Objections, countering, 135, 138−139
Of, have, 292
Organization:
  body paragraphs, 55, 63−68
  conclusions, 55, 66−68
  of essay examinations, 167
  introductions, 55−63
  outline of theme organization, 67−68
  of paragraph (*see* Paragraph organization)
  of theme, 55−68
  thesis, 55−60
  using an outline, 86−92
  (*See also* Outlining)
Outlining:
  essay examinations, 167
  final outline, 273−274
  form of, 86−87
  in organization, 86−92
  preliminary outline, 267−268

Outlining (*Cont.*):
  procedure for, 88
  purpose of, 86, 88
  twelve steps for writing a theme, 89−92

Paragraph organization, 35, 42−43
  body paragraphs, 55, 63−68
  the closing, 40−42
  supporting detail, 38−40
  topic sentence, 35−38
Parallelism, 239−243, 364−366
Paraphrasing in research paper, 269, 271−273, 275
Parentheses, 182, 183
Passed, past, 293
Peace, piece, 294
Person shift, 208−209
Personification, 18
Persuasion:
  countering objections, 135, 138−139
  gathering support, 135−136
  selecting a topic, 135, 136
  tips for handling, 136−140
Piece, peace, 294
Pierce, Kenneth M., "Rah! Rah! Sell! Sell!" 162−163
Plan for detail selection, 19−22
  (*See also* Detail; Thesis; Topic sentence)
Planning (*see* Outlining; Prewriting)
Possession, expressing, 218
Precise diction, 16, 26−27
Preliminary outline, 267−268
Preliminary reading, 263−264
Preliminary thesis, 89
Prewriting:
  answering questions, 7−9
  definition of, 6
  freewriting, 6−7, 53−55, 83

Prewriting *(Cont.)*:
  keeping a journal, 12,
    198–199
  letter writing, 11
  listing, 10–11
  talking to others, 12
  using a tape recorder, 12
Principal, principle, 294
Pronoun-referent agreement:
  in number, 206–208, 361
  in person, 208–209
  (*See also* Pronouns)
Pronouns:
  agreement with referents,
    206–209, 361
  ambiguous reference,
    210–211, 361–362
  avoiding sexist, 207
  implied reference, 210–211,
    361–362
  indefinite, 106–107,
    207–208, 218
  person shift, 208–209
  relative, 108–109, 179
  remote reference, 210–211,
    361–362
Proofreading, 91–92, 143
  checklist for, 316
  essay examinations,
    167
  for fragments, 77–78
  in-class themes, 173
  for run-ons, 101
Punctuation (*see* Apostrophe;
  Colon; Commas; Dash;
  Parentheses; Quotations,
  punctuating; Semicolon)
"Purse, The," 68–69

Questions:
  key words in, 166
  in prewriting, 7–9
  rhetorical, 236

Quit, quiet, quite, 294
Quotations, punctuating,
  71–73, 269–273, 275–276

"Rah! Rah! Sell! Sell!" 162–163
"Rainy View, A," 43
Reading, preliminary, for
  research paper, 263–264
Reason is because, reason is that,
  294
Reference works, general,
  317–318
Referents (*see* Pronouns)
Relative clauses, 179–181
Relative pronouns, 108–109,
  179
Relevance, 38–39, 56, 64
Remote pronoun reference,
  210–211, 361–362
Reports, 306–310
Research paper:
  bibliographies and indexes,
    selected list of, 319–331
  bibliography in, 262–267,
    344–345
  bibliography cards, 332–336
  end notes and footnotes, 276,
    337–344
  final draft, 276
  final outline, 273–274
  first draft, 275–276
  general reference works,
    317–318
  general topic, 263
  narrow topic, 264–266
  paraphrasing in, 269,
    271–273, 275
  preliminary outline, 267–268
  preliminary reading,
    263–264
  quoting, 269–273,
    275–276
  revising and editing, 276

Research paper *(Cont.):*
  six sins of research writing,
    282
  taking notes, 268–273
  working bibliography,
    266–267
Résumés, 293–301
Revising and editing, 19–20,
    91, 143, 276
  checklist for, 314–316
  in-class themes, 173
Rhetorical question, 236
Roberts, Paul, "How to Say
    Nothing in Five Hundred
    Words," 123–124
Roberts, Robin, "Strike Out
    Little League," 126–128
Role playing, 236–237
  sample theme illustrating,
    247
Run-on sentences, 93–101,
    349–351
  (See also Sentence fragments)

Semicolon:
  to correct run-on sentences,
    95–96
  with items in a series,
    102–103
  to separate complete
    thoughts, 95–96, 102,
    175
Sentence fragments, 74–78,
    346–348
  (See also Run-on sentences)
Sentence variety, 214–217
Sentences:
  closing, 35, 40–41
  run-on, 93–101, 349–351
  topic, 35–38, 63–65, 90
Sexism, avoiding, 207
Shift in person, 208–209
Shift in tense, 110, 352–353

"Should Instant Replay
    Cameras Aid in Officiating
    Football Games?"
    254–258
"Should Instant Replay
    Cameras Aid in Officiating
    Football Games?"
    (annotated), 277–281
Speech vs. writing, 85–86
"Strike Out Little League,"
    126–128
Subject-verb agreement,
    103–109, 351–352
  collective noun subjects,
    107–108
  compound subjects, 105
  definition of, 103
  indefinite pronoun subjects,
    106–107
  inverted order, 108
  relative pronouns, 108–109,
    179
  subjects with phrases,
    105–106
  there is, there are, 108
Subordinate clauses, 98–99,
    101, 176–179, 358–360
Subordinate conjunctions, 99,
    177–178
Subordination *(see* Subordinate
    clauses)
Support in persuasion,
    135–136
Supporting detail *(see* Detail)

Tape recorders, using, 12
Taylor, Deems, "The Monster,"
    232–234
Tense shift, 110, 352–353
Terminal subordinate clauses,
    99, 101
Than, then, 294
Their, there, they're, 294

Theme organization (*see* Organization)
Then, than, 294
There, their, they're, 294
There is, there are, 108
Thesis, 55–60
  narrowing, 58–60
  preliminary, 89
  (*See also* Introductions)
They're, their, there, 294
Three Sample Letters, 222–224
Threw, through, 295
Tips:
  for handling the essay examination, 164–167
  for writers, 141–146
  (*See also* Ideas about writing; In-class themes; Twelve steps for writing a theme)
To, too, two, 295
Topic:
  general, 263
  narrow, 264–266
Topic sentence, 35–38, 63–65
  preliminary, 90
Transitions, 146–151, 354–356
Twelve steps for writing a theme, 89–92
Two, too, to, 295

Updike, John, "Central Park," 14–15

Verb-subject agreement (*see* Subject-verb agreement)
Vocabulary:
  frequently confused words, 291–296
  how to build, 15, 205
  reasons for building, 15, 204–205
  simple, 16
  (*See also* Diction)
Vocabulary list, 311–313

Wear, where, were, we're, 295
Weather, whether, 296
Were, we're, wear, where, 295
Whether, weather, 296
Whole, hole, 293
Whose, who's, 296
Williams, Roger M., "Away with Big-Time Athletics," 130–133
Word choice (*see* Diction; Vocabulary)
Writing strategies:
  ideas about writing, 4–5
  in-class themes, 171–174
  tips for handling the essay examination, 164–167
  tips for writers, 141–146
  twelve steps for writing a theme, 89–92